THE
EXERCISER'S
HANDBOOK

THE
EXERCISER'S
HANDBOOK

How to Get More Out of the
Exercise You
Are Doing . . . Jogging,
Weight-Lifting,
Swimming, Tennis, Bicycling or
Any
Other Serious Exercise

Dr. Charles T. Kuntzleman

Arbor Press
SPRING ARBOR, MICHIGAN

To Beth

Lover
Critic
Wife
Friend

Library of Congress Cataloging in Publication Data

Kuntzleman, Charles T
  The exerciser's handbook

  Includes index.
  1. Exercise.   2. Physical fitness.   I. Title.
GV481.K82   613.7   78-9150
ISBN 0-940040-03-4

Acknowledgements

Acknowledgements are funny. They are seldom read, but no book would be complete without them. They are important to authors since we are indebted to so many people—people who give the moral support, love, and assistance. I have many to thank.

Lyn Cryderman: for ideas to stress in the book, suggestions on the manuscript, and excellent recommendations regarding the book's organization and thoughts.

Dan Runyon: for editorial assistance and objective criticism.

Lynette Van Alstine: for typing, typing, typing, and more typing.

Bob Rodale: for giving me a "break."

Debbie, John, Tommy, Lisa, and Becky: for trying to understand why daddy must write.

Beth: for love, patience, and understanding.

Thank you all. May God bless you.

CHARLES T. KUNTZLEMAN

Contents

Foreword: Everybody's Doing It!

Exercise. Suddenly, everyone seems to be doing it! Everybody is talking about it! People want to know more about it! Some are even exploiting it! At one time the domain of physical culturalists, it has become chic. People in all walks of life exercise. Construction workers, movie and TV stars, musicians, teachers, doctors, government officials, housewives, executives, and writers. A quick look around makes you think that every man, woman, and child in America runs, swims, lifts weights, does sit-ups, or hits tennis balls.

No wonder. In the past 10 years the medical profession and publishing industry have told us to exercise. It may prevent heart attacks, control our weight, reduce backaches, slow aging, improve our mental outlook, reduce our anxiety and depression, and enhance our sex life. Sixty million Americans have heeded this advice and started on the road to better health.

But it hasn't always been this way. When I was graduated from college in 1962, I was a lonely figure on the track. People would stop me and ask if I were training for the Olympics. Others would say, "Kuntzleman, stop trying to prove your manhood." A doctor friend told me I should be careful. I wasn't getting any younger (I was 22) and should be cautious about my heart. I told him I thought running was good for me. But he replied, "Who says so?" Being a novice in fitness I couldn't answer him. I was exercising on faith. I wanted an answer to that question and many more. I avidly read fitness books, magazines, and articles. I began a master's and doctoral program in exercise physiology at Temple University. I conducted research on the value of different fitness programs.

Tired of the abuse on the track, I started running in the early mornings. I also rode my bicycle to and from work. I lived in rural Pennsylvania and people would peek from behind their curtains and stare as I ran past in the early mornings. They smiled as I pedaled to and from work in suit, tie, briefcase, and top coat. I'm sure many wondered, "What is that guy doing?" I didn't care. I felt good. Then in 1966 I got a real break. Bob Rodale asked me to write a book on physical fitness. I jumped at the chance. Within a year he started a magazine and newsletter called *Fitness For Living* and *Executive Fitness Newsletter*. He asked me to assist in their publication. I acted as a consultant on fitness and exercise for Bob and the Rodale Press staff. He organized a group exercise program called Fitness Finders. He appointed me director. To make a long story short, Fitness Finders became part of the National YMCA movement and I had an opportunity to travel around the country to conduct workshops on fitness for YMCA personnel.

What an education I received. I met people of all ages interested in physical fitness. People who had all kinds of questions: How much exercise is necessary? Is there a best kind of exercise? Is exercise good for you? Can it control your body weight? I also had the chance to meet some pretty knowledgeable people in the fitness movement. I had many questions for them too.

My travels also gave me the opportunity to run in many cities. From Seattle to Miami; San Diego to Boston; and Edmonton, Canada, to Stockholm, Sweden; I ran and ran. During the early 1970's I was a lonely figure on those streets too. People would stop and ask, "Are you lost?" (My answer: Only in thought.) "Where's the fire?" (In my soul.) "Where are your pants." (With your wife.) I had things thrown at me—insults, rotten apples, obscene gestures, and even cars.

But around 1974 or so, things seemed to change. No longer were there insults. Instead, there were questions. How far did you go? How do you feel? Mind if I run with you? I'd sit on a plane with a fitness magazine or book. Invariably the person next to me would strike up a conversation. Are you a runner? How much exercise do you get? I think I should start, but I don't know how. Does the average American need more exercise? I delighted in answering those questions. For I felt they were sincere. People wanted answers.

During this same time I noticed another change. People became more informed medical consumers. They decided it was their responsibility to become healthy, not their doctor's. They concluded they would become fit and healthy, not by accident, but by resolve. They wanted to eat right, exercise, and ask their doctor intelligent questions. They even felt that they could take care of their own blood pressure and handle minor aches and pains without running to the doctor at the drop of a hat.

All this was new. At one time whenever we got ill, people ran to the doctor at the least little ache or pain. As a result, physicians obliged people with untold diagnostic tests and drugs. Even unnecessary surgeries were performed. But times change. Now people want to be masters of their own health. And they have questions. Questions that need and deserve answers. Questions about the weather and exercise. Who shouldn't exercise? How can I get more out of my favorite exercise? Can older people exercise safely? Should women run marathons? Questions, questions, and more questions. I like questions. Many times when you give a lecture you are not sure whether you are reaching people. But when the questions come to you thick and furiously at the conclusion of a presentation, you know you're getting to the listener. You are relating. You're answering their personal fitness problems.

As I traveled at least ½ million miles conducting over 100 workshops for teachers, physical directors, and medical personnel, I noticed there were always questions. So why not a book on these questions? *The Exerciser's Handbook* is such a book. It is based on my travels, workshops, lectures, and personal experiences. I want you to learn the real value of exercise and fitness. Learn how to get more out of the exercise you are doing. I hope you enjoy it. I hope your questions are answered.

C.T.K.

PART I

EXERCISING FOR THE HEALTH OF IT

"By chase our fathers earned their food,
Toil strung (improved) the nerves and purified the blood
But we their sons, a pampered race of men,
Are dwindled down to three score years and ten.
Better to hunt in fields for health unbought
Than see the doctor for a nauseous draught.
The wise for cure on exercise depend,
God never made his work for man to mend."

JOHN DRYDEN (1680)

CHAPTER

1

Who Needs Exercise And Why

Question: *Why do I need exercise, I'm healthy?*
Answer: If you decide NOT to exercise, see your doctor. Only he can tell you if your body can survive such a risky decision. You need exercise. No matter what your condition. Everyone does. Without exercise your body becomes sluggish—fat. Compare yourself with the wild animal brought to the zoo. When he arrives he is lean, healthy, and strong. He's had to lead an active life searching for food and protecting himself. Now that he is in a cage, his food is brought to him and he is protected from predators. After a few years, he is sluggish—fat.

Q: *Do I have to exercise daily to be healthy?*
A: First, let's realize that exercise is not a cure-all. Good health depends on many things including adequate rest, proper food, and avoidance of drugs, smoking, and pollution. But exercise is very important. I consider it pivotal.

Regular, proper exercise is basic to your health, longevity, and quality of life. Some physicians and scientists may criticize my fervor, but I think that for too long experts have chosen to ignore exercise or simply provide gentle lip service. They've not been specific in exercise's role in overall health and quality of life. They have directed more attention toward food, smoking, drugs, and the environment. It is my goal to make people re-think their priorities and to make them evaluate their way of life; to give you answers to questions on why and how exercise works in prevention and treatment of disease. Also, how to select activities based on their contribution to fitness and how to get more out of your physical activity. I also want to point out exercise's shortcomings, problems, and safety considerations.

Q: *Aren't Americans, as a whole, an active group of people?*
A: Americans don't like to admit that they're inactive. It implies that they are slovenly or lazy. Americans are not lazy. They are more active politically, domestically, educationally, and socially than any other group of people in the history of mankind. But when it comes to real physical activity, there has been a dramatic change over the years. It's reported that 60 million Americans exercise. But that also implies that 55 million do not exercise one bit. They are totally inactive. Furthermore, of the 60 million who do exercise, many exercise sporadically or improperly. Some experts say the figure of 60 million is inflated. That it's probably closer to 10 to 20 million adults who exercise regularly.

Regardless of who is right, one thing is clear. Many Americans do not exercise as much as their ancestors did. They also avoid the few opportunities they do have to exercise.

Q: *How do Americans avoid the opportunity to exercise?*
A: An observation by Jim Thatcher, a health educator for the Philadelphia Health Insurance Plan in Pennsylvania, illustrates my point. He stood at a huge office building on the first floor in downtown Philadelphia. There were an escalator and a stairway side-by-side. He decided to count 300 people going up to the second floor. Three hundred people who had a choice between using the escalator and the stairway. Two hundred and ninety-seven used the escalator, and only three used the stairway.

I was so impressed with his figure that when I was at Cleveland's Hopkins Airport recently, I tried the same thing. There were a stairway and escalator side-by-side next to the United Airlines counter. I counted the number of people who used the escalator or the stairs. Out of the 100 people, 89 used the escalator and 11 used the stairway. That may not be as impressive a statistic as Jim Thatcher's, but there's something else that happened while I was observing. I just couldn't believe it. It was poetic justice. The escalator broke down and people actually waited in line until it started again before they would go up the stairs. So help me.

The most unfortunate thing is that most people equate their busy life styles with being physically active. They also equate their two rounds of golf a week with a means of maintaining good physical condition. This attitude is most unfortunate because we need some form of exercise to replace our lack of activity in order to avoid hypokinetic disease.

Q: *What is hypokinetic disease?*
A: Hypokinetic disease refers to a host of ailments brought on by lack of motion. Hans Kraus, M.D., and Wilhelm Raab, M.D., two well-known preventive health physicians used this term to describe a process undergone by man in the last couple of thousand years. That is, man has changed from a highly active to a highly inactive fellow. A few thousand years ago man had to hunt or be hunted; a noticeable change from today's overfed, overprotected species. Since man has become sedentary he has been affected both physically and mentally. Heart disorders, ulcers, obesity, and muscular aches and pains are just a few of the physical problems man has "grown into." These diseases are one of the prices we pay for having achieved the "good life." Furthermore, neurosis, anxiety, depression, and maladjustment have crept into our mental/emotional side. This syndrome of inter-related diseases makes up what is known as hypokinetic disease. And these diseases are due in part to the fight or flight syndrome.

Q: *What is the fight or flight syndrome?*
A: For that we have to go back in time to when human beings had to hunt for their food and for this reason their very existence depended upon being physically active. In essence, the fight or flight theory refers to the way the human body reacted to threatening situations—by action. When an animal appeared, early man's first impulse was to size up the situation. If the animal was smaller than he, it was time for a fight. He probably figured here was a good meal. If the animal was bigger, it was time to "vamoose!" The early man's brain saw the threat and signaled

the hypothalamus of the brain. The ol' hypothalamus activated the nervous and endocrine systems. The nervous system in turn stimulated the liver which increased the blood's clotting time. (This, so that in case of injury there was less chance of bleeding to death.) Fat stored in the body was released for energy. The heart rate was speeded up to provide additional oxygen to the muscles. Blood pressure increased. Muscle tension was increased to facilitate quick responses. Copious amounts of hormones were released to allow the body to engage in long periods of intense activity. Fighting or fleeing. All this happened automatically in response to a real or imagined threat.

Q: *What are the problems that cause us to fight or flee in today's society?*
A: We're no longer challenged by man-eating tigers or invading barbarians. Instead, the boss yells at us or pressures us to meet a deadline, or we rush to catch a plane. We're confronted with frustrating domestic and social demands. We have to cope with stress brought about by money or other personal problems, overcrowding, unrelenting noise, anxiety over inflation, fuel shortages, crime and war. Since a purely physical response to threatening situations is inappropriate these days, we have to cope with our heads. So we usually adopt a grin-and-bear-it attitude, masking our anger, and internalizing our frustrations and anxieties.

It's hard work bottling up this physical response. It's a drain on our energy. It produces more stress and tension, which can ultimately lead to high blood pressure, elevated cholesterols and triglycerides, and blood sugar; overworked adrenal glands; *increased* muscle and nervous tension; as well as more frequent gastrointestinal upsets; and unrelenting depression and anxiety.

Q: *Are all of these diseases tension-related?*
A: Most are. Please note, however, I was referring to disease caused by tension *and* lack of exercise. That is an important combination. Drs. Raab and Kraus feel that a lack of exercise is crucial in this entire thesis. It goes something like this: underexercise provides no natural outlet for the fight or flight response. That is, our natural drive to respond physically is suppressed. Coupled with that is the fact that our body suffers from a disuse state which causes local (muscle) and general (body) fatigue. This

suppressed response to fight or flight and fatigue contribute significantly to stress. The stress in turn begets physical and emotional conditions which set us up for: internal disorders such as ulcers and heart disease; musculoskeletal disorders such as low back pain and tense muscles; and psychiatric conditions such as depression, anxiety, and alcoholism.

Q: *Couldn't I get the same benefits by just learning to relax and not being stressed?*
A: Not really. Practicing meditation and learning to relax are only part of the equation. I'm certainly not opposed to your learning good relaxation techniques and applying them. These will help you relax and reduce tension. But you are a physical being and your body demands physical exercise. As a sedentary person you have a higher heart rate because your heart is not as efficient as a trained heart. Your heart has to pump more blood with each beat to get the same amount of blood around your body. A trained heart is more ready to meet an emergency such as when you have to go up a few extra flights of stairs because the elevator broke down or shovel the driveway after a particularly heavy snowfall.

A fit person has more muscle strength and endurance than an unfit person. That means he or she can get through the day with less slouching and that 5 o'clock shadow of fatigue.

If you are not physically fit your lungs hold less oxygen. That may not sound significant, but the amount of air your lungs can hold correlates with the occurrence of heart disease. It seems as though the better the lungs can oxygenate the blood, the less demand is placed on the heart.

Nervous muscle tension can occur even if you are relaxed because the muscles demand some action on a periodic basis. Relaxation techniques may help you reduce tension but they fail to meet the demands of the muscles for motion.

Your muscles make up about 60% of your body weight. Muscles do more than make you move. The movement of the muscles also directly or indirectly influence circulation, metabolism, endurance, and nervous balance. Muscles directly influence the strength and integrity of your bones, your posture, and your body positions throughout the day. Besides these things, the muscles serve as an outlet for your emotional and nervous response.

And I still haven't said anything about the aging process. A sedentary life seems to accelerate the aging process or at least the appearance of aging. There are a lot of middle-aged people around who *look* old simply because their neck muscles can't hold their heads erect, their trunk and back muscles can't hold their bodies upright, and their weak legs let them do little more than shuffle along.

And as if this wasn't bad enough, it's important to point out that people who do not get an adequate amount of exercise usually function at what I like to call "6 feet under water." Their quality of life is not what it should be. They are in perpetual slow motion, and this applies to both young and old alike.

Q: *How can lack of exercise affect the* quality *of my life?*
A: Look at it this way. A doctor might be able to extend your life with miracle drugs. Let's suppose you have heart disease. A new drug may add years to your life. But is the drug really adding life to your years? Are you sitting in your chair simply waiting for the "grim reaper" or are you enjoying your life? You can't abuse yourself for 40 years, have a heart attack, and expect the doctor to fix you up. Your body doesn't work that way.

The conditions we are talking about are degenerative diseases; diseases which occur mainly because of age, but also because of poor health habits. They seem to be accelerated by our American life style. And regular exercise is crucial in slowing this process. My own feeling is that I don't care whether exercise improves my chances for living longer, but it certainly will improve my quality of life. You don't have a hernia operation to live longer. You undergo the hassle of an operation so you will feel better. It's the same way with exercise. You do it to feel better. But the important thing is that besides feeling better, you derive all these other benefits which build up an edge against the hypokinetic disease syndrome. And that's pretty good medicine.

And all you need is exercise. You can make 101 excuses, but the bottom line is that exercise is needed by all and no one can do it for you. You *must* do it for yourself.

Q: *What kinds of exercise help fight hypokinetic disease?*
A: All types of exercise will be of some benefit. Of course, some are better than others. Flexibility exercises, muscle strength and

endurance exercises, as well as cardiovascular or circulo-respiratory exercises are recommended. Of these, the most important are the cardiovascular-type exercises. Drs. Arthur Leon and Henry Blackburn from the University of Minnesota have said that 30 to 60 minutes of endurance-type exercise, 3 or 4 times a week "without question can improve health and quality of life for most people . . . and perhaps, increase longevity."

Q: *What are cardiovascular exercises?*
A: These are the kinds of exercises that get your whole body (or at least most of it) moving—exercises which get your heart beating faster, your lungs breathing deeper, and your body perspiring. Naturally, these exercises are not to be done to the point of exhaustion. Rather, they should be "pay as you go" type exercises: exercises during which you can take in enough air (oxygen) to keep you going.

Q: *What are some specific cardiovascular exercises?*
A: Walking, bicycling, jogging, and swimming are perfect examples of cardiovascular exercise. Others which qualify are rope skipping, running in place, some sports, and vigorous dancing. Notice all of them are nonstop. They are important because they improve your cardiovascular fitness.

Q: *What is cardiovascular fitness?*
A: Remember the last time the elevator broke down and you had to go up 5 or 6 flights of stairs? After the second or third flight you had to stop and catch your breath and relax. What you experienced was a low level of cardiovascular fitness. Or simply, you were unable to continue a muscular activity for a prolonged period of time. Your circulatory (heart, blood, and blood vessels) and your respiratory (breathing) systems needed major adjustments for you to continue such exercise.

Q: *Why is cardiovascular fitness important to me?*
A: Without a satisfactory level of cardiovascular endurance, performance in any activity drops off rapidly. You simply run out of steam quickly whether you are walking up a flight of stairs (assuming you got to the top), changing a tire, playing a round of

golf (and not feeling exhausted afterwards), enjoying sex, or even working overtime at your office. A proper level of cardiovascular endurance also means you will be more productive (at work *or* play) and you run a smaller risk of tangling with the whole Pandora's box of cardiovascular disease. Dr. Ernst Van Aaken, the world famous German doctor who has coached many record holders says it best. "True health starts with endurance." And that's what cardiovascular fitness is all about.

Q: *How do I go about improving my cardiovascular fitness level?*
A: I discuss this more thoroughly in a later chapter. Let me say here, however, that the key is teaching your body to handle a certain amount of exercise over an extended period of time. This is done through a regular program of exercise that gets progressively harder as your fitness improves. Let's say you try to jog a half mile (I wouldn't advise that now if you haven't been running regularly) and you quit after 100 yards because your heart sounds like a Buddy Rich drum solo. If you keep that up for two weeks or more, you would soon find that the run gets easier and easier until one day—Wow! It's easy! Your cardiovascular system will have adapted to this level of exercise. That ½ mile isn't exactly a high level of endurance, so you increase the dosage to maybe 1 mile. Eventually you're adding more distance or shortening the time it takes you to run a certain distance. So your cardiovascular fitness increases. Remember, exercise doesn't always mean jogging. The same principle holds true for other enjoyable activities such as bicycling, walking, swimming, rope skipping, or dancing. These are activities which help you improve your aerobic fitness.

Q: *What is aerobic fitness?*
A: Your aerobic (air·o'·bik) fitness is your ability to engage in activities that place a reasonable amount of stress on your heart and lungs. The term aerobic refers to oxygen, an element your body thrives on. Aerobic fitness is the heart, blood, and blood vessels doing "their thing" of providing the body with oxygen, and doing it efficiently when you are engaged in physical activities such as walking, running, cycling, and swimming. In other words, you participate in activities that have you breathing deeper and stronger but do not leave you breathless. Activities that leave you

huffing and puffing (and totally gassed out) are called anaerobic exercises. That is, exercises without oxygen.

Q: *I walk quite a bit on my job. Does that qualify as aerobic exercise?*
A: The big problem is that most of the time walking on the job is not continuous. It's stop and go. You have to check on the people you supervise or talk to the boss. Or you must observe the machines in operation. As a result, you're caught in a pattern of exercise which is not continuous and therefore does not build cardiovascular endurance.

There's another problem here also. The activity on the job may not be as beneficial as your activity away from the job. A study conducted by Dr. Charles L. Rose of Boston in 1965 bears this out. After analyzing 200 factors relating to longevity such as drinking habits, eating habits, occupation, physical exercise, and the like he found:

    a. Physical exertion during leisure hours benefited people more than physical exercise during working hours.
    b. Physical exertion off the job, particularly during the years 40 to 49 years of age was among the best of all longevity predictors.

If you walk non-stop for 30 minutes at a brisk pace, 3 or 4 times a week, and if your heart beats faster, or your lungs breathe more fully and deeply and your body begins perspiring, then ok. You might get sufficient exercise. Unfortunately, most of us do not walk in that manner on the job. Plus you shouldn't forget Rose's conclusion: off the job activity seems more important than activity on the job!

Q: *I think I understand cardiovascular or aerobic exercise. But what about flexibility exercises?*
A: The best illustration I can give you is yoga-type exercises or positions. These are exercises which focus on stretching of selected muscle groups. Inflexible muscles bother us quite readily. That's because we feel it many times (occasionally painfully). Try sitting on the floor with your legs out in front of you; knees locked, and toes straight up. Now, slowly bend forward and try to

touch your toes. Don't lift those knees! If you had difficulty doing it (or couldn't do it at all), it's because the muscles, tendons, and ligaments in your lower back and legs aren't flexible enough. Muscle flexibility is the range of motion possible at the joints (or bending places) of your body.

Q: *Is it important to have good flexibility to prevent injuries?*
A: Absolutely. An inflexible person frequently pulls or strains muscles or tendons when he tries to do something physical like getting a cat off the roof, bending under a table or desk to pick up a piece of paper, or mowing the grass. If you don't have the proper range of motion, you may reach too far and *zingo*. There goes that pain, which is usually followed by weeks or even months of disability, pain, or dull aches.

Q: *Are people who are tense more prone to a lack of flexibility?*
A: When you are under pressure, there is a tendency for the muscles to contract. Repeated tension causes the muscles to shorten considerably. The shortened muscle gets tired after a period of time and soon lets you know about it with pain. The result is a stiff neck or backache.

Q: *I have another question that I think is related to flexibility. What is a double-jointed person?*
A: There is no such animal. But there are people with extremely flexible joints. They have a high degree of range of motion at one or several joints. A number of factors are believed to be responsible for permitting this extreme mobility. Bone structure, muscles, ligaments, soft tissues, temperature, and lack of adhesion all contribute. That's understandable since the movement possibilities of a joint are determined by the shape of the bones, the disposition of muscles, ligaments, and cartilage, and the way in which they fit together. The type, direction, and extent of movement are uniquely determined for each joint by a complex interweaving of the above factors.

Exercise can increase the range of motion of joints. But it appears that the type of exercise is crucial and that lack of exercise (or movement) results in a reduction in their range of motion.

Extreme ranges of motion are achieved by hurdlers, high jumpers, gymnasts, and ballet dancers who perform highly specific exercises. However, when these exercises are no longer practiced, the gains are lost and the range of motion becomes restricted.

Q: *What is the best type of exercise to increase the range of motion in my joints?*
A: Slow yogic stretching exercises are much better than ballistic-type movements for improving flexibility. For example, let's assume you're going to try to touch your toes. Go down very gradually. Go to the point where you feel pain or are just ready to feel pain. Now concentrate on relaxing those muscles and you'll find that you are able to slip down just a little bit further. For some people it may be a quarter of an inch. For others it may be several. That is a slow, yogic stretch. That is better than a forceful movement in which you try to touch your toes and find that you can't get down so you forcefully bob your way down. The bobbing or forceful movement can cause problems. The yogic stretch is best.

Q: *Why is the yogic stretch best for increasing flexibility?*
A: Receptors located in the muscles and joints are stimulated by specific kinds of stretching movements. If you use fast, jerky, bouncing movements, the muscles you are stretching contract quickly after the stretch. Physiologists call this a stretch reflex. I guess you might say it's like stretching a rubber band and then letting go. The quick contraction after the forceful stretch reduces the effectiveness of your stretching and may cause muscle soreness and tightening.

By using a slow, sustained stretch, the receptors cause the muscles to relax and lengthen and thus aid in obtaining true increased flexibility. Much of the muscle soreness is prevented or alleviated by this type of movement.

When performing flexibility exercises, use a slow, sustained stretch.

Q: *What kind of muscles do body builders and weight lifters have?*
A: Big! But they're really working on the development of muscle strength. Any time a muscle in your body is called upon to

move something, it contracts. Muscle strength is the maximum effort made with just one of these contractions. For example, if you wanted to lift a heavy box, either you would have adequate strength in the flexors of your arms or you would not. The ease or the difficulty you experience in doing this type of activity demonstrates your muscle strength. Strength is measured by the amount that can be lifted in one attempt and is developed by exercising the muscle against strong resistance for a few repetitions. In other words, a program of weight training.

Q: *Do the weight lifters also have strong hearts?*
A: Weight lifters and body builders work on the muscles near the surface of the body. These are the muscles which allow you to lift and carry things. However, this type of exercise does very little for the most important muscle of your body—the heart. If the good Lord had made us in such a way that we had a window in our chest, the weight training people would do a heck of a lot more aerobic exercise. Weight training may do wonders for your physique, but it does very little for your heart and blood vessels.

Q: *Why doesn't weight lifting help my heart?*
A: To develop aerobic fitness requires that the heart, lungs, and blood vessels of your body be worked steadily for a period of at least 15 to 30 minutes per day, three to four days per week. That is, you must do exercises which will get your heart rate up to a certain point and keep it there. Exactly how high will be discussed in a later chapter.

If you exercise through weights, you will find that you'll lift intensely for 30 seconds to a minute, rest, then go back to the lifting. The exercise is not sustained. There's too much pausing for station identification. The fact that weights make nice muscles to show on the beach does very little in the way of helping your heart.

Q: *Does that mean I don't have to worry about my muscles?*
A: No. But you don't have to carry it to an extreme. Some muscle strength is necessary for your health. Sufficient arm, shoulder, and back strength is needed for good posture. Abdominal strength is needed to help avoid a bay window and therefore

possible low back pain. Good muscle strength of the body is also necessary for such tasks as carrying out the garbage, pushing the car when it is stuck in the mud or snow, or moving a piano across the hall.

Closely allied to muscle strength is muscle endurance. Although muscle strength is necessary for correct posture, muscle endurance is essential to maintain that posture throughout the day. You will find that many jobs require muscle endurance. Typists need good forearm, shoulder, and back muscle endurance to type all day. Bricklayers need a high degree of muscle endurance to perform continuously. Many of you need enough muscle endurance to stand or sit at your job all day without becoming tired. Without muscle endurance, you tire rapidly and your efficiency level drops. You develop a typical 4 o'clock slouch position.

Q: *What kinds of exercises are best for improving muscle strength and muscle endurance?*
A: You can use the weight training exercises listed in Chapter 10. You might also try some of the calisthenics found in Chapter 11. There you'll find specific exercises described for different areas of the body. It's up to you which you'll want to use, because most calisthenics are sufficient for improving muscle strength and muscle endurance.

Q: *Can I store my exercise?*
A: It would be nice, perhaps, if this were true; but unfortunately the benefits of exercise cannot be stored for any great length of time. The simple fact is that you never graduate from the school of physical conditioning. A regular schedule (at least 3 to 4 times a week) is necessary to maintain a proper fitness level. A heavy workout once every 2 weeks is not good. It may be dangerous. Don't be a weekend athlete.

Q: *Is it too late for me to begin to exercise?*
A: Absolutely not! No one is beyond (i.e., too fat or too old) the effects of exercise. Ben Franklin lived to be 84, a long life by even today's standards and he swam regularly for 80 of those years. Thomas Jefferson jogged regularly during the late 1700's and early

1800's. He lived to be 83. I know several people who didn't start exercising until their 60's, 70's, and 80's. I'll tell you about several of them throughout the book, but one is worth mentioning here. George Dowling is a volunteer fitness leader for the Central Branch YMCA in Milwaukee, Wisconsin. I was introduced to George at one of my YMCA workshops. George, a retired CPA, started exercising in January 1976 at the age of 77. He began in a YMCA starter fitness program. During the 10 week starter program his percent body fat and weight dropped, while his aerobic capacity increased significantly. After that George gradually started increasing his running mileage so that now he is running 2 to 3 miles a day, 3 to 5 days a week. He also learned how to swim at the age of 78! So he added swimming to his exercise regimen. The Milwaukee Y contracted him to lead fitness classes for senior citizens. He's a super floor leader. His doctors are amazed at his stamina and physical well-being. Back in January of 1976 his resting heart rate was 92. Today it is 58. His most recent goal is to complete 500 miles in a year. Keep it up George, you're an inspiration to all. It's never too late, but the sooner you begin, the better. You'll gather more benefits. The next few chapters will show you why.

CHAPTER

2

Fitness For A Better Sex Life

Q: *Can exercise improve my sex life?*
A: Yes, I believe it can. In fact, several years ago the former Surgeon General of the United States, Dr. Jesse Steinfeld, said, "Those people who are in good physical condition even enjoy sex more. If that isn't a motivating factor, I don't know what is."

Q: *Why is sex improved through exercise?*
A: There are many good reasons. Although I wouldn't be presumptuous enough to say it's all physical, I'm sure psychologists would not say sex is all emotional. Let's face it, sex is a physical act. Some people call it the best exercise. Others call it the perfect exercise. Whatever, you must admit it is a beautiful gift. We should treat it as such. Unfortunately, most of us do not.

A lot of people let themselves go to pot. There's an old saying that the honeymoon is over when the husband starts shaving in the morning. I have another: the honeymoon is over when your waistline starts to expand. To me it's a sign that you may no longer care. I realize it's not as simple as that. But I bet you 9 times out of 10 you were first attracted to your spouse for physical reasons.

Furthermore, when you first made love you delighted in looking at each other's bodies. Now what do you think? Do you still

look? Or worse still: Are you ashamed of the way you look? I
hope not.

Exercise will help you keep that slim waistline. Proper exercise
will keep your muscles taut, hips narrow, and body attractive. It
gives you good body tone. Proper exercise keeps your body fat
low. That too is important. No one likes to see gobs of body fat.
Exercise will give you a more attractive and desirable body.

Q: *This discussion of sex goes beyond just how you look, doesn't
it?*
A: It certainly does. Dr. T. K. Cureton, professor emeritus of
physical education at the University of Illinois, reported many
times that one of the basic complaints of middle-aged men starting
in fitness classes was a lack of sexual vigor. Many felt they just
didn't have it any more. So they no longer tried. Interestingly,
after going through Cureton's training program many of the men
claimed that they had an increased sex drive.

David H. Pain, a lawyer from San Diego, California, and the
main force behind the Masters Olympic program, agrees. He says
that exercise, particularly running, can act as an aphrodisiac. "It
can help men with their sexual problems. Men who turn 40 frequently have real ego problems associated with sex and approach-
ing inadequacy. In my law practice, I've handled hundreds of
divorce cases. Very frequently, the woman's complaint is that her
husband, even while very young, never got any exercise. He just
let himself turn into a vegetable."

Q: *Why do you think exercise increases sex drive?*
A: I think that, through exercise, men lose their timidity. One of
Cureton's pet comments about sedentary males was that they
were afraid to be physical beings any more. They were afraid they
might get hurt, have a heart attack. When they became more fit,
their courage returned. So did their interest in physical things.
And sex is physical—sooo. Cureton also felt that the increased
sex drive was due to a change in stress.

Q: *How does stress affect sex drive?*
A: Stress drains your energy. It makes you more tired. So you
are no longer interested in doing anything extra. After a full day

on the job or doing housework, the thought of going dancing is just too much. It's the same way with sex. "Why bother, I'm too tired. Besides, I have a headache." Soon you become less active and your body starts to go down the tube. When the body starts to lose its attractiveness, there is less stimulation to start the sex act, and you're even too tired to get started. So sleep, TV, or books become the replacements.

I asked a cardiologist friend of mine why he thought more men were becoming impotent. Was it women's lib? He said that was a possibility. But to the cardiologist, the primary reasons were stress and lack of physical fitness. Men were too tired or stressed to "make it." The great majority of his patients had to be counseled along these lines. The lack of sexual drive leads to more stress, which leads to less sexual drive . . . and on and on and on.

Q: *How else does physical activity help to reduce stress?*
A: I'll discuss this later. But let me say here that physical activity seems to help people who are depressed. It helps them overcome their feelings of depression and anxiety. Dr. Thaddeus Kostrabula, a psychiatrist whom you'll hear a great deal about in the following chapters, uses running to help his depressed patients. Other researchers say exercise helps people overcome anxiety. And the conclusion is apparent: less depression and anxiety—less stress.

Q: *How else can exercise help my sex life?*
A: Sex therapists say that one of the many reasons men and women no longer have a successful union is because they have too much fat on their bodies. Maybe being that fat is an exception.

But I don't think the following conditions are exceptions: First, a low degree of fitness sets a person up for low back pain. And there's nothing like a pain in the back to slow or stop intercourse. Second, as your fitness level declines, so does your flexibility. And a lack of flexibility makes it difficult for some people to assume a desirable coitus position. Third, when you engage in intercourse your heart rate and blood pressure increase dramatically. If a person has a poorly conditioned heart, the sex act may be difficult and scary because of a racing heart.

Q: *Can exercise increase a man's sex drive physiologically?*
A: A male's sex drive is influenced by the level of the hormone testosterone. In the past, it was assumed that men inherited a tendency to produce more hormones. But there is evidence now that lifestyle may also contribute greatly to the production of testosterone. Although scientists still disagree, there is evidence that different factors in life may influence testosterone. One of these factors seems to be physical exercise. Dr. J. R. Sutton and his colleagues at the Gavin Institute of Medical Research, St. Vincent's Hospital, Sydney, Australia, studied two groups of athletes—14 oarsmen of a rowing team and seven swimmers. These were not typical college athletes, but highly trained men who had achieved Olympic standards. The training was rigid, involving two sessions daily—one all out and another somewhat less demanding.

Sutton tested blood testosterone levels for all men before and after each of the two sessions. He found that when the exercise was less than maximal, there was no change in testosterone levels, but when the physical effort was all out, the testosterone levels increased dramatically.

Q: *Does a man have to train as hard as an Olympic athlete to increase his testosterone level?*
A: No. Dr. Sutton conducted further investigations, with more reasonable levels of exercise. He selected 4 more subjects— medical students in good health, but not athletes. He had them exercise for 20 minutes on a stationary bicycle, and he collected blood samples before, during, and after their performance. After 10 minutes of activity, testosterone levels began to rise, reaching their peak at 20 minutes, when the exercise was discontinued.

Q: *Why does a man's testosterone level increase after exercise?*
A: For one thing, studies show that exercising muscles can store energy in the form of glycogen. But to do that they need more testosterone. The hormone may also help increase carbohydrate metabolism in the muscles. In both cases, the body "asks" for more testosterone and the glands usually respond with increased production. Also, testosterone secretions are dependent upon blood flow surrounding the testes. Testosterone is secreted

through the walls of the glands and goes directly into the blood. If it is not swept away through adequate blood flow, the testosterone molecules back up. Much like passengers waiting to get on a train. Apparently this "crowding" of testosterone molecules backs up within the gland, and the cells are told to stop producing testosterone. So decreased blood flow produces decreased testosterone production. Fortunately exercise increases blood flow. In addition, exercise causes the adrenal glands to secrete more hormones, some of which have been shown to stimulate secretion of testosterone by the testes. All of these things encourage production of greater amounts of testosterone in the body.

Q: *How can exercise increase a woman's sex drive, physiologically?*
A: Not as much research has been done with women as with men. But Dr. J. Sonka and associates did an experiment involving hormone levels of obese women. These researchers found that obese women who dieted had a drop in certain hormones. While those who dieted *and* exercised did not have this reduced production. Which, of course, suggested that exercise may slow the destruction of certain sex drive hormones.

Also, as people get older there is a tendency for them to do less. While that may be ok for a car or motor, it is not good for the human body. There is a standard principle which every student of physiology learns: "Use it or lose it." The more an organ is used the better it will function. The application for a husband and wife here seems obvious.

Q: *How is circulation involved in the improvement of sexual performance?*
A: As the average sedentary American grows older, his or her blood vessels lose their flexibility. The walls tear and thicken with plaques so that the vessels themselves are narrowed. The blood must push with greater force to continue circulation. This is called peripheral resistance. The heart is forced to work harder. Blood pressure increases. Sometimes smaller vessels are entirely blocked, and circulation to these peripheral areas of the body are cut off. Thus the poor circulation and "cold feet" of old age may occur.

Far tinier than the blood vessels to the feet are the capillaries serving the testes. Gonads of most older men are critically deprived of essential oxygen and nutrients. Inevitably they waste away and function is lost.

Q: *How else does circulation affect sex performance?*
A: As a person gets older and more sedentary, the circulatory system gets more sluggish. Heart rate and blood pressure start to rise. The blood vessels become less elastic and breathing becomes more shallow. In short, cardiovascular fitness drops and early fatigue sets in. Physical effort becomes a chore, even if it is done lying down. Many times extra effort coupled with an emotionally charged situation causes a very high heart rate and blood pressure. People feel uncomfortable—dizzy or "shaky." Many may be frightened. Consequently, less physical work is done. With less exercise there is a further decrease in cardiovascular fitness. A vicious cycle ensues: less work, less fitness, more fatigue, less work. Soon people become so unfit that they avoid exercise at all costs—including sex. They simply don't have the stamina to keep it up any longer. On the rare occasions they do attempt the act, they become exhausted and quit before reaching orgasm. All of this because of poor physical fitness and sluggish circulation.

Q: *What is the oldest age that a person can remain sexually active?*
A: I don't have a specific age. But sex therapists say people can stay sexually active until their eighth or ninth decade of life. Although this is rare, it does occur. Later in this book I'm going to introduce you to the long living Russians who reside in the Caucasus (Abkhasia). In that part of Russia it is not unusual for people to live to be 100. These vigorous people have excellent fitness levels and remain physically active right up to their last days. Dr. Lawrence Lamb, M.D., former professor of medicine at Baylor University, notes that the Abkhasian male expects to remain sexually active to the age of 100. Notice I said expects. One of the men studied in Russia, according to Dr. Lamb, is said to have fathered 9 children, the last of whom was born when the father was over 100. Additionally, he was tested at the age of 119 and found to be potent and producing sperm. Contrast that to the

fact that about half the male population of the United States by the age of 75 is impotent. And the other half probably fear they are going to lose potency soon.

Q: *Are there other ways that exercise can improve a person's sex life?*
A: I would be remiss not to mention that sex begins in the head. It is involved with your attitudes and self-esteem. Your attitudes about the opposite sex and your self-esteem are crucial. If you don't think much of yourself, you may be slow to get involved. Furthermore, if you don't think much of the opposite sex and/or want to dominate, you may find that your sex experience is far from satisfactory. I'm a physical educator, not a psychologist, so I won't go into all kinds of psychological details. But I would like to mention that if you have poor self-esteem, you may be hesitant to participate in sex. One of the major benefits of exercise is improved self-concept. Why self-concept improves has not been determined. It may be because you are pleased that you are disciplined enough to exercise on a regular basis. It may be you like the way you look. Consequently, you feel better about yourself. It's also just possible that exercise produces some little-known or -understood changes in the brain due to better circulation or transmission of nerve impulses. Of course, it may be that you have taken some time to do something you enjoy. Researchers just don't know. Whatever the reason, improved self-esteem is a by-product of proper, regular exercise. How much improvement will depend upon the individual.

If you have greater self-esteem, you have helped to take care of one side of the equation of sex starting in the head. Now, it's time to work on your attitude toward others.

Q: *Is sex a good way to burn off calories?*
A: There is a great deal of confusion over how many calories are expended in sex—foreplay or coitus. Part of the problem stems from the fact that some partners are passive, while others would put an Australian tag wrestling team to shame.

Most authorities agree that the average person burns the number of calories listed in the following chart. Notice that the number of calories you burn depends on whether you are the aggressor or the submissor. You'll also find that the number of calories burned is a lot lower than most people expect. But sex is still a good activity. Dr. Theodore Rubin the formerly-fat psychiatrist used to say: "Next time you're hungry, reach for your mate instead of your plate." That's good advice.

Calories Used Per Hour* During Sex

WEIGHT (IN POUNDS)	110	150	200
Foreplay	80	100	115
Intercourse			
a. Aggressor	235	300	350
b. Submissor	105	135	155

* These calories refer to calories used per hour. If the sex act lasts 15 minutes simply divide by four; 20 minutes by three; 30 minutes by two; and so on.

Q: *Is sex a good way to keep the heart in shape?*
A: Not really. You need to participate in other types of cardiovascular exercise to maintain good sexual function. Of course, after the sex act is completed there is a feeling of complete relaxation, so it may help the heart in that regard.

Naturally, some people may be disappointed that sex as a primary exercise does not burn up many calories, and that it does not condition the heart. But look at it this way: it sure beats watching TV!

CHAPTER

3

The Battle Of The Bulge

Q: *Everybody talks about obesity and weight loss these days. Just what is obesity?*

A: Obesity is a bodily condition caused by excessive generalized distribution of fatty tissue. Or to put it more bluntly, obesity means being too fat. Being called obese bothers people and brings out a lot of negative vibes. People will tolerate being called big boned or chunky. If they can't be chunky, they'll accept overweight. If not overweight, then they'll accept the term fat. But under no circumstances does anyone want to be called obese. As my seven-year-old Becky would say, "Dad, that's gross."

Unfortunately, a large percentage of the population *is* obese. At one time obesity was considered a sign of success and well-being, so fatness in men was a sign of prosperity. When it was fashionable, plumpness was thought to enhance a woman's charms. Children who were fat were considered to be healthy. Today, however, Americans are becoming increasingly conscious about their weight. They realize not only that it looks bad on them, but also that it is a health hazard.

Q: *What's the difference between being overweight and being obese?*

A: Plenty. Obesity refers to the percentage of fat which is on your body. Overweight is what you weigh according to the height/weight charts put out by insurance companies. And there's a big difference. For example, you can have two men who are 6'2" and weigh 235 pounds. One man plays halfback for the Los Angeles Rams and the other is a typical male citizen of the United States. According to the height/weight charts, both are overweight since they shouldn't exceed 198 pounds. However, when you tell both men to take off their shirts, there is an obvious difference between the two. The professional football player has minimal body fat and a high distribution of lean body tissue. He looks very good. The other gentleman carries a large amount of fat and low lean body tissue. He doesn't look good.

For some reason I've had less difficulty explaining this concept to men than to women. Women panic at the sight of an unwanted pound. They are a slave to scales. Don't let the scales be your master. They are deceiving. Trust me. Muscle tissue weighs more than fat. When you exercise you lose the fat stores on your body and increase the muscle tissue. Consequently, there may be no change on the scales. Women of America do not dispair. Fat is the problem, not pounds. Lean body tissue is what gives you an attractive body—male or female. I wish I had a dollar for every woman who has told me "I haven't lost a pound with exercise but I dropped a whole dress size." I'd be rich! Remember: Behind every curve there is a muscle!

Q: *What is lean body tissue?*
A: Lean body tissue is the bone, organ, and muscle tissue of your body. Your body is composed of two types of tissue—fat and lean body tissue. A person who is in good physical condition will have a high distribution of lean body tissue and a low distribution of fat. On the other hand, a person who is unfit will have a reverse distribution. It is most unfortunate, but as we grow older, changes occur. Our lean body distribution drops and our percentage of body fat goes up. Ex-President Ford is a perfect example. Early in his presidency he claimed that he weighed only 4 pounds more than when he played football at the University of Michigan. That doesn't sound too bad, except for the fact that his waist measurement jumped from 32 to 38 inches. What happened was that his lean body tissue decreased as his percentage of body fat had gone up.

I'm a pretty good example myself. I'm 5'11" and weigh 185 pounds. That's too much according to the tables. But only 10% of my total body weight is fat. Which is well below the recommended level of body fat.

Q: *What is the recommended level of fat for adults?*
A: For men it should be around 15% body fat and for women around 19 to 23% body fat. If a male exceeds 25% and a female exceeds 30%, they are considered obese.

Q: *What is the recommended level of fat for children?*
A: They should be around 12% body fat. And if they carry more than 20% body fat they are obese.

Q: *Can I rely strictly on the height/weight charts to determine if I'm overweight?*
A: No, not entirely; they're a very rough guide at best. They don't tell the whole story. As I indicated before, you can have people who weigh what they're supposed to but are a disaster because their percentage of body fat is too high.

Q: *Can a person be underweight and obese?*
A: Yes, it is possible for a person to be underweight, or right where he's supposed to be according to the height/weight charts, and be obese. I have examined many men and women and have found this to be true. A woman in one of my classes is a perfect example. She was 5'3" and weighed 112 pounds. According to the height/weight charts she was right on the money. In fact, she weighed the same as she did 20 years ago. She was quite proud of that. But when I checked her percentage of body fat I found she had 30% body fat. She was obese. And very upset. She didn't speak to me for a week.

When she was 15, she had a higher percentage of lean body tissue. But somewhere along the line it gave way to body fat. It was all due to sedentary living.

A study done by Dr. Ancel Keys at the University of Minnesota also showed this. He ran a series of tests on adult males and found that 20% of his subjects fell into the "underweight but too fat" category. At the same time, somewhere between 20 and 30% were overweight but within the normal range of fat distribution. Many were, in fact, extremely lean. From this same study came another interesting finding: the men who were both obese and overweight led very sedentary lives, while the men who were overweight but not fat engaged in heavy labor. Because of this I think the height/weight tables should be taken as something less than the last word. Don't be misled. Don't be one of the many Americans who use the tables to put one over on themselves. It's so easy to do!

Q: *Do people really cheat on height/weight charts?*
A: Of course they do. I could give many examples, but a friend of mine is a classic. When she was editing a previous book of mine she came to a discussion I had on obesity and overweight. At that time she told me that when she was 20 she weighed approximately 116 pounds. She is 5'6" tall and back then she classified herself as having a "small frame." Over the years she put on weight. In her late 20's she was hovering about the 135-pound mark. She really didn't look fat, she said, and since all height/weight tables indicated that 135 was not a bad weight for a 5'6" woman of medium frame, she relaxed and decided that a medium frame was what she had after all. In her mid thirties, this same woman weighed around 143 pounds. The height/weight tables say that this is ok for a woman of her height with a "large frame." She re-evaluated the situation and concluded that, yes, she had been a "large-framed" person all along. After all, her wrist was rather large. So she must have big bones.

It was only when she hit 150 pounds and ran out of frame categories that she finally faced up to the fact that she had a problem.

Q: *Do men cheat on height/weight tables?*
A: Men tend to manipulate the tables a little differently. Instead of reclassifying themselves by frame, they add inches to their height. One guy I know "grew" 1½ inches over the years: At 20 his height was measured with his shoes off; at 30 or so, he had himself remeasured, wearing shoes with one-inch heels and straining to stand at tall as he possibly could. By reclassifying himself by height, he was able to justify an accumulation of 19 pounds of fat.

Q: *If height/weight charts don't give the whole story, why do people rely on them in the first place?*
A: Tradition. They fail to understand that weight is not important. Fat is. But the concept of weight is ingrained in us from a very early age. Young girls are told that they're supposed to weigh such and such. Women's magazines tell them that they're supposed to be the slender model and not to exceed a certain weight. It's all ridiculous. In the United States, the height/weight charts exercise a kind of tyranny not seen in other countries. And it's a cultural phenomenon, and a rather curious one. In Scandinavia, for example, a fit and attractive body is emphasized; pounds are just numbers on a scale and relatively unimportant. There it's how you look that counts, not what you weigh! Here, though, I've known people who have almost a fanatical desire to weigh what the tables say they ought to—unaware, for the most part, that the indicated "ideal" weights may not be at all ideal in terms of their structure and the composition of their own individual bodies.

Q: *If the height/weight tables are so misleading, how can I know what weight is best for me? How can I tell whether I'm obese or not?*
A: The quickest, easiest way I know of is so obvious I almost hate to mention it, except that I've discovered through past experiences that lots of people really are expert at ignoring the obvious. So, for test #1, you can get undressed and stand in front of a full-length mirror. Be critical. If you look fat, you can reasonably conclude that you are fat, i.e., that the poundage of the total percentage of fat on your body is greater than it should be— regardless of whether you presently weigh what the tables say is "right" for you. Don't be too hard on yourself, though. Younger women, especially, are apt to want to measure up to a fashion-model-ideal figure, which, unless one is built along long, lean ectomorphic lines, is probably not possible, nor even desirable. If this test doesn't tell you too much, you might try running in place. If you can see your body jiggle anywhere where it shouldn't, you also can conclude that you are too fat.

A second test is to think back to what you weighed when you were 18, if you are a woman; or 21, if you're a man. (If memory fails, see if you can dig up old medical records.) You can assume that each pound gained since then represents an accumulation of fat. You can also assume that your percentage of fat has increased if your waist has gotten bigger.

Q: *What is the most accurate way for someone to determine his percentage of body fat?*
A: By far the most accurate method yet devised for estimating body composition is hydrostatic weighing. For this you are immersed and the amount of water displaced is determined—and other measurements—lung volume, body weight in and out of water, etc., are made. Hydrostatic weighing requires some rather elaborate and expensive equipment. Obviously, this is not a do-it-yourself project, unless you have a very large bathtub and some fancy equipment.

Recently, physiologists and nutritionists have used a device called the skinfold caliper to estimate a person's percentage of total body fat. It is practical for a physician or a clinician to use, but rather expensive for the layman—it costs around $150. Therefore, it is not readily available to most people. But you may be able to have someone determine your percentage of body fat at your local YMCA for a reasonable fee.

There is another technique which you can use if you do not have access to a skinfold caliper. And that is the pinch test. With the pinch test you simply try to find if you have an excessive amount of fat folds on your body. As a general rule of thumb, if you're under 16 years of age and you can pinch more than ½ an inch of fat on the back of your arm, you can consider yourself obese. If you are an adult male, one inch is a sign of obesity. For a female an inch and a half.

There's one final point I'd like to mention and that's that a high percentage of body fat (obesity) is the real culprit in all types of ailments. So if a person has a high percentage of body fat, regardless of what the height/weight charts say, he's more apt to be unhealthy.

Q: *If an obese person doesn't exercise, can his condition be dangerous?*
A: There's no real doubt about it. Obesity *is* dangerous. It is a disease and like many diseases, if allowed to progress without

treatment, it can kill you. The old bed-ridden geezer who comically gasps, "It's not those cigarettes that are killing me, it's the coughing that's doing me in," may be able to illustrate my point. Being fat in itself is not fatal. But being obese leads to numerous other life-shortening conditions and diseases that may, as the old guy said, "do you in." Medical science has found that being obese puts stress on the body's systems. This stress can lead to heart disease, vascular problems, diabetes, kidney afflictions, digestive disorders, cancer, arteriosclerosis, high blood pressure, arthritis, and other disorders. Surgeons have even said that they have more difficulty in surgery with the obese, and that obese people have less likelihood of survival. In fact, most life insurance companies charge higher premiums for fat people. But, unfortunately, they rely strictly on the height/weight charts. I'd like to reiterate, obesity is a dangerous disease and can be fatal when not treated.

Q: *Just how does obesity cause so many health problems?*
A: When fat is put on, there is more body tissue to take care of. Your skeletal and muscle systems are under strain to support the additional load. Your heart and lungs must work harder in order to assist your muscles in moving all that weight around. Added to that is a more subtle, but very dangerous strain placed on the cardiovacular system. All that fatty tissue can mean an increase in blood pressure, which causes the heart to work harder. Muscle tissue, which normally aids blood flow, is minimal or has been replaced by fatty tissue. (Remember the decrease in lean body tissue and the increase in fat tissue?) In obese people, the blood vessels become less elastic and lose some of their ability to aid circulation. Rather than receiving help from the blood vessels and muscle tissues (as in normal people), those vessels and muscles just lay there, causing the heart of an obese person to work much harder to pump the blood throughout the body.

Closely allied to this is a build-up of fatty substances in the blood vessels themselves. Doctors know that fat circulates throughout the body at all times. This allows fat to be deposited in the fat cells of the body, which transport fat back to the liver so it can be broken down into energy and for several other important purposes. This fat must be transported by the blood vessels, but it is possible for these fatty materials to be deposited on the inner lining of the blood vessels. Because of this, the blood flow in that particular vessel is restricted. It's much like an old pipe which is starting to clog up with rust and mineral deposits. In the very worst stages of this condition, solid parts of the deposit may break off from the lining and be carried throughout the vessels until they become lodged somewhere, causing a blockage. Or the vessel itself may become blocked simply because of the "clogging up" of the vessels. If the vessel serves a major organ of the body such as the heart, brain, or kidney, the condition can be fatal. So immediately you can see how it is implicated in heart disease, kidney affliction, arteriosclerosis, and high blood pressure.

Q: *How can I avoid the health problems caused by a high percentage of body fat?*
A: Exercise!

Q: *How does exercise help me lose weight? Don't I have to go on a diet to lose weight?*
A: No. It's all a matter of calories.

Q: *What is the definition of calories?*
A: Unfortunately, most people think calories and food are synonymous. Therefore, they rely on diets to keep their weight down. Actually, a calorie is a unit used to measure heat. The body needs those calories to supply energy. It receives calories from food and either releases them through energy or stores them. When they are stored, they become fat. One of the reasons you picked up this book, perhaps, is because your body has become quite a warehouse.

Q: *If I have a surplus of calories, don't I have to go on a diet to cut down on that surplus.*
A: No. Keep in mind we are talking about a surplus of calories, not food. To maintain a steady weight, your intake and output of calories must be the same. For example, if a normal day's eating takes in 3,000 calories, you must expend enough energy to use those 3,000 calories. If you have 100 calories "left over" they go into the warehouse. After you have stacked 3,500 calories in the

warehouse, you've gained a pound. Now one way to get rid of those calories is to reduce the intake. But that's no fun, and it doesn't always work. How many people do you know who are always on a diet but always look the same? They lose weight but they gain it right back. Dr. Jean Mayer, former professor of nutrition at Harvard, and now president of Tufts University, has said this pattern of losing and gaining weight is "the rhythm method of girth control." By the way, some doctors report that only 8% of the obese are able to lose weight *and* keep it off. That's the bottom line. I've known hundreds of people who've said, "I lost 50 pounds on such-and-such diet." Unfortunately, they gained it all back—and then some.

Q: *If dieting doesn't work, what can I do to use up excess calories?*
A: Another more sensible and certainly more enjoyable way is to be just a little more active and "burn" those calories. Not only will it tackle your weight problem, but it will make you feel better too. So I like to place the emphasis on weight control through exercise rather than through dieting.

Q: *Why is exercise more effective than dieting for weight control?*
A: Because activity is the most natural way of controlling body weight. Activity—using your body the way it was meant to be used—is the key to weight control. Fat accumulates not so much because of overeating, but because of underdoing.

You probably know someone who claims to "eat like a bird" but gains weight anyway. And someone else who "eats like a horse" but never puts on an extra ounce. There's a tendency to disbelieve both stories, because until very recently in our society, the accepted "cause" of overweight has always been "eating too much."

Chances are, however, that both these people are telling the truth about how much they eat. We now know that many people who are too fat eat no more than the "lucky" ones who have no problem with their weight, and that most people—fat and thin— eat somewhere between 2,500 and 3,000 calories worth of food a day. So, it's beginning to look as though the reason one person gains weight while the other one doesn't has less to do with relative amounts of food consumed than was previously suspected.

Somehow, it doesn't make much sense to assume that soft,

round people are just naturally attracted to sedentary occupations, while lean, wiry people like to be active. It is more logical
to conclude that when people sit around a lot, they get fat, and
people who are active, stay lean.

Q: *Have there been studies done on the benefits of exercise vs.
dieting?*
A: Yes, several. A particularly interesting one was made of an
industrial population in Calcutta. At one end of the scale were the
sedentary workers—office personnel, merchants, etc.—who sat
during their working hours. Next came the mechanics, drivers,
weavers, and others whose work called for an average amount of
activity. Finally, there were the ashmen, coalmen, and
blacksmiths—extremely active people who were forced to carry
their body weight for 8 to 9 hours a day.

The results of the study were fascinating. The sedentary merchants and clerks ate about the same as the moderately active
people, but weighed considerably more. While the very active
blacksmiths, coalmen, and others ate as much as the sedentary
workers, they weighed significantly less.

Dr. Jean Mayer, the world-famous nutritionist, also concluded
that inactivity is indeed the primary cause of obesity. His study of
overweight high school girls indicated they ate no more and some
ate less than their normal-weight classmates. But they exercised
far less and went in for "sitting" activities. In fact, they spent 4
times as many hours watching TV as the others. Similar studies
done with boys revealed the same pattern.

Q: *Is it true that stepping up your physical activity is an ineffective
way to fight excess poundage, and that the only real way to lose
weight is to diet?*
A: I'm not sure why this pro-diet, anti-activity bias should exist.
But it does. I only wish I had a dollar for every magazine and
newspaper article, every pamphlet and book, stating the rationale
behind this kind of thinking. Usually, it's presented something
like this: "In order to burn off one pound of fat—3,500
calories—you'd have to walk 35 miles, or split wood for 7 hours,
or play volleyball for 11 hours."

Strictly speaking, the equations are correct. But it is just as misleading to say that in order to lose 10 pounds by limiting your food intake you have to fast for 14 days.

In other words, the pro-diet argument ignores the cumulative effect of physical activity—which is the key to the entire national obesity dilemma! While it may indeed take 6 hours of handball to burn off one pound of fat, you certainly don't need to play six consecutive hours of the game in order to do so. You could, instead, play an hour a day for six days. Or a half hour a day for 12 days, or a half hour every other day for 24 days. At that rate you'd burn off 25 to 30 pounds in a year.

Q: *Is there any truth to the argument that physical activity does not use a lot of calories?*
A: If you're out of caloric balance by 10 calories a day, that means you will gain about a pound a year. So if you would be out of caloric balance by 100 calories a day, you would gain an extra 10 pounds a year. It's just that simple. Most of the time, to get yourself in caloric balance does not require a tremendous amount of physical activity. Many times a 30 minute walk a day is all you need to get yourself into caloric balance and to start losing weight. You can look at it another way. The World Health Organization of the United Nations and the United States National Research Council say that a "sedentary man" requires approximately 2,400 calories a day to maintain his weight, while an active man needs about 4,500 calories. Laborers, soldiers, and athletes may have to consume 6,000 calories or more a day in order to keep from running away to nothing.

I should also point out that the National Research Council publication can be taken one step further. Back in the 1930's the Research Council indicated that the average sedentary man needed 3,000 calories to maintain his body weight and the average woman around 2,400 calories. Today, in the 1970's, the average male needs 2,400 calories to maintain his body weight and the average female around 2,000 to 1,800. Somewhere along the line we've cut 600 calories out of our life. We burn 600 fewer calories. Lack of activity is the culprit.

It's obvious that activity does make a difference. If intense physical activity results in a need in one person for almost twice as many calories as a less active person, then activity is certainly a major factor in determining whether weight will be gained, maintained, or lost.

Activities burn calories and calories do count, although not necessarily in the same way as many people think they do. If you're concerned about weight, then the number of calories you burn off is more important than the number you take in.

Q: *But won't exercise increase my hunger?*
A: It all depends. If you're a young and vigorous athlete and you step up your activity, you'll probably find your hunger increasing. On the other hand, if you're sedentary, you'll find that more physical activity will decrease your hunger.

Studies done by Dr. Jean Mayer and several other nutritionists have demonstrated that phenomenon. In fact, an increase in activity decreases hunger for sedentary people. Remember the Calcutta study and Dr. Mayer's work with high school girls on the previous pages? I think these studies illustrate the point. But you may also be interested in Mayer's work done with rats. Here he studied the food intake of these animals and how it varied with exercise. To do the experiment, the researchers divided the rats into several groups. The groups ran on a treadmill for 1, 2, 3, and up to 10 hours daily. The doctors measured food intake and noted weight changes in the exercised rats. They then compared the active animals with those left unexercised in their cages.

Surprisingly, the rats that ran 1 to 2 hours daily did not eat more than the inactive rats. In fact, they ate somewhat less. By comparison, the sedentary animals gained more weight. The animals who exercised more than 2 hours a day ate more food, but their weight stabilized at a lower level than that of the restricted rats.

Q: *Is the reason for decreased hunger physical or mental?*
A: It's probably both. Increased activity probably depresses the hunger responses. On the other hand, if you're more active there's less likelihood of being bored. So you probably won't grab an extra donut, potato chip, or glass of soda.

Q: *Why does it seem that some people are more hungry than others?*
A: There are really three reasons. There is a physiological drive,

a psychological drive, and a cultural dependency for more food. It all relates to weight control.

The physiological drive focuses on a center in the brain called the appestat. If you had lived in this country 2,000 years ago, your life would have been quite different. Life would have been physical. You also would have had a little center in the brain called the appestat that regulated the number of calories you needed to feel comfortable. Some people in those days had a low-set appestat and some had a high-set appestat. Regardless, they had an appestat which dictated the amount of food they needed.

The person with a high-set appestat was the one who was always "stalking the wild asparagus" and actively pursuing food. As a result, he carried a little extra tissue on his body. This tissue was muscular because he was so active. The low-set appestat guy could take or leave food. He didn't really care and so he was a lot leaner.

At that period of time there was much famine. And the famine did not last just a week or two. It may have lasted months or years. There was no way food could be shipped in from outside the country. Unfortunately, the person who was lean didn't survive; the person who carried a little extra weight would survive even though he was gaunt, emaciated, and drawn. Yet he did survive until another period of plenty.

Now jump to today. We still have appestats. Again, some people's are set low; others rather high. High-set appestat people are constantly looking for food. The doctor tells them to cut out calories and they try to. However, this gnawing desire for food overwhelms them. They start to raid the refrigerator and get a glass of milk and a chocolate eclair to satisfy their appetite. And if they don't have any food in the house, a quick drive (almost never a walk) to the supermarket takes care of it. So, the person with a high appestat setting is at a disadvantage. He or she still quietly harbors the ancient desire—instinct, really—to eat more in order to survive a food crisis, which almost certainly never will come. The appestat—indeed most of the systems and organs of the human body—is centuries behind the times.

So, unless the will is truly Spartan, any diet is doomed to be an exercise in frustration, at least in the long run. When high appe-

stat people diet, they are literally fighting their own instincts for
more food. It's one thing to live with constant hunger when food
is not available, but when it's all around us—sitting there in the
refrigerator, displayed in the stores, staring out in glorious four-
color detail from the pages of magazines, being eaten and gloated
over on TV—well . . . that's an altogether different story.

Q: *How do emotions play a part in overeating and obesity?*
A: I can illustrate the answer with my own personal experiences. When I was about two years of age, I fell and scraped my
knee. I ran into the house crying. Quickly, my mother held me on
her lap and said, "That's ok Charles. Here's a lollipop." Soon
everything was beautiful. A few days later I was outside playing
with my sister when WHAMO, she hit me right on the nose.
Soon I was comforted with a lap, cookie, and love. Still later,
I was supposed to go to the doctor. "I don't want to go to the
doctor's!" My mother told me that if I didn't put up a fuss we'd
go to the ice cream parlor afterwards.

Slowly, I started to equate food with stress. Now that I'm an
adult I'm subjected to pressures, but they are no longer little
scrapes and being hit on the nose. I've got job, domestic and
social pressures. Or I may even be bored (I should be so lucky).
Because of that, I overeat. Since I overeat there's a weight gain.
With the weight gain I become less active and because I become
less active, I have no natural outlet for stress. Consequently, I
tend to eat even more. It's a vicious cycle.

Q: *It seems impossible to eliminate stress from our lives. Won't
dieting help eliminate the weight gained as a result of stress?*
A: No. Dieting produces even more stress.

The doctor tells you to get your weight under control. To do
that you're not supposed to eat many kinds of foods. So you try.
Oh how you try! Soon there's an overwhelming desire for food.
Donuts are an example. You decide: "Today I *earned* this donut
because I worked so hard." You eat one donut. And you think,
"Gosh, I went off my diet so I might as well eat another." After
the two donuts you say, "What the heck. I might as well finish the
whole box." You feel awful. Vaguely guilty. But the next day it
hits you. "Why in the world did I ever eat all those donuts. You

ding-a-ling!'' You start to feel badly about yourself. Your self-esteem is reduced, which in turns produces an even greater amount of stress. Frustrated, you eat more.

Q: *What can I do to avoid the vicious cycle of diet—weight gain—diet—weight gain?*
A: Step up your activity. A good walk or a favorite exercise every day will nullify the weight gain. It also helps to provide a natural outlet for stress. With activity the natural response is no longer bottled up. Here the natural biological response for anxiety—the impulse to use one's body—is directed into constructive channels and stress is relieved. With the reduction in stress and tension comes a reduction in the desire to overeat. (At least for those people who have been conditioned to use food as a tension relieving device.) What follows is an increased capacity for more activity, which results in the burning of more calories and loss of weight. So the syndrome is reversed.

You'll also find that the person who exercises has fewer hang-ups. He starts to feel good about his body, he feels like he's able to discipline himself, his self-esteem increases, and so he's able to get his weight under control. It's a neat thing to see happen.

Q: *Can friends influence a person's eating habits?*
A: Yes. To illustrate this let me ask you a question. Have you ever spent a weekend with your spouse or another group of people? It seems as though the entire weekend is centered on where you're going to eat, what you're going to eat, and how much you ate. Other examples are: Have you ever invited somebody over to watch the NFL game of the week and then offered them only a drink of water? You just don't do that. How many times have you been to a church meeting which only focused on the greeting and meeting of your committee members? I'm sure you also did some eating. You were experiencing the ''greet, meet, and eat syndrome.'' When you were at the church meeting you raved over someone's luscious desserts and drooled over the delightful pastries that your next-door neighbor made.

Food is a focal point in our society. We're continually trying to con our kids into eating more than they need or want and usually they do it to avoid negative consequences: "If you don't finish your dinner, dear, there'll be no TV tonight." Or to get what they want: "If you finish your soup, I'll take you to the park after lunch." Or to win adult love and approval: "Such a good girl; you ate all your mashed potatoes."

You can even go back earlier than that. Very often a child's first exposure to "forced feeding" occurs during the first few months of life. Many times a baby cries because it wants cuddling, companionship, a change of diapers, or a change of scene. But the new mother has a tendency to interpret any kind of crying as a demand for food, and if she is "modern" she will immediately attempt to gratify the child with breast or bottle. Thus, very early in life, the child learns to associate gratification of all emotional and physical needs with eating. Placating the baby with food, when it is attention or stimulation it wants, may also discourage the child's budding interest in actively exploring the outside world. Because with eating there is encouragement for sedentary, less active activities.

Q: *How can I avoid the cultural tendency to overeat?*
A: You know that you're going to be bombarded with cultural cues to overeat. And if you try to restrict your food by diet, you know that physiologically you have road blocks and psychologically you have hang-ups. Even if you were able to get through these road blocks and hang ups you have to recognize an important fact. You are a social being. You like to associate with people. So if you try your best to stay on the diet, you will find that eventually cultural pressures force you to succumb. If you exercise, you can compensate for it.

Q: *Will exercise make me feel less guilty when I do overeat?*
A: Yes. I know a woman in one of my wife's fitness classes who said that this past year was the first Thanksgiving and Christmas she ate a full meal during those holidays without feeling guilty. The guilt was gone because she knew she could go out and burn it off with a several-mile walk. She'd caught the right idea. She had broken the chain of feeling guilty. And that's one of the most crucial things in weight control. I don't care if you don't learn anything else from this chapter but I do want you to understand

that you should have no more guilt feelings about food. You should do something about it and exercise. And don't blame anyone or anything else. It is your responsibility.

Q: *Which activities are best for controlling my body weight?*
A: I like to call them the Big Four. Walking, bicycling, swimming, and jogging are perhaps the best. But you can try rope skipping, tennis, handball, racquet ball, and dancing—anything that burns a lot of calories and does not take a lot of time and equipment. The important thing is that the activity be efficient, effective, entertaining, and emotionally sound.

Q: *Which method is faster for losing weight, exercise or dieting?*
A: Dieting *is* faster than exercise. But remember, jogging and exercise are for more effective because once the weight is off, it's off for good. And physical activity is good for you. Not all diets could make that claim.

Q: *Which exercises are best for burning calories other than walking, bicycling, swimming, and jogging?*
A: There are many good activities. I think the following chart summarizes them best.

Calories Used Per Hour In Different Activities

ACTIVITIES	Weights (in pounds)		
	110	150	200
Badminton			
a. Singles recreational	275	350	405
b. Doubles recreational	235	300	350
c. Competitive (vigorous) singles	480	610	710
d. Competitive doubles	360	460	535
Basketball			
a. Game (full court, continuous)	585	750	870
b. Nongame, ½ court, etc.	435	555	645

Calories Used Per Hour In Different Activities (Continued)

ACTIVITIES	Weights (in pounds)		
	110	150	200
Bicycling			
a. 5½ mph	190	245	280
b. 10 mph	325	415	475
c. 13 mph	515	655	760
Bowling	150	190	220
Dancing			
a. Fox trot	195	250	295
b. Rock	195	250	295
c. Square & western	330	420	480
Fencing			
a. Recreational	235	300	350
b. Competitive (vigorous)	480	610	710
Football			
a. Playground (touch)	470	600	695
Golf			
a. Twosome 9 holes in 1½ hours etc. (carrying clubs)	295	380	440
b. Twosome 9 holes in 1½ hours (pull clubs)	260	335	385
c. Foursome 9 holes in 2 hours (carry clubs)	210	270	310
d. Foursome 9 holes in 2 hours (pull clubs)	195	250	295
e. Cart	175	220	260
Handball			
a. 2 people	610	775	905
b. 4 people	400	510	595
Horseshoes	180	230	270
Judo & Karate	620	790	920
Pool	120	155	180
Racquetball			
a. 2 people	610	775	905
b. 4 people	400	510	595

Calories Used Per Hour In Different Activities (Continued)

ACTIVITIES	Weights (in pounds)		
	110	150	200
Rope skipping			
a. 50–60 skips left foot only (per min.)	400	510	595
b. 90–100 skips left foot only (per min.)	515	655	760
Run in place			
a. 50–60 steps per min. (left foot only)	400	510	595
b. 90–100 steps per min. (left foot only)	515	655	760
Running			
a. 5.5 mph	515	655	760
b. 7.2 mph	550	700	810
c. 8 mph	625	800	930
Skating (leisure)			
a. Ice	275	350	405
b. Roller	275	350	405
Skiing			
a. Downhill (continuous riding and lifts not included)	465	595	690
b. Cross country—5 mph	550	700	800
c. Cross country—9 mph	785	1000	1160
Squash			
a. 2 people	610	775	905
b. 4 people	400	510	595
Stationary bicycle: resistance sufficient to get pulse rate to 130			
a. 10 mph	330	420	490
b. 15 mph	515	655	760
c. 20 mph	700	885	1030

Calories Used Per Hour In Different Activities (Continued)

	Weights (in pounds)		
ACTIVITIES	110	150	200
Swimming (crawl)			
a. 30 yards per minute	330	420	480
b. 40 yards per minute	470	600	695
Table tennis			
a. Recreational	235	300	350
b. Vigorous	355	450	525
Tennis (singles)			
a. Recreational	335	425	495
b. Competitive	470	600	695
Tennis (doubles)			
a. Recreational	235	300	350
b. Competitive	335	425	495
Volleyball			
a. Recreational	275	350	405
b. Competitive	470	600	695
Walking			
a. 2½ mph	200	255	300
b. 4 mph	270	345	405
Yoga	180	230	270

Q: *What are some of the other reasons why exercise is better than dieting?*
A: Exercise is good preventive medicine. Not only does the exerciser feel better than the dieter who is starving, but he also looks better. Many dieters come through their ordeal looking loose and flabby. Flab is definitely not beautiful. When a person exercises, his muscles become firmer. And more fat is lost through exercise than through dieting, which is what this whole discussion was about from the beginning—reducing percent of body fat or obesity.

Speaking of flab or obesity, a study conducted by Dr. Larry Golding, of the University of Nevada at Las Vegas, and Bill Zuti, Assistant Professor of Physical Education at the University of Kansas, yielded some interesting results.

In the study, 25 women volunteers between the ages of 25 and 40, and all 20 to 40 pounds overweight, were separated into three groups. The first group reduced their caloric intake by 500 calories a day and made no changes in their level of physical activity. The second group cut their caloric intake by 250 calories daily and increased physical activity so that they burned 250 extra calories a day. The third group ate as usual but stepped up their activity level to where they burned 500 extra calories daily.

By the end of 16 weeks, the women in all three groups had lost weight. But, upon measuring differences in body composition, it was found that the women in the exercise-only group and in the combination exercise-diet group had lost significantly *more* fat and *less* muscle tissue than the women in the diet-only group.

The implications are clear: when people exercise, or use diet and exercise in combination, their muscles will be firmer, their bodies less flabby—better looking—than if diet were the sole means of losing weight.

Golding and Zuti concluded that activity has a more desirable effect on body composition and physical fitness than dieting—which sums up what I've been saying.

A strong case can also be made for the fact that when you exercise you build up your muscle mass. Because there is an increase in muscle there is more functional tissue on the body. Consequently, you will probably end up burning more calories simply because you have more muscle tissue than fat tissue. It's a complicated mechanism but it certainly is an added advantage. It means that you'll burn more calories in everything you do. All because you have more muscle tissue. It may not mean much each day, but over the years it becomes significant.

Q: *What happens when a person really doesn't like to exercise and yet he needs to exercise to lose weight?*
A: I've known very few people who didn't like to exercise at all. Unfortunately, most people think in terms of participating in an activity they don't like—the old physical training approach to fitness. The point is, if they pick something they enjoy, they'll stay with it. If gardening is their thing, then they should garden. It will be great for weight control if they do it on a regular basis. If bicycling is their thing, then they should cycle. It's also great for

weight control. The point is to do something you like. You don't read books you dislike, you don't watch TV programs you dislike, so why should you pick an exercise program you detest?

Of course I will accept the premise that there is a person who hates exercising. So I give them a choice. You can diet to lose weight but you have to put up with it 24 hours a day. I'm sure you'll hate it. Or you can exercise, and you only have to put up with that for a half hour. The choice is yours.

CHAPTER

4

You're As Young As Your Arteries

Q: *What is a heart attack?*
A: A heart attack is really a condition of the arteries—the coronary arteries—that supply the heart muscle with blood. A heart attack occurs when one of these arteries is blocked, causing the muscle in that particular area of the heart to die. Some people have the mistaken impression that the heart receives its blood supply from the blood that it pumps constantly. The heart, just like any other muscle, receives its blood supply through the arteries. Remember, it does not receive its blood from that which flows through it.

In the anatomy of the heart is an extensive network of arteries which grow out of two main trunks, the right and left coronary arteries. These main coronary arteries branch in much the same way as a tree. Every branch is smaller than the main trunk, and each one soon subdivides into smaller branches. Those in turn divide into still smaller ones. They divide into such small compartments so that every part of the heart, no matter how small, is supplied with blood and oxygen through its system of coronary arteries. As long as those arteries are allowed to bring blood to the various parts of the heart muscle, the heart can do its job effectively.

Q: *What does the medical term "arteriosclerosis" mean?*
A: For some reason there has been a communication gap between doctors and lay people on heart disease. Below are definitions of a few of the medical terms which confuse people most.

ARTERIOSCLEROSIS—a general term for various types of arterial illness. The phrase "hardening of the arteries" is often used synonymously with arteriosclerosis. It is associated with a gradually increasing brittleness of arteries.

ATHEROSCLEROSIS—a slowly developing disease process of the coronary arteries. In atherosclerosis, the passageways through the arteries become roughened and narrowed by fatty deposits that harden into patches along the inner lining of the artery. Consequently, the channel is gradually narrowed, and there is less room for blood to flow through.

CORONARY OCCLUSION—a severe narrowing of some coronary artery to the point that blood can no longer pass through.

CORONARY THROMBOSIS—a coronary occlusion caused by the formation of a blood clot (thrombus) which completely blocks the flow of blood to some part of the heart muscle.

MYOCARDIAL INFARCT—the condition when the blood supply to a portion of the muscle is blocked, causing the muscle directly around the blocked artery to die.

ANGINA PECTORIS—commonly called "angina," an uncomfortable sensation of pressure, tightness, or pain in the center of the chest. The discomfort often spreads to the left shoulder, arm, or hand, where it may be felt as a sensation of numbness. This feeling is a sign that the heart is not getting enough oxygen through its blood supply. Angina may occur in people who have recovered from a heart attack, in people who are going to have a heart attack, and in some people who will never have a heart attack.

COLLATERAL CIRCULATION—the opening of new or dormant arteries which seem to offset the effects of atherosclerosis. It is fortunate that the coronary system is able to grow and repair itself. When some of the coronary arteries become narrowed by gradual development of atherosclerosis, nearby arteries get wider and even open up tiny new or dormant branches to bring blood to the area of the muscle that needs it. Collateral circulation explains why many people who have narrowed arteries do not have a heart attack and also accounts for some of the excellent recoveries from heart attacks.

LOAFER'S HEART—a term coined by Dr. Wilhelm Raab to describe the weakening of the heart muscle as a result of a lack of exercise. This degenerating, inadequate loafer's heart is cause for concern.

Q: *What are the main types of heart attacks?*

A: There are two primary types, but the most common is a blood clot (thrombosis) forming in a blood vessel and blocking, partially or completely, passage of the blood. Sometimes this clot (an embolus) may break off from the wall and lodge in a vital area of the body. Death or serious impairment can result. If a blood clot blocks an artery in the heart, brain, or kidney; a coronary thrombosis, stroke, or uremia can result. Atherosclerosis is the most common cause of this circulatory disorder and occurs when yellowish and whitish spots accumulate on the walls of the arteries. Those small spots protrude into the inner surfaces of the vessels themselves.

At the outset of this disease, these atheromas are very small and may appear to be little more than marks on the inner lining of the vessels. In a period of years, however, the atheromas enlarge substantially until there is little room for the blood to flow through. These atheromas may occur in the arteries of any part of the body.

When the atherosclerosis occurs in the coronary arteries and develops into later stages, a coronary thrombosis with myocardial infarction (heart attack) occurs. The heart has an extensive network of arteries that supply it with blood. The left and right coronary arteries, which arise from the aorta and then develop into an amazing capillary network, literally bathe every fiber of the heart with blood and, therefore, provide oxygen for the chemical process of muscle contraction.

In coronary thrombosis with myocardial infarction, the clot blocks the blood supply to one part of the heart muscle. When the supply is blocked, pain may or may not be present. Sometimes the chest pain is very severe and may extend to the neck, arms, or shoulders. In other individuals, however, the pain is virtually nonexistent. But there may be an unexplained weakness, sweating, or breathlessness.

At the point of blockage the "heart attack" has occurred. A pain or ache may persist sometime after the initial blockage, for the fibers of the heart not receiving the oxygenated blood stop contracting; then, the fibers become swollen and die. At this point, the pain subsides. The part of the heart that does not receive oxygen suffers an actual injury, and therefore requires time to heal. The rest of the heart (unless the attack is so severe that the heart muscle is damaged and causes death) continues to struggle along in a limited capacity.

Once the attack occurs, the heart begins to repair itself. First, leukocytes are sent to the damaged area to clear away the muscle fibers that are no longer able to contract. This removal must occur before the tissue can heal and form a scar—a process that takes about a week. For the tissue to heal, nearby arteries must open up new branches to deliver blood to the area of the heart that needs it. These new vessels that supply blood to the area around the injury produce what is called collateral circulation. If the healing is normal and continuous, the person who suffered a moderate to fairly severe attack may leave the hospital after two or three weeks. If complications develop, the healing process usually takes longer.

The second general type of degenerative cardiovascular disease is a breaking of a blood vessel. It results in a loss of blood to a vital area of the cardiovascular system and is caused by a sudden increase in blood pressure often brought about by excitement or unusual exertion.

The brittleness of the vessels is called arteriosclerosis, or "hardening of the arteries." It is actually the artery walls that become thick and hard and lose their elasticity. The lack of elasticity is a common cause of high blood pressure. Moreover, the diseases mentioned earlier—heart attack, angina, stroke, loss of kidney efficiency—may all be a result of hardening of the arteries. The most common cause of strokes or apoplexy is arteriosclerosis.

Q: *Is a stroke the same as a heart attack?*
A: No. A heart attack concerns the heart muscle. A stroke re-

fers to the blood vessels in the brain being broken or blocked by a clot. In a stroke, a part of the brain is affected. The brain does not receive sufficient oxygen and blood, causing weakness, numbness, or loss of sensation or movement in some part of the body. The extent to which the above occurs depends upon the area and side of the brain and the size of the vessel that is blocked or broken.

Along these same lines, reduction of blood supply to the kidneys through a narrowing of the vessels that supply these organs will reduce the efficiency of the kidneys as a waste remover. If the damage is severe enough from the blocked arteries, poisons may pile up in the bloodstream and produce uremia. So, many times you will see conditions listed as degenerative renal disease, kidney failure, and the like.

Q: *What causes heart attacks? Is it diet, or smoking?*
A: I wish it were that simple. Everyone recognizes that the major killer in this country is heart disease. It is the major factor in reducing Americans' longevity and quality of life. Many people are stricken at the prime of life, between 35 and 55 years of age. All too often the disease strikes with such severity that it reduces productivity and curtails many activities. Modern science is making long strides in treatment of those afflicted with coronary disease. But if the disease is to be halted, emphasis must be placed on prevention.

To prevent or slow down the progress of the disease, scientists have tried to find out what causes it. To date, no one factor has been identified. Doctors say several factors put a person at a greater risk of having an attack. They are called coronary risk factors. Doctors also feel that when two or more of these factors occur in combination, there is an even greater chance of a heart attack occurring.

Q: *What are these coronary risk factors?*
A: The list seems endless. Some of them you have heard of before and a few of these you probably haven't. So here goes: 1. sex; 2. race; 3. ethnic background; 4. body build; 5. family history; 6. economic status; 7. social class; 8. emotional tension; 9. occupation; 10. catacholamines; 11. personality type; 12. uric

acid; 13. caloric intake; 14. total fat intake; 15. cholesterol intake; 16. saturated fat intake; 17. fatty acid content in diet; 18. sugar consumption; 19. salt; 20. softness of water; 21. deficiency of vitamins or minerals; 22. blood cholesterol levels; 23. blood triglyceride levels; 24. free fatty acids; 25. beta lipoproteins; 26. hypertension; 27. ECG abnormalities; 28. diabetes; 29. obesity; 30. smoking; 31. age; and 32. physical inactivity.

Even though there is some overlapping, you might try to arrange these 32 risk factors as follows: The first 7 factors might be listed as *heredity*. I like to call this risk factor #1. Factors 6 to 12 might be listed as *stress and personality type* or risk factor #2. Factors 13 through 21 would be noted as *diet or nutrition* (risk factor #3). Factors 22 to 25 would be listed as *lipid (fat) abnormalities* (risk factor #4). The remaining factors would then be listed as #5 *hypertension*, #6 *ECG abnormalities*, #7 *diabetes*, #8 *obesity*, #9 *smoking*, #10 *age*, and #11 *physical inactivity*.

Not surprisingly, these 11 factors identify very closely with the well-documented Framingham Study on cardiovascular disease and the list published by the American Heart Association. So, while the list is still complicated, it is not as mind-boggling as first indicated.

Q: *Why is heredity such an important factor in the development and occurrence of heart disease?*
A: Since heredity has an effect on every part of a person's body chemistry, it is logical that one may be predisposed to coronary heart disease. For example, Chuck Hughes, the professional football player of the Detroit Lions died of a massive coronary a few years ago during a Sunday afternoon game. Quite frankly, he was clobbered in terms of heredity. At 28 years of age he had the circulatory system of an old man.

Some people, of course, tried to use the Hughes case as an example that exercise does not work in preventing heart attacks. But the detractors failed to point out that when we talk about risk factors we are speaking about statistical probability: the odds you have of having a fatal or crippling heart attack.

Some people may escape a heart attack even though they do everything wrong in terms of keeping their risks low. They are lucky. Their parents gave them good genes for survival. But they are exceptions.

On the other hand, you can have people who try to do everything right and still die of a coronary. For example, I know of a man who did just that. He wanted to prevent a heart attack. He didn't smoke, he was extremely careful in his selection of foods, didn't drink, took vitamins and minerals, walked at least an hour a day, and kept his blood pressure under control. Yet he died at the age of 71 with a massive coronary. Many people said, "See I told you all those health habits didn't work. Old _____ died of a heart attack even though he practiced all those good things you preached." What the critics failed to realize was that no one in his family—mother, father, sisters, or brothers had lived beyond the age of 57. In other words, he was a victim of his heredity, and the fact that he made it to 71 is a tribute to his good health habits.

As far as I was concerned, my friend came closer to his potential for longevity than most of the pessimistic critics. Furthermore, he was an extremely alert, vibrant, and creative person right up to his death. The bottom line on heredity is that a person who has a family history of this disease should be extra careful about his health life style. Sound health and fitness practices may contribute to warding off or slowing the progress of heart disease. Or next time around pick parents who lived to be 120!

In regard to what you start with at birth, you should also understand that men are much more likely than women to have a heart attack. It is not clear why this is so. It may be that the female hormone, estrogen, provides women a measure of protection. Interestingly, after menopause, the mortality rate of women increases dramatically and starts to approach that of men.

It is also important to note that black Americans are twice as likely as whites to have high blood pressure. And high blood pressure is one factor which contributes to heart attacks and strokes. Blacks suffer more strokes at an earlier age and with more severity. Again, the reason for this is not clear; but heredity, life style, diet, and stress may contribute.

Q: *Why are stress and personality such important coronary risk factors?*
A: Stress has been associated with heart disease for several years. Back in the 1930's Dr. Hans Selye, the world-famous endocrinologist, noted that psychological stress of long duration

produces a syndrome that can cause excessive hypertension, colitis, gastric ulcers, chronic diarrhea, heart disease, and death.

Stress is a feature of many occupations. It is connected with long hours, pressure to meet deadlines, and demanding job and domestic obligations. Stress is also common among those with a driving personality. The latter is the individual who is aggressive, conscious of deadlines, and never relaxes. You may have heard of this type described as Type A Personality. He is the person who squeezes 25 hours into a 24-hour day. He has an intense desire for recognition and a profound sense of obligation. He is unable to relax during his leisure hours because he has a feeling of guilt that he should be doing something.

Dr. James Lynch of Johns Hopkins Medical School, has stated that loneliness, a lack of sound relationships, and high social mobility are also related to coronary heart disease. Lynch's factors, I think, are intimately tied into the stress and personality risk factor. Many times the lonely person who does not develop sound, close relationships is hostile, angry, and frustrated. It is also possible that a person may be such a workaholic that he doesn't take time to develop sound relationships.

Stress, whether it is the result of fear, anxiety, frustration, fatigue, or hostility, can produce an increase in heart rate, blood pressure, and blood cholesterol. Those increases are attributed to the release of adrenalin. The central nervous system is also affected. If the stress and resulting release of adrenalin and the stimulation of the nervous system continues repeatedly over extended periods, the heart muscle and blood vessels are adversely affected.

Q: *Should stress be entirely avoided?*
A: Not really. Dr. Hans Selye has said that "Stress is the spice of life. Without it you would be a vegetable—or dead." What you must do is learn to control it. You must learn to use stress as a positive force for personal achievement and happiness.

Q: *Does exercise play a role in reducing stress as a risk factor?*
A: Yes. Dr. Selye notes that "a voluntary change of activity is as good or even better than rest. . . . For example, when either fatigue or forced interruption prevents us from finishing a mathe-

matical problem, it is better to go for a swim than simply sit around. Substituting demands on our musculature for those previously made on the intellect not only gives our brain a rest but helps us avoid worrying about the frustrating interruption. Stress on one system helps to relax another." I say amen to that!

Q: *What about risk factor #3—Diet? How does diet affect my chances of having a heart attack?*
A: This is a tough one. There is so much controversy in this area I sometimes would like to avoid it. Doctors disagree, nutritionists disagree, food faddists disagree, and journalists disagree. I'll try to summarize very briefly what the research is at the present time. I have broken it down into four categories.

Fat
a.   Most researchers feel that Americans should cut back on their saturated fat intake. They also feel that cholesterol intake should be lowered. Cholesterol and saturated fat are not synonymous. Cholesterol is a fat-like solid alcohol that is almost insoluble in water. It is found in such things as egg yolks, butter, cream, and the fat of meat. In other words—animals and animal products. Saturated fat, on the other hand, is found in plants and animals. People who eat high amounts of saturated fats and cholesterol tend to have higher blood cholesterol levels. Generally, those people who have higher cholesterol levels are more prone to heart attacks.
b.   Americans' total fat intake should be reduced substantially. Currently it's around 40 to 45% of the diet. It should not exceed 30 to 35% (the lower, the better), with one third coming from saturated fats; one third from unsaturated fats (chicken, turkey, nuts); and one third from polyunsaturated fats (most oils, fish). Again, this ties in very closely with point a) above. Diets high in saturated fat may raise cholesterol levels. Diets high in unsaturated fats tend to stabilize cholesterol levels and diets high in polyunsaturated fats tend to reduce cholesterol levels.
c.   Polyunsaturated fats in our diet should be increased. It is

felt that the American diet should have a substantial increase in polyunsaturated fat since this seems to reduce cholesterol levels. The most logical way of increasing your polyunsaturated fat intake is to make sure you cook with safflower or corn oils, use special margarines that are made of vegetable oil (not coconut and not hydrogenated), and also eat large amounts of fish (not shellfish).

Sugar
a. Although it is still a minority opinion in medical circles, more and more researchers are criticizing the large amounts of sugar eaten by modern-day Americans. Twenty percent of your diet contains plain old table sugar or sucrose. Ten percent or less would be better for you. The average American eats about 100 pounds of sugar a year. Or two pounds a week. Quite a change from the 1600's and 1700's when only 2 to 4 pounds were eaten in one year's time. Some physicians feel that a high sugar intake increases triglyceride levels, cholesterol levels, and blood glucose levels. They also feel that people who have a carbohydrate metabolism problem are more prone to develop diabetes if they eat large amounts of sugar. Diabetes, of course, is a risk factor in heart disease. The consensus is that our sugar consumption should probably be reduced to half.
b. Sugar is also dangerous because it significantly increases the total number of calories that a person eats and again this has been implicated in heart disease.

Total Calories
As mentioned above, the total number of calories a person eats seems to increase a person's chance of a heart attack. Though the reasons are not clear, it is probably related to fat deposits on the body.

Salt
I think that every book that has been written on high blood pressure and heart disease has suggested that people cut back on their intake of salt. High blood pressure drops dramatically with a low salt (sodium) diet. Doctors feel that a reduction in salt will reduce a person's

chances of hypertension and a relationship to heart attacks.

You should understand that certain foods have a tremendous amount of salt in them. Foods such as pickles, olives, luncheon meats, crackers, and canned fruits and vegetables.

All this is not the final word on nutrition. But it is important for you to realize that if you reduce your total number of calories, watch your sugar and saturated fat intake, increase your polyunsaturate intake and cut down on your salt intake you're doing a good job in reducing the diet risk factor.

Q: *How can exercise help improve my diet?*
A: Usually people who start exercising also change their eating habits. Most doctors say it is because they are more health conscious. I'm not sure that's the answer. I think there's more to it than that. People who exercise have a better feeling about themselves. They feel good about exercising. Their self-esteem improves. They are improving physically with exercise. Now they want to improve in many other ways. And diet is one of them.

Q: *What is the difference between risk factor #3—Diet—and risk factor #4—Lipid Abnormalities?*
A: Lipid abnormalities refer to blood fat levels that are higher than normal. The blood carries different types of nutrients including fats and sugars. These nutrients must be kept in proper proportions. For some reason, fats, or lipids as they are called, may exceed recommended limits. Doctors often test the blood for such lipid abnormalities. They do this because people who have high levels of triglycerides and cholesterol seem to be predisposed to heart attacks, much more so than people who have lower levels of these fats. In fact, a person with a cholesterol reading of 260mg% is more than twice as likely to suffer a heart attack than a person with a normal reading of 150-250mg%. Personally, I like to see readings of 180mg% or lower.

A great controversy rages at the present time in the medical community regarding lipid abnormalities. Some say it is caused by heredity, others by diet, some say lack of exercise, others smoking, and still others blame emotional stress. In reality, it's probably a combination of all five. With some people heredity may predispose them to produce excessive amounts of blood fats, particularly cholesterol. Or one's body may have difficulty utilizing it properly. My advice: Don't smoke, plan your rest and break periods satisfactorily, exercise vigorously and regularly, and eat the right kinds of foods. And don't get upset about your ancestry. You can't do anything about that!

Q: *How does exercise help reduce blood fats?*
A: Perhaps no other area has been subjected to more controversy than the effect of exercise on triglyceride and cholesterol levels. Until very recently, the consensus was that endurance-type training and conditioning programs *may* play a role in stabilizing cholesterol levels and possibly reducing these levels if accompanied by weight loss. But there was much confusion about whether exercise reduced cholesterol levels. Doctors couldn't agree. With triglycerides it was the same. Doctors couldn't agree on cholesterol and triglyceride. There was a tremendous amount of controversy. Sometimes cholesterol and triglyceride levels changed with exercise, sometimes they didn't.

Recently, however, things have changed. Doctors now know that it's not how much cholesterol that's important but how the cholesterol is carried. The jigsaw puzzle is finally starting to fall into place.

In the bloodstream, cholesterol is contained within several different types of large conglomerates of proteins and fatty substances. And cholesterol only misbehaves when it falls in with the wrong crowd.

A cholesterol molecule that is bound up with a high-density lipoprotein (HDL) is probably on its way back to the liver to be excreted back into the intestinal tract and eliminated from the body. Cholesterol carried by a low-density lipoprotein (LDL), on the other hand, is meant to be taken up by the body cells as a building block for hormones and cell membranes. And, as necessary as this type of lipoprotein is, when there's too much of it in the blood, chances are that some of it will end up contributing to the buildup of atherosclerotic plaques on the inside of the arteries.

Dr. William P. Castelli, laboratory director of the famous

Framingham Heart Study group in Massachusetts, thinks that HDL cholesterol can actually interfere with the process of atherosclerosis. The HDL's may pick up the extra cholesterol in the blood and take it back to the liver for removal from the body. A "garbage collector." He points out that persons with low levels of HDL cholesterol have 8 times the rate of heart disease as those with higher levels. He thinks that it is best to have a high amount of HDL's and a low level of LDL's. Fewer LDL's mean less cholesterol is carried and more HDL's mean more cholesterol is carried for removal from the body. He recommends that physicians testing cholesterols use a slightly more complicated test in which the high-density lipoproteins are separated from the low-density lipoproteins in order to obtain separate measurements for HDL and LDL cholesterols.

Dr. Peter Wood and his associates at Stanford University in Palo Alto, California have been keeping records for 8 years on HDL's and LDL's. Their research shows that long-distance runners have a much lower frequency of heart disease than the average American. They also have very high levels of HDL and lower levels of LDL. This ratio is most favorable, for it increases protection against heart attacks.

Q: *What kinds of exercise help reduce blood fats?*
A: It seems as though all types of regular, vigorous exercise are helpful. Dr. Castelli mentioned that "you do not have to run marathons to get a protective effect. When a group of medical students in New Orleans participated in an exercise program which combined jogging, bicycling, and calisthenics for 30 to 40 minutes 4 times a week, their HDL levels began to climb after only 7 to 10 weeks."

Q: *How is high blood pressure related to heart attack?*
A: High blood pressure is closely associated with emotional stress. When the heart contracts, blood is forced out into the arteries, which expand in response to this contraction. The force or pressure of the blood vessels on the blood as it circulates throughout the body can be measured. Those numbers (like 120 over 80) that the nurse writes down really *do* mean something. In a person who has normal blood pressure the systolic (the upper

reading) pressure will have a reading of 120 to 140 millimeters of mercury and the diastolic (the lower reading) blood pressure will measure from 70 to 90 millimeters of mercury. (These figures refer to the height in millimeters to which the pressure of blood can lift a column of mercury.) In cases of hypertension, however, the blood pressure is permanently above this range. Systolic blood pressure will be over 150 and diastolic will exceed 100.

This kind of chronic high blood pressure is attributed to an increase in peripheral resistance (and/or constricting of the arterioles throughout the body). Because of the abnormal narrowing of the arterioles, greater pressure is required in the arteries to force the blood through. Even though the heart may not beat faster, it does have to work harder and the blood pressure rises. The reason for the increase in peripheral resistance has not been definitely established, although body chemistry, lack of exercise, heredity, emotions, and poor diet play critical roles.

Research has shown that people who have high blood pressure are more than 2½ times as likely to suffer from coronary heart disease than people who have normal blood pressure levels. Even slight increases in blood pressure can increase a person's chance of having a heart attack.

Q: *What does exercise do for high blood pressure?*
A: Exercise seems to keep it under better control. A person who exercises on a regular basis with proper exercise tends to have lower blood pressure—at rest, when exercising, or when under pressure.

My mother-in-law is a good example. A few years ago her blood pressure was 180/110. In fact, the blood pressure was so high one day that the doctor was afraid to let her drive home from the office. She was placed on medication and told to take it easy. So she came home and worried. She felt awful.

Beth, my wife, advised her to start walking. At first she could only walk a few minutes. She would have to stop and rest quite frequently. Gradually she increased her distance over the months and years and today she walks 6+ miles a day, 7 days a week. She even jogs a small part of her walk! Neither sleet, nor rain, nor gloom of night will stop Nathalie from her appointed walk. Her husband calls her walk a "walkie-talkie." Let me tell you this, she walks. The talking is only secondary.

Q: *But you didn't tell me about her blood pressure.*
A: Are you ready for this? She has a blood pressure her doctor would like to have. It's 120/75—without medication. Not bad for a 67-year-old woman.

Q: *What is involved in the 6th risk factor, electrocardiographic abnormalities?*
A: Electrocardiograms are used to demonstrate how the electrical impulse travels over the heart muscle itself. If the heart muscle is normal, the electrical impulse will pass in a normal fashion. However, if there is some damage to the muscle—such as that caused by an insufficient blood supply—the electrical impulse will not travel over the heart properly. This irregularity will show up on the electrocardiogram, or ECG. If the pattern is abnormal, the doctor will say you have electrocardiographic abnormalities. Research studies have shown that people who demonstrate these abnormalities are more prone to develop heart disease than people with normal ECG readings. There is one sidelight here however.

For some unknown reason, some endurance-trained athletes will show abnormal electrocardiograms. This has been called the "Wilt Chamberlain Syndrome." Since Wilt's electrocardiogram is so bizarre, doctors who didn't know his case history would place him in coronary care right away! Physicians have been unable to explain why this phenomenon occurs. They do note, however, that if a person is tested and has an abnormal ECG wave, it is important for the physician to request information about the person's activity patterns and do further testing before making a positive or negative diagnosis. Some physicians feel that the abnormal electrical impulse comes from the heart muscle getting larger in the course of endurance-type training. This is purely speculative.

Q: *Why do some doctors now recommend electrocardiograms when exercising?*
A: It's one thing to check your heart at rest and another to check it when exercising. It's like checking your car when it's idling versus traveling at 55 mph. Problems can show up at higher speeds that would not be revealed when the car is parked. It's the same way with your body. At rest, your heart may be ok. But

when you are exercising, under stress, or eating, your heart may be in trouble. Abnormal tracings may appear. So by giving you an ECG when exercising, your doctor can see how your heart works in "action." Doctors call this ECG when exercising a stress test.

Q: *Can a stress test determine whether I have heart disease or not?*
A: No one can deny that stress electrocardiograms have led to the discovery of untold cases of latent heart disease. It is also true that many perfectly normal people use the "need to get a stress test first" as an excuse not to exercise. Also, it's not usually the guy who takes up jogging and gradually conditions his body out of an undetected cardiac abnormality that ends up a coronary statistic. The fellow who might benefit from a stress test is the one who clings to his sedentary ways except when a snow blizzard forces him to shovel out from under.

One of the main complaints about the stress electrocardiogram is its inaccuracy. For instance, of documented coronary disease patients given a stress test, 54% had false negatives. That is, the disease was not detected by the electrocardiogram.

One reason for this is that the electrocardiograph abnormality of coronary artery disease does not always show up during exercise, but may show up only during certain daily activities such as climbing stairs, watching TV, or simply sleeping.

The artificial conditions surrounding the test are one of the problems. Dr. George Sheehan, the well-known long distance runner and cardiologist says that the problem is "the test is done at 70 degrees and 40% humidity. The patient has not eaten for 2 or 3 hours, and he is mildly interested in the proceedings. That's a far cry from jogging in 90 degree heat on a full stomach after a heated argument. The results of the stress test may simply not be valid under such conditions."

Despite the shortcomings, I should note that a stress electrocardiogram is probably a good idea for anyone over 35, particularly if you have vague chest pain, irregular pulse, inappropriate fatigue, shortness of breath, or if there's a family history of heart disease or high cholesterol. If you lead a sedentary life style and have a diet high in cholesterol and saturated fats, it would also be advisable. Furthermore, if you're a smoker, are obese, have diabetes, or high blood pressure, there's no question that you should have a good cardiologist examine you. And the examination should include a stress test.

The stress test will tell you how much exercise you can safely withstand.

It's also very important that the stress test be given by a physician who understands exercise physiology. My feeling is that a stress test is beneficial only if it's given by someone who himself is a regular exerciser. It's also important that the test be considered in light of all other information that was taken about you. If the doctor notices some abnormal squiggles and you have some other suspicious tests, then the stress electrocardiogram may be helpful.

Q: *Does regular exercise help improve abnormal electrocardiogram readings?*
A: Some studies have shown that people who start on cardiovascular fitness programs have improved their exercise electrocardiograms. That is, they have fewer, or no longer have, abnormal squiggles on the ECG graphs. Some doctors feel this happens because new vessels appear or become functional on the heart muscle. Others aren't sure why this happens. For whatever reason, the changes can and do occur, thereby reducing this particular risk factor.

Q: *What is involved in the 7th risk factor, Diabetes Mellitus?*
A: Research has demonstrated that people who suffer from diabetes are far more likely to develop coronary artery disease than people who do not have this disease. As a result, researchers have started to look at carbohydrate metabolism—that is, how people digest and use carbohydrates. They feel that mix-ups in this metabolism may be a factor in heart disease. Since diabetics have trouble with carbohydrate metabolism and also have a high incidence of coronary heart disease, it seems likely that there may be some relationship between carbohydrate metabolism and heart disease in non-diabetics.

Q: *How is obesity related to heart disease?*
A: Obesity is a risk factor. People who are obese have a significantly greater chance of having a heart attack than those

who maintain a good body weight and a low percentage of body fat. In fact, some researchers say that your chances of having a heart attack double if you are obese in comparison to people who are not obese. Obesity, of course, was discussed in greater detail in Chapter #3. Interestingly, it was concluded there that exercise was the most important ingredient in reducing obesity.

Q: *How are smoking and age related to heart disease?*
A: Excessive cigarette smoking has been linked to degenerative heart disease for several years. Studies indicate that people who smoke 20 or more cigarettes daily run a greater risk of suffering heart attacks than those who do not smoke. Figures place it at 2 to 5 times greater. This higher incidence is prevalent regardless of high blood pressure and cholesterol, though if a person has high blood pressure and cholesterol and smokes, he is significantly increasing his chances.

Q: *Why does smoking increase my chances of having a heart attack?*
A: When a smoker inhales, his heart rate and blood pressure increase. The cardiac work increases and removal of oxygen from the blood is lowered. Dr. Kenneth Cooper, author of *Aerobics* has noted: "The carbon monoxide and smoke, like that in your automobile exhaust diminishes the red blood cells' capacity to carry oxygen. The result: the heart has to pump more blood to get the same amount of oxygen to your system. Cigarette induced emphysema results in an increased work load for your heart: more blood has to be pumped through less resilient lungs to pick up the same amount of oxygen. And amyl hydrocarbons from the smoke may act as mutagens for the arterial wall cells, accelerating the process by which atherosclerotic plaques are formed." Naturally, all these things make the blood more likely to clot and constrict the blood vessels.

Smoking is one thing you're going to have to do something about if you plan to reduce your incidence of cardiovascular disease. Though it is not always as easy as it sounds, you must stop smoking and either ask the person next to you to stop smoking or leave the room.

The next risk factor is age, and until someone invents a time machine, you can't do anything about it. It is apparent that as we get older the rate of heart attacks increases. Three out of every four heart attacks occur after the age of 65, and 5 out of 6 strokes occur after the same age. The seeds for the disease are planted in childhood. It has been estimated that over 60% of the children between the ages of 7 and 12 have one risk factor and about 35% have two or more risk factors. Quite frankly, fatty deposits of the arteries are common in young men from industrialized nations. Atherosclerosis of the coronary arteries was observed in nearly 80% of young American men, average age 22, killed in the Korean war. In fact, about 10% of the GI's had one of the three major coronary arteries of their heart nearly blocked. Obviously, as a person gets older the chances of his getting a heart attack increase dramatically. That's because he has a greater chance of being exposed to these risk factors over a lifetime. And the disease is degenerative. My advice on the age factor, however, is don't sweat it. Just don't fight age. There is nothing you can do about it and worrying about it will produce greater amounts of stress and increase another risk factor. Accept your age and be happy with it.

Q: *How does lack of physical activity increase the chances of heart disease?*
A: I'll try not to get too fired up, but this is an area all of us can really *do* something about. Lack of physical activity appears to be strongly related to heart disease. According to recent research, regular participation in suitable exercise and a high degree of body fitness appear to have significant importance in charting the progress of this disease, possibly preventing or slowing and definitely aiding in recovery.

Numerous studies have been conducted to compare sedentary occupations and their relationship to the incidence of heart attack and cardiovascular disease. A study in England classified 2½ million people according to occupation—sedentary and non-sedentary—and compared the percentage of deaths from heart attacks in each. The findings revealed that people engaged in occupations requiring only light physical work had a much higher percentage of deaths from coronary heart disease than people engaged in heavy physical work.

Another study compared the incidence of that disease among several hundred adult men living in Ireland to its presence among brothers who had migrated to the United States and settled in Boston. The Irish-Americans were less active and heavier than their Irish brothers. It was found that the Irish-Americans had a much higher incidence of coronary disease even though they had the same heredity and background.

Other studies on London employees revealed that: 1) Conductors who frequently walked around the double-decker buses and continually climbed stairs had a lower mortality rate and a higher recovery rate from heart attacks than the bus drivers. 2) Postmen delivering the mail had a significantly smaller percentage of heart attacks than the postal executives whose work was sedentary. The famous Framingham Study (5,127 men and women were followed for 16 years) and the study of San Francisco longshoremen (6,351 men were followed for 22 years) found sedentary people have double the number of fatal heart attacks as active people.

Over the last 20 to 30 years, studies have been conducted which indicate that exercise plays a role in reducing obesity, high blood pressure, and several other risk factors. The results all show that active people have about half the number of heart attacks of inactive people.

Recently, Dr. Kenneth Cooper, M.D., conducted a particularly relevant study. Dr. Cooper compared a person's level of aerobic capacity or his fitness level with selected coronary heart disease risk factors. The unmistakable conclusion of his study indicated that as a person's fitness level improves, his coronary heart disease risk factors drop substantially. The heart disease risk factors affected were cholesterol, triglycerides (lipid abnormalities), glucose, uric acid, systolic blood pressure, and body fat measurements. His study showed that men who were in very poor or poor aerobic fitness showed poor results. Men who had fair aerobic fitness levels appeared to be better than those in the very poor or poor categories, but not as good as those in the excellent category. Those people who had scored good and excellent in the aerobic fitness test scored the best of all and had the lowest scores on selected heart disease risk factors. And Cooper wasn't talking about just a few subjects. His study involved 2,998 men with an average age of 44.6 years. His study summarizes what I have been telling you all along: exercise reduces heart disease risk factors.

A recent meeting of scientists in New York City which addressed itself to marathon running concluded that people who adopted the life style of a marathon runner (able to run 26.2 miles non-stop, trained 36+ miles a week, and a non-smoker) had very little likelihood of developing a coronary. One person, Dr. Thomas Bassler, a pathologist in California, even went so far as to say that this type of life style provided immunity from coronary artery disease. It's a pretty strong statement for him to make and it's obvious when you are talking about humans it is best never to say never about anything. But the general trend does seem to indicate that a marathon runner who is a non-smoker and trains as indicated above has little likelihood of developing a coronary.

Q: *Why do you think exercise is so important in preventing heart disease?*
A: Exercise is important because it is something positive. It's something you do and not something you avoid. More importantly, exercise reduces *many* of the risk factors, not just one. If you kept a score card, you would find that exercise may affect 8 of the 11 risk factors. Remember I said the 11 risk factors were: 1) heredity, 2) stress, 3) diet, 4) fat abnormalities, 5) hypertension, 6) ECG abnormalities, 7) diabetes, 8) obesity, 9) smoking, 10) age, and 11) lack of physical activity. Of these 11, exercise may improve all except age and heredity. Of course, smoking and diet are not altered by exercise itself. Usually, people who exercise on a regular basis adopt more healthful life styles. They often stop smoking (or cut back substantially) and start eating less. They also tend to eat more wholesome foods.

Q: *Exactly how does exercise help the heart, blood, and blood vessels?*
A: There are a lot of theories. But the following chart shows you how exercise influences your circulatory system in a healthful way.

How Exercise May Improve Your Heart, Blood, and Blood Vessels

EXERCISE MAY:

1. Increase the number and size of your blood vessels (better and more efficient circulation).
2. Increase the elasticity of blood vessels (less likelihood of breaking under pressure).
3. Increase the efficiency of exercising muscles and blood circulation (muscles and blood better able to pick up, carry, and use oxygen).
4. Increase the efficiency of the heart (able to pump more blood with fewer beats—better able to meet emergencies).
5. Increase tolerance to stress and give you more joy of living (this means you will be less likely to be caught in the stress/pressure syndrome).
6. Decrease triglyceride and cholesterol levels (less likelihood of fats being deposited on the lining of the arteries).
7. Decrease clot formation (less chance of a blood clot forming and blocking blood flow to the heart muscle).
8. Decrease blood sugar (reduce chances of blood sugar being changed to triglycerides).
9. Decrease obesity and high blood pressure (most people who are obese and have high blood pressure are more prone to heart disease).
10. Decrease hormone production (too much adrenalin can cause problems for the arteries).

Exercise won't take care of everything with respect to heart disease. People must make other modifications in their living patterns to reduce their coronary heart disease risk factors. You must remember that foods are to be selected with care, stress should be dealt with in a positive manner, and smoking is to be stopped. But I feel quite strongly that exercise is extremely important. Recent statistics released by the National Institute of Health (NIH) revealed that the incidence of fatal heart disease has decreased by about 14% among Americans. Dr. Theodore Cooper, former Assistant Secretary for Health in the Department of Health, Education, and Welfare, said 3 factors contributed to improved heart health. They were better dietary habits, less smoking, and more exercise. Significantly, he noted that the most important change was in exercise habits.

Exercise is a positive approach to better quality of life and health. Exercise is something you can actually look forward to. So it's important to select an activity you enjoy. That way you will participate on a regular basis.

Q: *What are varicose veins?*
A: The veins are vessels that collect blood from the various tissues and send it back to the heart. Getting the blood from your legs up to your heart forces the blood to be pumped against gravity. Fortunately, your veins have valves surrounding them that help keep the blood from slipping back down to your big toe. The condition of varicose veins develops when these valves in the vein walls become weakened due to the pooling of blood against them. They simply give way to the pressure of the blood, sag, and lose their elasticity. It seems as though some people are more prone to this. In other words, they may inherit this tendency.

There are many ways to treat varicose veins including special elastic stockings, avoiding periods of standing, refraining from wearing elastic girdles, and sometimes surgery. Doctors also suggest exercise for varicose vein patients because the movement of the leg muscles while walking, jogging, swimming, and bicycling all help to push the blood upwards. In fact, exercise helps the veins by massaging them so the blood can get back to the heart more readily.

In the more advanced stages, varicose veins can be both unsightly and painful, but they should not stop you from exercising. You should continue in your exercise and be regular about it. Just be glad you're not suffering from intermittent claudication.

Q: *What is intermittent claudication?*
A: Like varicose veins, intermittent claudication is a leg disorder, but it affects the large iliac or femoral arteries of the legs and results in severe pain while walking. The pain, when it strikes the lower legs, is severe and cramp-like. Rest brings relief, but only until the victim walks again. Intermittent claudication gets worse without treatment and frequently indicates heart involvement. In

many ways it resembles the heart ailment angina pectoris in that circulation is impaired, usually because of stricture or arteriosclerotic blood vessels. The muscles suffer from oxygen starvation. Lactic acid builds up causing severe pain.

Until very recently doctors usually prescribed surgery, drugs, and "complete rest" or, at best, mild exercise. But in 1966, two British researchers found that a program of vigorous walking over a period of 6 months increased threefold the patient's ability to walk. In 1970, three Swedish doctors detailed studies showing that muscular exercise definitely increased the patient's ability to walk without pain. In one program, the patients were required to walk for one hour (rest not included), even though some were able to walk only 50 yards. The patients walked until they felt pain, rested, and then walked again.

Exercise as therapy for intermittent claudication is far from painless—to be effective, the patient must walk through the pain. When the cramp-like pain strikes, he must continue to walk as long as possible. Walking is the most effective exercise for overcoming claudication but there are other leg exercises to supplement it, including cycling, swimming, and the upside down pedaling exercises. Vitamin E therapy with exercise has also been used with some success.

CHAPTER
5

Oh, My Aching Back
And . . . !

It's amazing how exercise can help people overcome, better endure, or control certain ailments. Exercise has been used in the treatment and rehabilitation of so many conditions that the list seems endless. It doesn't mean that if you have a certain affliction you should rely entirely on exercise. What it does mean is that you should consider it a possible adjunct to your current therapy. If exercise can improve your quality of life, then it has contributed significantly to your health. Furthermore, everything that I talk about in the following pages has been used by physicians. Some quite successfully. For those in which it's on the fringe area, I'll let you know.

Q: *Can exercise help cure backache?*
A: Exercise is extremely effective in treating backaches, particularly low back pain. Dr. Hans Kraus, the world famous back specialist who has treated thousands of people—world leaders, writers, movie stars, athletes and maintenance men—feels that therapeutic exercise is effective in 80% of all low back pain cases. The medical consultant to the President's Council on Physical Fitness and Sports feels that most back pain is caused by a lack of physical fitness. In addition, Kraus says that most surgeries on the back are not necessary. Of course, his comments have raised the ire of many physicians, but he does have pretty much clout to back up the importance of exercise.

Q: *What are the specific ways in which exercise helps reduce low back pain?*
A: Dr. Kraus notes that most of the pain in the lower back is muscular in origin. You may think that's nothing new. Except for the fact that it's usually the stomach muscles rather than the back muscles which are at fault.

Studies have demonstrated that in the majority of cases, the abdominal muscles of persons with chronic back conditions are less than ⅓ as strong as their back muscles. The prevention and treatment of potentially disabling back disorders is so simple, it is often overlooked, according to Dr. Kraus. And the major culprits as you may have guessed are inactivity and tension.

Seventy million Americans will have some back pain sometime during their lifetime. New York's executive health examiner's report states that at least 25% of the sedentary, middle-aged executives they examined had some form of back trouble. The problem is that the business of making a living while sitting down makes us particularly susceptible to the low back syndrome. A lack of physical activity causes our abdominal muscles to weaken and sag. Because these muscles sag, we develop a "pot belly." To compensate for this sagging waistline we have to shift our weight to the back. Consequently the pelvis tips forward, the derriere sticks out, and the last joints of the spine require a lot of muscle to hold them up. Eventually, the muscles in the lower back tire of carrying the load and begin to hurt.

To add to this problem, day-to-day tensions caused by traffic jams, late trains, office and family worries, aggravate the problem. Tension makes the muscles tight and short. And when the muscle is tightened beyond a certain point it starts to hurt. Back pain results.

Q: *What can I do to avoid low back pain?*
A: To offset the adverse conditioning imposed by our life style, you must learn to live sensibly. That is, to rethink those actions which have become second nature. It's not that difficult. It's simply an awareness of the way you move, sit, and stand. Remember, everything affects the health of your back, even the way you stand to brush your teeth, shine your shoes, or eat.

Take stock of your posture. Do you slouch, stoop, or lean to one side? Or does your stance reflect the unnatural straightness associated with the military? In either case you're doing your back a disservice. You should strive for a compromise between the two extremes. You want to keep your lower back flat. And to do that you have to tuck your buttocks in to straighten out the small of your back. Under no circumstances should you assume a ramrod stance. Good posture varies from person to person. But authorities generally agree it is the most vertical position you can achieve comfortably. It should not make you tired.

Q: *What is the best way to avoid low back pain if I stand for most of the day?*
A: Long hours of standing put a strain on your spine. If it's necessary to stand for a long period of time, try to vary your position as much as possible. To relieve tension on the lower back, rest one foot a little higher. A brick or telephone book will do. And then lean on the raised knee. Some people might even say that the brass rail along the base of most bars is there for that reason. They're probably right. If it's there, use it.

Q: *What would happen to my back if I sat all day?*
A: Even sitting can cause problems. Be certain that you choose a properly-fitted chair, that is, one which does not cause you to slouch. The best chair has a low, straight back, a firm seat that is not too deep, and armrests, if the nature of your work makes that possible.

It is also best if the height of the seat is adjustable so you can find a comfortable position for writing and reading. When you're sitting, it's good to sit with the small of your back snugly resting against the chair's backrest or if the chair has a cushioned seat, lean slightly forward rather than sitting backwards into it. It is also a good idea to get up and move around whenever you can or rest one foot on a stepstool or telephone book.

Q: *How can I avoid low back pain if I drive for most of the day?*
A: If your job keeps you on the road a good bit of the time, invest in a hard seat-and-back-rest combination which fits over the seat in your car, or a contoured back cushion which may be placed at the small of your back. These devices provide support

for the lower back. You should also sit close enough to the steering wheel so that your arms remain bent and your legs do not fully extend when you work the pedals.

You may even have to do something more vigorous. Let me give you an illustration. Back in 1969 I took my family for a summer vacation across the United States. We hauled a trailer and did a lot of camping. Obviously we also did a lot of driving. On the way home while driving through Wyoming, my son John, who was then 5 years of age, complained of a backache. In fact, he complained of a backache for 3 days. I went through the customary procedures of making sure he had gone to the bathroom, that he had not been kicked in the back by one of the other children. All to no avail. The further we drove the more he complained of his sore back. At one point when we got out of the car for a rest stop he couldn't move. We happened to be in the town of Laramie so I took John to the local hospital. The attending physician was just super. He put John through a full series of tests all afternoon. About 4 hours. While he was doing these tests all kinds of thoughts raced through our heads. What was John's problem? He seemed so healthy and vigorous just a few days before. He's a perpetual motion machine. At 5 o'clock the physician came to me and he said, "I've checked your son over thoroughly. He's in fantastic shape." Then he said: "How much driving have you been doing?" I told him we had been driving steadily for the last three weeks. He said, "That's your answer. John has just not had enough exercise. The back pain is due to a lack of physical activity!" Boy, was I embarrassed. We changed our entire itinerary for the rest of the trip. We made sure that the kids got 2 to 3 hours of vigorous activity each day.

Q: *What other things should I be careful about to avoid low back pain?*
A: Be careful when lifting objects. If you're not in the best physical condition, don't try to lift heavy things. At least not without assistance. Also, don't lift things at a distance from your body, like pulling a bookladen briefcase out of the trunk of your car. Remember, whenever you choose to tackle a heavy weight, bend your knees and lift with your leg muscles. Your leg muscles, not your back, should provide the lifting force.

Dr. Leon Root, a well-known New York orthopedic surgeon, has said that even sneezing can aggravate your back. Believe me, there is a proper way to sneeze. You should bend your knees as you sneeze. If you're in a standing position when you feel a sneeze coming on, lean over and put your hands on the knees. If you're lying down, simply draw your knees up to your chest.

Q: *What sleeping positions should I use to avoid low back pain?*
A: You spend ⅓ of your time in a bed. You should select a mattress that is firm. If you find that your present mattress is too soft or sags in the middle, place a ½ inch plywood board between the mattress and the box spring.

The wrong sleep position can also cause low back pain. According to most authorities, sleeping on the stomach puts a strain on the spinal column, and sleeping on the back is not much better unless you place a very flat pillow under your head and a thicker one under your knees. The ideal position involves lying on your side with both knees flexed.

Q: *What exercises should I do to strengthen my back?*
A: Hit it in the gut! You must condition your tummy muscles. Some of the abdominal exercises as outlined in Chapter #11 are good for you. I would suggest the *look up* and *curl down* as good beginning exercises. They will help to firm up the tummy muscles. Get yourself involved in walking or some other exercise which will help reduce your body fat. Remember, part of the problem is not only weakened tummy muscles but an accumulation of too much body fat. You must whittle your middle.

Dr. Arthur T. Michele, professor and chairman of the Department of Orthopedic Surgery at New York Medical College, has some exercises which I think are good. The first is to lie on your back with a pillow under your head, your hands folded over your stomach, knees bent, and feet flat on the floor. Keeping one leg and the knee in up position, roll the other knee out to the side, then back to the original position 10 to 20 times. Repeat with the other leg.

In the same position as above, pull one knee up to your chest with both hands, keeping the other leg in that position. Repeat 10 to 20 times with both legs.

Again in the same starting position, place your left hand on your left knee, lift your left foot off the floor and move your knee out to the side and around in a circle 10 times clockwise and 10 times counter-clockwise. Repeat with the other knee.

And before you begin exercising you should take a few minutes to relax. Lie on the floor and concentrate on relaxing different muscles.

Q: *Can shoes also cause back problems?*
A: They sure can! Poor-fitting shoes and particularly high-heeled shoes can lead to foot and leg deviations that can cause pelvic misalignment. For example, if you put on high heels (and this can include anything from an inch on up) they tend to throw your posture forward. The result is you try to compensate with balancing a little bit and you tip your pelvis. Go barefooted whenever you can and wear shoes with low heels.

Q: *What about shoes with negative heels? Are they good or bad for your back?*
A: It depends upon which authority you ask. "Earth" shoes are a most peculiar style of footwear, readily distinguishable by a thick contoured sole which gently slopes downward from the toe to a lowered heel. Its creator, Anne Kalso, a Danish yoga instructor, first came upon this unique idea as she studied the pattern of bare feet imprinted on a sandy beach.

Many podiatrists feel that the heavy construction and lack of flexibility of shoes with negative heels restrict the motion of the foot. Others warn that the rigid contours of the arch make the shoe uncomfortable for persons with very flat feet or extremely high arches. And still other authorities argue that the negative heel throws the entire body off balance. Exponents of the negative-heel shoe claim that the lowered heel tends to improve posture. Slipping the weight back onto the heels causes the wearer to stand more erect.

Try it yourself: standing in front of a full-length mirror, take off your shoes, plant your heels on the ground and slightly raise your toes. This causes your pelvis to rotate forward, flattens your stomach, and forms a vertical line along your spine from the neck downward. If the shoes help rotate your pelvis in this manner, they may be good for you. But don't be misled. The strengthening of the abdomen is more important than simply wearing corrective shoes. But these shoes may help you.

Q: *Are there any other precautions regarding negative-heel shoes?*
A: Should you decide to wear this type of shoe, consider this— the shoes require breaking in. This usually involves a two-week adjustment period of gradually increasing the wearing time, similar to the adjustment period experienced with contact lenses. During this period you may have heel pain and mild stiffness or cramps in the calf. But don't get discouraged. If you still feel this sensation after one month's time, take the hint. The negative-heel shoe may not be for you.

Q: *Can low back pain also be caused by arthritis?*
A: Arthritis is a disease and inflammation of the joints. It is often used synonymously and erroneously with the term rheumatism. Rheumatism refers to a broad group of diseases affecting body tissues that have to do with moving about, such as the muscles, tendons, ligaments, and joints. Many times the back is affected. Arthritis is only one aspect of what doctors call the rheumatoid diseases. There are a whole host of them. Here I'd just like to talk about rheumatoid arthritis and osteoarthritis for a moment. Rheumatoid arthritis occurs more frequently in women than in men. Why this is so is not clear. Doctors aren't sure exactly what the cause may be but it has ranged everywhere from an infection to emotional shock. Whatever the cause, there are several signs that are easily recognized. The hands feel numb, the skin is cold and clammy, and the person may feel "under the weather" with digestive upsets and emotional depression.

Although the entire body suffers, the joints cause the most discomfort. Usually the smaller joints such as the fingers are affected first. Later, the larger joints such as the hips and knees may be affected. Occasionally, the first sign of rheumatoid arthritis may occur in the larger joints. Regardless of where the pain occurs, you'll know it. For it comes slowly and with sharp twinges. Swelling may also appear.

Q: *What can be done about rheumatoid arthritis?*
A: Continuous medical supervision is very important. Although there is no complete cure, prompt medical attention and the patient's cooperation will go a long way in limiting the malady. The most commonly prescribed medication is aspirin. Hormones, carefully prescribed, may also be used. Treatment consists of much more than a few aspirin tablets, however. The doctor will set up a well-balanced diet for the patient and in a few instances nutrients may be added—such as vitamins and minerals. It is important that the overweight person lose weight.

Q: *Can exercise play a part in curing rheumatoid arthritis?*
A: Exercise will play a role in the treatment of rheumatoid arthritis once the condition of the patient improves. The exercise will be initiated by a physical therapist and conducted under medical supervision. Usually the exercise involves limited exercise of the joints. The person may do some himself or someone else may move the joint for him. After a period of time if sufficient progress has been made, a person may exercise by himself.

The primary objective of the exercise is to re-establish the full range of motion of the joints. This may take several months or longer. It is also important that the muscles be developed and maintained. For if they are weakened, additional stress or pressure may be put on the afflicted joints.

Q: *What are the best exercises for someone who suffers from arthritis?*
A: I think the best type of exercise for the arthritic is swimming. The next best is bicycling, and this is followed by walking. For most arthritics, jogging is out. Although I know a few people who staunchly persist in jogging. One man had degenerative arthritis of the hips. He found that cross-country skiing was more suitable than any other kind of exercise since his hips did not experience any bouncing trauma. His doctors, from the Mayo Clinic, encouraged him to be as active as possible and endorsed cross-country skiing.

Naturally, the time that an arthritic can exercise is when the acute stage of pain has passed. He is not to engage in exercise

during a flare up. But when it's in a state of remission or quies-
cence, then it is ok.

One of the confusing things is that some people who have joint
pain blame their condition on rheumatoid arthritis when it is really
osteoarthritis.

Q: *What is osteoarthritis?*
A: Osteoarthritis, sometimes called degenerative joint disease,
is a breakdown of the cartilage and other tissues which make the
joint move properly. It is a wear-and-tear disease. Some doctors
have said that over 95% of the people past the age of 60 show
signs of it. Osteoarthritis is most common in the hips, knees,
spine, and the base of the big toe and thumb. The cause is not
clear, although heredity may be a factor. A joint that has received
particular stress may also be a cause.

A person with osteoarthritis may not even know that he is
suffering from the disease. But when there is trouble, the most
prevalent symptom is pain. Generally, it is only a mild ache or
soreness on movement. In other cases, the pain may be constant,
even at rest. Another sign is loss of movement. Although that is
usually not severe, it inhibits the ability to perform easy, comfortable movements of the joints.

Q: *Could I tell the difference between rheumatoid arthritis and
osteoarthritis?*
A: No. A doctor must make the diagnosis of whether it is osteoarthritis, rheumatoid arthritis, or something else. But here are
a few differences.

1. With osteoarthritis, the pain is usually mild and can be
relieved by small amounts of aspirin.
2. Usually with osteoarthritis the pain will go away if you
rest the joint. That does not occur in rheumatoid arthritis.
3. Usually with osteoarthritis there is stiffness after sitting.
After you use the joints for a short time, the mild stiffness may
disappear. In rheumatoid arthritis the pain is much more pro-
nounced and persistent.
4. In osteoarthritis the joints develop spurs and there may
be knobby joints. And when the joint is moved, it can make

grating or loud noises. Rheumatoid arthritis does not cause this. Rheumatoid arthritis may cause swelling and involve the finger joints where they attach to the body of the hand.

5. With osteoarthritis there is no fever or indication of illness whereas with rheumatoid arthritis there is.

Q: *If osteoarthritis can be caused by a joint receiving a particular amount of stress, aren't people who are more active also more susceptible to osteoarthritis?*
A: It would seem that way since we're talking about osteoarthritis being a wearing-out disease. Many people feel that since the jogger is running constantly, the hip joints would be more susceptable to osteoarthritis. Dr. Lowell Lutter, an active member of the American Medical Jogger's Association decided to investigate whether this was so. He did a computer search of the medical literature on hip osteoarthritis. Of all the studies reviewed, no reports were found to support the theory. And one study, done on 74 world-class distance runners, showed the exact opposite effect. According to x-ray examinations, the hip joints of these distance runners, after an average of 20 years of distance running, showed only half as many instances of wear-and-tear osteoarthritis as the hips of a control group of non-runners.

Doctors are not sure exactly why this occurred but they do recommend that physical therapy and exercise be used along with the previously mentioned techniques for treating arthritis and osteoarthritis patients. In fact, some doctors think activity may be the most valuable treatment.

Q: *Why is physical therapy a valuable treatment for osteoarthritis?*
A: Muscle weakness and loss of normal joint motion are serious end results of osteoarthritis. They disable the patient. The main objective of rehabilitation is to keep the joints flexible, maintaining strength of the muscles so that the joints retain their stability, and protecting the joints from further injury. It is important that the exercise be carried on continuously. Osteoarthritis is a progressive disease.

The key idea in exercise is to see that the joints are moved through the entire range of motion, several times a day. This is extremely important. If one joint of the body has restricted movement, it affects another part of the body. For example, if one hip joint is stiff, the patient may favor that side. Consequently, posture is affected and abnormal stress is placed on joints of the body. The pattern of walking is seriously affected. This increases the possibility of developing osteoarthritis in other joints.

Again, the exercises selected for the osteoarthritis patient should be gentle rather than vigorous. I would suggest swimming at first, followed by bicycling and then walking. These kinds of activities will not only improve patients' strength but will maintain their aerobic capacity, that is, the heart-lung function.

Q: *Can the bones themselves be hurt by too much exercise?*
A: No. As you get older your bones tend to become more porous and thus more brittle. Your bones start to lose their strength. Exercise seems to slow this process. The constant tug and pull of the ligaments on your bones during exercise stimulates bone thickness and strength. In fact, the astronauts are plagued by bone demineralization when subjected to long periods of weightlessness. So physicians require that they exercise during their travels through space. Apparently exercise helps maintain the integrity of the bone.

Carl Abendroth, vice president and controller of the Milwaukee Transit Company, is a good illustration. Carl, about 60 years of age, has been running 2,000 to 3,000 miles a year for the last 12 years. In October 1977 the Milwaukee YMCA had a big celebration that announced Carl's having run 25,000 miles (one time around the world). Over the years Carl suffered a lot of abuse. He had critics who claimed that all his running would harm his leg bones—wear them out prematurely. Ironically, because of the October publicity, Carl was asked to participate in an aging study conducted by the Reno Orthopedic Clinic in Reno, Nevada. There the doctors did extensive tests on Carl, including x-rays of his legs. At the conclusion of their study one of the doctors sent a letter to Carl and said: "Your bone age is approximately 12 years less than your chronological age. This indicates to me that your exercising has been effective in slowing the aging process as far as your bone structure is concerned." Carl's critics are strangely mum.

Q: *What can exercise do for the asthmatic?*
A: You may be surprised that exercise *does* help asthmatic patients. For too long, asthma patients were restricted from such normal activities as baseball, running, gymnastics, and dancing. Physicians used to insist on long periods of rest for asthmatics. More recently, however, that trend has stopped. In the 1972 Olympics, five medal winners were asthmatics. Doctors have learned the value of exercise in helping the asthmatic toward a more enjoyable and productive life.

The National Jewish Hospital in Denver, Colorado, is a case in point. They discovered that 60 minutes of calisthenics such as sit ups, push-ups, pedaling a stationary bicycle, and weight lifting allowed two out of three of their patients to improve in physical endurance, and three out of four had better heart-lung efficiency. Improvement, once obtained, lasted for about 3 months. The controlled physical activity did not harm the asthmatic's bronchial tubes.

In another survey, Dr. Thomas R. McElhenny, of the University of Texas, conducted a study on asthmatic boys, ages 8 to 13. He found that after the children had instruction in breathing exercises and running, throwing and catching, their lung capacities were increased by 20%. They also had improved performance in the standing long jump, sit-ups, agility run, grip strength, and the 50-yard dash. Most importantly, 90% of their teachers noted that the boys' emotional stability improved. The doctors reported a 40% decrease in both the duration and the severity of their asthmatic attacks. The results were triple barrelled—improved physical performance, better mental outlook, and less severe attacks. That's pretty good medicine. Other studies have shown similar results.

It is becoming increasingly apparent that exercise is now recognized as an important adjunct for asthmatic treatment. It is not a panacea, but it should not be neglected. It has both psychological and physiological values.

Q: *What are the best exercises for asthmatics?*
A: Some asthmatics get what is called "Exercise Induced Asthma." Their attacks are unlikely to occur with only two or three minutes of fairly vigorous exercise. It usually takes five to eight minutes of heavy exertion to cause an attack. So the best

activities are those that permit pauses. The pause may be easy walking or jogging. The important thing with children is to encourage activity since half of them will outgrow asthma.

Swimming is a particularly good activity for the asthmatic, provided he is kept from being exposed to too much cold.

One more thing—the usual attitude of a parent, teacher, and physician with an asthmatic is either to be overprotective or hardnosed. Balance is the key. Experimentation is necessary. Have the asthmatic try interval-type exercises. That is, work for two minutes, slow down, work for two minutes, etc. He should listen to his body.

Q: *What is emphysema?*
A: Next to heart disease, emphysema disables more working men than any other disease. And the number of cases of emphysema is increasing dramatically. Unfortunately, more and more women are also plagued with this disease. Doctors suspect that the reason for the increase is increased smoking among women. ("You've come a long way baby.")

As you probably know, emphysema causes an increase in the size of the alveoli in the lungs and the destruction of the capillaries. Because of the size of the alveoli, the total lung volume is increased. But the effective lung tissue and vital capacity are reduced because of the loss of pulmonary capillaries (less aeration of the blood) and restricted exhalation.

Emphysema is sneaky. It begins with occasional spells of coughing and a buildup of phlegm. Tragically, this deceptive beginning allows the condition to progress to a more critical state.

Now don't get too shocked if you have experienced some of those symptoms. Special tests are required to make a definite diagnosis, but if those conditions persist, you should ask your doctor about them, especially if you have trouble blowing out a candle.

Q: *Can a person with emphysema exercise or not?*
A: Both absence of activity and overexertion are dangerous for someone with emphysema. A lack of activity will make a person greatly dependent upon others, while over-exertion will make breathing excessively difficult and frightening.

Although exercise will not restore lung function, it will improve the circulatory system. This will allow the emphysema patient to do more work. For example, Dr. Lazlo Ambrus and his co-workers at the Veterans Administration Hospital in California, have experimented with an exercise program which combined breathing, relaxation, and general conditioning exercises. Besides traditional exercises such as relaxation and the like, he did weight training exercises for the upper body and also had people walk and climb stairs each day.

At the beginning of the program, the 43 emphysema patients were tested for labored breathing, breathing function, and various activities. They also walked, walked stairs, and walked on treadmills. They were then placed on the training program. At the end of the study, Dr. Ambrus found that the men were able to breath easier, their weights stabilized, and their strength returned. Their endurance also increased. They were able to walk for longer periods of time, from 3½ to over 7 minutes. Their ability to climb stairs, exercise on the Exer-Rower, and walk on the treadmill also improved a great deal.

But just as with the asthmatic, the thing most exciting about the study was the fact that the people said they felt better, enjoyed the exercise program and increased activity, breathed easier, and worried less about their condition. They even claimed that the food tasted better, and their outlook on life improved. The improved mental state was probably the most important result of the study.

Dr. John Boyer, a San Diego cardiologist and past-president of the American College of Sports Medicine, achieved similar results with a group of emphysema patients. He noted that although he could not produce any significant changes with respect to breathing function, he found that the people were able to tolerate greater amounts of exercise (due to better circulation) and they felt better. They felt they could accomplish a great deal more work. They felt less dependent upon other people.

I've personally seen these kinds of results. I've worked with emphysema patients who were not able to tolerate much exercise on a bicycle or treadmill. But with a regular, progressive training program we found that there were significant changes. Again and again, the people kept saying the thing they liked best was their improved mental attitude. It took 6 months or longer, but they started to feel better about themselves, less dependent upon others, and had a much better attitude about their condition.

More and more physicians are recommending exercise as a means of helping emphysema patients. It's not always easy, however. The emphysema patient often feels so poorly that the additional exercise wipes him out. But if he can begin walking gradually, even if it's only a few feet, he will soon find that by gradually increasing the distance he will be able to walk 10, 15, or even 30 minutes comfortably. This will improve his ability to cope with the disease. Again, it is not something that is achieved overnight. It may take months or even years.

Q: *Can exercise help prevent cancer?*
A: I don't think I can make that statement but there is some interesting research about exercise retarding tumor growth. Research shows that people and animals who are more active are less prone to the development of tumors.

Drs. Dennis Colacino and Bruno Balke, of the Department of Physical Education at the University of Wisconsin, are a case in point. They started cancer growths by placing a cancer-causing chemical on the backs of mice. Half the rodents were then forced to run 20 minutes a day on a treadmill for 17 weeks. The other half just sat around. At the end of the study the researchers found that although there was no difference in the food intake or weight, the number of tumors in the inactive group was twice that of the exercising mice. In fact, two inactive mice died of cancer during the observation period, but none of the exercised mice did.

The studies done by Colacino and Balke were by no means the first. At least five studies on animals have supported their work. Their conclusion: mice that were exercised had a lower incidence of cancer than those who were inactive. Not surprisingly, the length of life was also longer in the exercising animals.

Q: *Have there been any exercise/cancer tests done on humans?*
A: Very recently Dr. Ernst vanAaken of Germany examined whether endurance type exercise continued over many years could protect a person from cancer. To investigate that possibility, Dr. vanAaken sent a questionnaire to 1,000 senior (over age 40) distance runners all over the world. A total of 454 ques-

tionnaires were returned to him. Some had been answered with the backing of family doctors or specialists.

The men were between the ages of 40 and 89 years of age, with the average age 53.8 years. Each was active in sports for an average of 32.4 years and most of them had been running for 19.6 years. Those who filled out the questionnaires were not a "physical elite." Seven of them had had a heart attack and 74 had severe circulatory disturbances before they began long distance training. (Only two of the 74 were still suffering from those ailments.)

The runners also had other kinds of diseases including bronchitis, dysentery, and malaria; many had had operations of various kinds. According to Dr. vanAaken, the most important finding of the project was, "That altogether only four cases of tumor formation were determined." None of these cases resulted in death. And one tumor growth was really questionable. Two of the three other distance men recovered after treatment. In fact, one of them was a 71-year-old internist who was back to running three miles a day.

Dr. vanAaken then compared these 45 senior runners with the same number of 40- to 90-year-old patients in his practice. These patients were non-athletes, some were heavy smokers, some alcoholics, and every fifth person was heavily overweight. Among them Dr. vanAaken found 19 verified and 10 probable cases of cancerous tumors.

When comparing the two groups, Dr. vanAaken found that, of the 454 fit senior runners, the incidence of cancer was less than one percent. The 454 men from a country practice between 40 to 90 years of age had 29 tumors. That means 6.4 percent of his practice had cancer. That 6.4 percent is still well below the American average—20 percent of the people in this country will get cancer sometime in their lifetime.

Dr. vanAaken suggested that this study "can serve as clear proof that a healthy way of living, continued for years, with fasting, non-smoking and daily running training does not only give extensive protection from cancerous diseases, but preserves a performance capacity on into old age which even some trained athletes cannot show."

Dr. vanAaken concluded: "That an optimal running training with eight-fold increase in endurance function of the biological oxidation process, carried on for years, prevents cancer with 99 percent certainty."

Although I cannot be as definite as Dr. vanAaken is about the effect of exercise on cancer, a review of current research lends considerable support to the theory that both exercising and the control of body weight may lead to a reduction of the number of cancerous tumors.

Q: *Why do you think that the exercising people in this study had less cancer?*
A: There are a few theories. VanAaken proposes that the cells are better oxygenated and hence are healthier and less susceptible to cancer growth.

Some doctors have theorized that the reduction in cancer might be due to improvement of metabolism, a positive effect on the DNA (genes), better capillarization of tissue—hence, a healthier tissue more able to compete for available nutrients and ward off cancer growth.

As early as 1921 Dr. I. Sivertsen, M.D., felt that the incidence of cancer was a direct result of the advent of the "age of machinery." He set forth a very interesting hypothesis. He noted that human cancer "may be the reaction to and the result of chronic irritation of the adult epithelial tissue bathed in body fluids formed by certain metabolic products as a result of deficient muscular activity."

Of course, Dr. Peter Wood, of Stanford University, may have the best answer of all. He thinks that exercise helps prevent cancer for another indirect reason. Most exercisers do not smoke. And many of the people who become more active give up smoking in the process.

Although it may take 100 years or more to determine whether exercise can slow down or prevent tumor growth, it does seem wise to engage in aerobic-type activities—running, brisk walking, cycling, and swimming every day. Quite frankly, the investment is minimal in light of the potential returns.

Q: *Can exercise do anything for the diabetic?*
A: At one time it was about the only thing doctors could do about diabetes. Before the discovery of insulin in the summer of

1921, diet plus exercise was the only treatment available for diabetes. Along with a list of dietary do's and don't's, the patient was advised to "get plenty of exercise." And although the command was general and lacked scientific or specific direction, exercise was still considered essential.

But exercise was forgotten as insulin proved its worth and greatly extended the life span of diabetics. Insulin was a remarkable discovery for the diabetic and I would certainly not reject its value. But exercise can and should be a part of a diabetic's life style.

Q: *Why is it important for diabetics to exercise?*
A: Many diabetics develop heart disease. According to Dr. Rachmiel Lavine, Executive Medical Director of City of Hope Center, California, "70% of all diabetic deaths are the direct result of vascular diseases." So exercise is important in providing some insurance for the diabetic.

Q: *How does exercise affect diabetics?*
A: Diabetes is the direct result of a metabolic malfunction. When everything is going smoothly inside of you, carbohydrates are converted into glucose (sugar), some to be used immediately for energy, the remainder for future needs. Without insulin, a hormone produced by the pancreas, sugar never reaches the cells. It builds up in the blood only to be excreted through the urine.

It has been shown that during exercise the insulin requirement drops below the usual amount needed. It appears that increased muscle activity increases the transport of glucose into the muscle cells even in the absence of insulin. Exercise produces an insulin effect.

Dr. Lawrence Kinsell stated that exercise is essential for diabetics and cited that the average diabetic child who gets to camp in the summer will find his insulin requirements decreased by more than 40%. Some other factors may play a part in this remarkable change, but it seems reasonable to assume that increased physical activity is the factor that is most responsible. Study after study supports the fact that when a diabetic patient becomes less active his insulin requirement increases while those same requirements decrease when that patient becomes more active.

Q: *Should a diabetic who exercises stop taking insulin or oral drugs?*
A: No. I'm just saying that there is every indication that virtually all diabetics should begin exercising. Cycling, jogging, tennis, rowing, or similar forms of exercise that increase the heart beat and intensify breathing should be included in the workout.

Physicians should provide the encouragement and careful guidance needed, for once a diabetic begins exercising, insulin dose levels will decrease.

Q: *Can exercise prevent headaches?*
A: As Cervantes said, "When the head aches, all the body is out of tune." I'm sure most of you have experienced the dull throbbing pain of the simple headache, though it's not so simple when you're having one. Many of us feel helpless and in our desperation swallow a couple of aspirins and hope for the best. Aspirin seems to be a good pain killer but it's also a good producer of gastric bleeding or anemia, or even another headache.

Even though it seems as though your whole brain is hurting, actually your brain is incapable of feeling pain. The pain of a headache is from the sensitive blood vessels surrounding the brain. When they become enlarged they push against nerves and cause pain.

What causes that pain? Perhaps more important than physical cause is the psychological cause. The late Dr. Harold G. Wolff described headaches as a "red flag" run up by nature which signals that something is wrong, usually in the life style, emotional reaction, or life situation of the patient. The two most common types of headaches—migraine and muscular contraction, are almost always caused by excessive stress and tension. It follows that avoiding stress and tension is the best way to avoid a headache.

But we all know that it is not always possible to get away from those situations that create stress and tension. Something extra is needed. Recently, exercise has been found to be that something extra. Dr. Walter C. Alverez tells the story of a headache victim he treated at the Mayo Clinic. After every drug tried failed to be effective, the patient pointed out that after a fast game of handball he was always free from headaches for two or three days. The physician suggested that he continue this vigorous therapy and he did, with good results. Dr. Alverez also treated a man who had suffered frequent headaches until he discovered that a routine of calisthenics could prevent attacks. From these and other similar cases, Dr. Alverez concluded that: "Perhaps many people could get relief from their headaches if only they would exercise actively every morning."

Quiet, relaxing activities like hiking and bicycling can also serve as a change of pace from hurry-up living—and that prevents tension from building up and causing headaches. More vigorous sports like swimming and tennis can drain off the excess physical and emotional energy which might otherwise lead to headache pain. A good swat at a ball may also be a great way to release pent up hostility and frustration.

CHAPTER

6

Good Health, Lousy Shape

Q: *Is it true that Americans live longer and are healthier today than ever before?*
A: America is the most affluent, industrialized, and scientific nation in the world. It also has the top physicians, hospitals, and medical research centers. Billions of dollars are spent each year to perform intricate surgery which extends people's lives. Research is progressing so rapidly that science and technology seem to have extended the lives of people suffering from cancer, strokes, and heart disease. Microsurgery saves many young children who would have died at birth or during the first few months of life. The knowledge explosion in the area of medicine and health-related fields has been astounding. Physicians, scientists, and hospital staffs are justifiably proud of much of the progress which has been made in the treatment of disease.

With all this progress, you would think there would be no unhealthy people around to work on. You and I know, of course, that that's not true.

If television advertising is any barometer of our health, America might be a nation of "sickies." You are told to pep up with Geritol, relieve pain with Midol, fight fevers with Tylenol, clean your breath with Cepacol, wash your ears with Oticol, and solve indigestion with Pepto-Bismol. Write down all the TV ads for medicine and health placed on the airways. After a few hours you will probably give up. But the advertisers don't think it's ridiculous. Someone's buying all those products. And that's not all they're buying. Between 1950 and 1977 the annual cost for health care in the United States jumped from $12 billion to $180 billion. And most of that increase came in the past 5 years. Currently, health care accounts for over 10% of our gross national product.

A lot of this money is spent on trying to keep us alive. Diseases such as heart disease, stroke, and cancer are rampant. These degenerative diseases account for over 71% of all deaths. Heart disease alone, the biggest killer and crippler of them all, accounts for over 50% of all deaths. What's shocking is that I'm not talking about a lot of old people dying, but about people in their 40's and 50's. How many times have you said, "Why, he was so young to have a heart attack?"

When the United States is compared to other countries in terms of longevity, we do poorly. The American male ranks 22nd and the American female ranks 10th. That means 21 and 9 countries respectively outrank us in staying alive longer. A pretty poor showing for a country with our medical expertise.

Today, an average one-year-old American girl or boy may have a life expectancy of 75+ and 69+ years respectively. Quite a change from 1900 when the typical one-year-old lived about 46 years and in 1776 about 34 years. That seems great.

Unfortunately, these figures are deceptive. They might make you feel comfortable until you analyze the figures carefully. Let me explain:

The life expectancy figures do not give the actual age when most people die. Instead, the figures simply tell you that when you lump all ages of death together, that is the average. Of course, many men die older than age 69 and many die younger. Therefore, in those countries whose infant death rate is very high, the average life expectancy will be quite low. And it will remain low even though many people live to an advanced age. But when medicine can save the lives of small children, the life expectancy figures for the entire population soar.

For example, until the 1850's only half of all the children born in the United States reached the age of 5. Today, almost 98% make it to that age. In 1790, a 60-year-old veteran of the American Revolution had a life expectancy of around 15 more years. Incredibly, in 1970, his 60-year-old counterpart had almost the same number of years to live.

Q: *Do you have other statistics on longevity?*
A: If you visit an old cemetery, you will notice several things:

1. A large number of children between the ages of 1 and 10 years are buried there.
2. A high number of women 20 to 40 years of age are also buried. Typically, these women died during childbirth.
3. Very few people buried are 35 to 47 years of age (the average age in 1770 and 1900). Many people died at age 70, 80, or 90+.

Next, check the ages at death of the first 7 Presidents of the United States. Compare them to the last 7. The first seven lived an average of almost 80 years. It would have been around 83 if Washington had not been bled to death by his doctors at the age of 69. The last 7 Presidents, excluding John F. Kennedy, lived 72 years.

The preceding statistics are not meant to be an indictment of the medical profession. They simply indicate that Americans are not as long-lived as they like to think they are. The figures also point out that something is wrong. Life expectancy has increased, but true longevity has not.

Q: *What do you mean by the statement "life expectancy has increased but true longevity has not"?*
A: To understand this it is necessary to consider the history of disease in technological countries. Modern scientists and physicians have increased life expectancy by stopping death due to such things as influenza, polio, pneumonia, smallpox, and other contagious diseases that used to kill children. If you were a little tyke before the 19th century, you just didn't have much of a chance. In previous centuries, most early deaths were caused by infections of this type which had been carried from one place to another by animal and human "hosts."

Our Yankee ingenuity (with ample help from Europe and Great Britain), came up with improved health measures that brought outbreaks of these and other diseases under control. Along with innoculations and vaccinations to produce artificial immunity, we quarantined suspect ships offshore and told them "get well or get lost!"

Thanks to vaccines, American children are free from the polio that menaced their parents' childhood. Even measles can be avoided. Because of modern medicine, microbes kill far fewer of their victims. In 1971, for example, only 30 out of every 100,000 American deaths were caused by pneumonia or tuberculosis. Both were once major killers.

Nevertheless, technology's victory over some of the fatal diseases that still ravage some primitive populations must be considered a qualified triumph. In our zealousness to claim medical sophistication, we often overlook two important considerations. First, although we have virtually solved the problem of treating scarlet fever, diphtheria, and other bacterial infections, some types of acute viruses play havoc with us. The common cold, mononucleosis, and hepatitis are examples. Child health experts tell us that the average two-year-old has 5 to 7 colds in one year, while college students are beginning to think that "mono" is an institutional requirement for graduation.

A second cause for concern is the fact that rather than wiping out disease, we have simply traded one type for another. As the pattern of life has changed, the pattern of disease has also shifted. Almost all of our deaths in 1750 were the result of communicable diseases—diseases you got from the guy next door. (Even though you didn't ask for them.) In that same year very few deaths resulted from degenerative diseases such as heart disease, diabetes, and cancer.

By 1850, outbreaks of communicable diseases had been reduced significantly. And this happened even though individuals were living in the city in crowded and unsanitary conditions. At the same time, cases of degenerative diseases had increased to the point where they were taking about the same toll as communicable diseases had. Today, the situation that prevailed in 1750 is completely reversed. Communicable diseases are pretty well under control but degenerative diseases are causing the great majority of deaths.

Just as disturbing is the fact that since the 1920's the frequency of degenerative diseases has been skyrocketing. In 1966, over 13 million Americans were suffering from various forms of arthritis. In 1973, the figure was over 17 million, with 2.5 million of the victims under 45 years of age. Twelve million working days each year are lost to arthritis. Heart disease was around in the early 1800's but it was a medical rarity. Today, over 600,000 people die each year from heart attacks and perhaps another 14 million are being treated in one form or another for the disease. It is estimated that another 12 million may have the disease and not know it!

The common backache, far less dramatic than the heart attack, has been increasing by leaps and bounds. It is difficult to determine how many people are afflicted with this malady, but demographers speculate that 1 out of 3 Americans will suffer from low back pain sometime in his life. Dr. Hans Kraus, the back specialist of Chapter 5, says that 28 million are severely afflicted.

All this reveals that something is radically wrong with our health. It seems that science is merely allowing children to live long enough to fall victims to chronic degenerative diseases which often show up in middle age. Prize-winning biologist Dr. Rene Dubos has said that although medical sciences have "done much in the prevention and treatment of a few specific diseases, they have so far failed to increase true longevity or to create positive health."

Q: *Do people who live in less advanced countries get these kinds of ailments?*
A: Degenerative diseases occur much less frequently in primitive societies. It is possible to argue, of course, that the only reason people in underdeveloped countries suffer less from heart disease, cancer, arthritis, and back aches is that they don't live long enough. That may be true.

It's equally true, however, that in a number of underdeveloped societies, the longevity of those who live past childhood compares very favorably or even better with that in medically-sophisticated America. The most widely-studied of these places are an Andean village in Ecuador, the land of Hunza in Kashmir, and the region of Abkhasia in the Soviet Union.

If your goal is to live to be 100, you might consider a transfer out of the country, for in the U.S. a mere three people out of every 100,000 live to be 100 years of age or more. In Abkhasia, however, careful research has established that as many as 63 individuals out of 100,000 are centenarians. In Hunza, which has a completely unique language with no written form, establishing ages is much more difficult. However, physician Alexander Leaf discovered that the ruler of the country could confirm ages in relation to the state's history. Dr. Leaf himself had a "definite impression of an unusual number of very vigorous old folks clambering over the steep slopes." In the Latin American village of Vilcabamba, church baptismal records have helped to confirm that there are at least 9 centenarians out of every 100,000 people. That's 6 more per 100,000 than the United States. On the basis of these statistics, it seems clear that with all its technology, the United States cannot assure its citizens of the quantity and the quality of life they would receive if they were living in a remote mountain village.

Q: *Why do you place such importance on the "quality of life"?*
A: Because many Americans who are living longer may be enjoying life less. You probably have seen older people who have simply wasted away because they have become ill or have lost their place in life. The families of some of these people stick them in nursing homes, where they die of psychological as well as physical ailments. While they are "waiting to go," such older people are confined to wheelchairs or rocking chairs and soon refuse to do anything. Because they have no purpose in life, they are literally just existing. This kind of helpless, futile old age is one of the real tragedies of our society.

It is especially tragic when you realize that the oldest people in Abkhasia, Vilcabamba, and Hunza are able to participate fully in life right up to their last days. Working as farmers, goat herders, or tea pickers, these hearty men and women continue to contribute to the economy. It seems no coincidence that they also enjoy very high social status and have a privileged position in the family group.

For these older people, advanced age is far from a curse. Its pleasures are considerable enough for a 123-year-old Vilcabamba man to tell Dr. Leaf, "I would not like to be young again, but if I could take 15 years from my age—wonderful!" As one 117-year-old women declared, "Youth extends up to the age of 80. I was still young then." And all of this without Geritol!

Q: *What makes these people live longer?*
A: Doctors just don't know. But Dr. Leaf has said that their level of activity, meager but adequate diet, relative isolation, and increased social status as they became old were factors. Dr. Alex Comfort and other researchers have said the real job of research on aging should be into prolongation of youth, such as these people experience, instead of lengthening senility. Medical science "should aim to extend our period of more vigorous and active life by keeping us biologically between say 25 and 35 until we are chronologically 50."

Without such a breakthrough in gerontology, it seems as though mature adults will be experiencing chronic degenerative diseases at ever-younger ages. For example, among American men between 25 and 44, the coronary death rate has gone up 14% since 1950. Equally alarming is that as of 1961, one in every five Americans under 15 years of age had at least one chronic disorder.

It's small wonder, then, that the failing health of most Americans convinces them they're ready to get out of the running and into the rocking chair by 63 or 65. Since productivity and self-reliance are traditional values in our society, these inactive senior citizens are not respected. Deprived of their vigor, usefulness, and social status with years still to be lived, too many older Americans look on the end of life as something to be endured rather than enjoyed. As long as this continues to be so, it is premature for us to rejoice at extending the average life expectancy of our people. What's so great about giving someone another a year or two in bed? Instead, we need to eliminate some of those chronic ailments that make living so tedious. To do that, we need to look first at how we fall victim to those diseases.

The degenerative diseases that plague us in our middle and later years are caused by many factors. As we have seen, they include heredity, physical activity, diet, stress, drugs, smoking, and pollution. These are all factors which are potent forces acting on our health. Ideally, each factor should be explored carefully, but that is not the intention of this book. As I've told you time and again, it is my personal feeling that *exercise is crucial to health*. It is a vital part of our biological heritage. I feel a strong case can be made that regular exercise is basic to our health, longevity, and quality of life.

Unfortunately, many Americans have what Dr. George Sheehan, the guru of long distance runners, calls good health, lousy shape. The average American can pass a physical exam at the doctor's office but has a difficult time passing an escalator because the stairway will exhaust him.

Modern diseases and poor quality of life may be due partly to civilization's failure to meet the basic needs for physical activity that were encoded thousands of years ago. Dr. Hans Selye's classic research on stress supports the idea that maladaptation is an important factor in many contemporary illnesses. He suggests that good health involves learning "to express our vitality through the particular channels and at the particular speed which nature foresaw for us." Dr. Robert D. McCracken, a noted anthropologist, has stated if you had lived 10,000 years ago, you would have been healthier than you are today. "Cave people were much healthier and in much better physical shape than we are. Cave people ate natural foods while modern people eat mostly processed foods and a lot of refined sugar. Cave people also got a lot more exercise on a regular basis. They walked miles a day instead of sitting in a car on a smoggy freeway. They didn't smoke or drink. They may have had to worry about freezing to death or getting eaten by saber-tooth tigers, but they had absolutely no worries about heart attacks, getting run over by automobiles, air pollution, or getting mugged in an alley."

Q: *With all the things that Dr. McCracken mentioned, why do you recommend physical activity so highly?*
A: Before the advent of technology, life called upon the body as well as the brain. In pre-historic times, people perished if they weren't physically strong. Every daily task required the vigorous use of their versatile bodies. Success in life meant being able to run fast enough to hunt, walk far enough to gather nuts and berries, and strike hard enough to defend one's self against attack. Those primitives who failed such tests didn't survive. The body developed the unique combination of physical characteristics that

enabled early people to do their jobs supremely well. Their minds grew in strength along with their bodies. As early societies evolved, people began to use both physical and mental skills to alter their environment. These skills raised their standard of living above that of the animals.

But on the giant clock of recorded history, only a few brief moments have elapsed between a life style based on physical strength and endurance and today's living by our wits. This historical interval has been too short for the slow mechanisms of biology to work their miracles of adaptation. As a result, civilized people doing "brain work" continue to inhabit bodies which nature forged to do physical labor. Quite frankly, we're going downhill.

Q: *Aren't the new records established by athletes proof that America's health is getting better?*
A: I like to look at it another way. There's no better example of our heritage of great strength than the outstanding performances of today's athletes. Records for speed, endurance, and skill are continually being broken by young people. And their marks will be excelled in the future.

But in highly-industrialized countries there are far more examples of people of all ages who seek to live by their minds alone. They fail to use the physical potential which is in them. These individuals have chosen to be sedentary. Unfortunately for them, limbs that are not used become weak. Bodies which are not flexed become stiff. Food energy which is not used turns to fat and is carried through life as a useless and unattractive burden. Organs of the body designed for intensive use begin to atrophy and create serious health problems.

This process of physical debilitation has been dramatically documented by researchers studying Eskimos in the North Canadian Arctic. In the old days, these hearty people lived a nomadic, self-reliant life. In numbing temperatures of $-50°$ Fahrenheit, the men hunted and fished, while the women fished through the ice, tanned skins, and made clothing.

Today, the airplane links Eskimos everywhere with the 20th century. For all but a few of them, driving dog sleds and living in snowhouses are only a memory. Today's Eskimos drive snowmobiles and live in electrified wooden settlements built by the government. Once left to die in times of famine, infants and the elderly are now protected by welfare payments and old age pensions.

But if the Eskimos are further from death than they used to be, they are also further from fitness. Since they live in settlements, the men no longer hunt for food. Instead, they work at sedentary factory jobs and take their meals in the company cafeteria, where they overeat. The women can now purchase what they once made, and now have nothing to do but eat sweets and go to the movies. Bored with the tameness of settlement life, teenagers educated in Bureau of Indian Affairs Schools solace themselves with sedentary activities.

As a result of this sheltered, inactive life style, in one generation the Eskimos have begun to develop degenerative diseases at a frightening rate. Obesity, diabetes, heart disease, and other ailments are starting to "rust out" bodies that at one time thrived on the challenge of the frozen North.

It is revealing to contrast the Eskimo with the oldsters in Hunza and Abkhasia. Just climbing over the slopes of their mountainous homelands has given these people a high degree of cardiovascular fitness. Tests by cardiologist Dr. David Kakiashvili showed that although these old people have forms of heart and blood vessel disease, the oxygen supply to their hearts is so good that heart attacks go unnoticed and do little harm.

The daily activities of these hardy people are astonishing. They scramble after goats and walk up and down steep hills to gather food or bathe in a stream. In most parts of the world technology has made this kind of vigorous living obsolete. Most of us do not have to do much physical work, either in our occupations or at home. The only muscle that gets much work is the one in the finger that pushes all the buttons. Factory managers have found that production is most economical when the brain power of people is used to guide the forceful action of machines. At work, human muscle power is now used only for the miscellaneous tasks which are too random or unimportant to be mechanized.

Machine power has also been put to use at home. Mechanization has made household work easier. The vacuum cleaner has replaced the broom, the washboard has yielded to the automatic washer and the clothesline to the automatic dryer. The result has been a lowering of our vitality. We're tired before the end of the day. Our waistlines sag. Our hips spread. We suffer heart attacks while shoveling snow. Our weight escalates. We're short of breath after two flights of stairs. We're uptight, nervous, and have mysterious aches and pains. Life for many of us is a "bummer" because the prescription for a healthy life is exercise and plenty of it.

From this awareness that lack of exercise is contrary to our need to move, the concept of fitness has emerged. We must use our muscles and preserve a healthy balance between our mental and physical development. Evidence is rapidly accumulating that proves we should strive to condition our bodies to enable us to withstand the stresses of life. With all our achievements, progress, and development, we have not been able to find a suitable replacement for the benefits of regular, vigorous exercise.

Q: *Where are the healthiest people in America?*
A: The healthiest people are those people who live on farms and are much more active than the typical American. Also, white men and women who live in the West North Central United States, where agriculture still dominates, generally live longer than other Americans.

Q: *Can people who do not live in these areas become healthier and live longer?*
A: Of course, the benefits of a more physical way of living are available to those "other" Americans too. It's just a matter of choosing an activity and performing it 20 to 30 minutes every day, 3 to 4 days a week.

The so-called "big muscle work" will strengthen your heart, lungs, liver, and endocrine system. It will help to prevent or slow the degenerative diseases that cause premature, "pathological" aging and help to slow down the natural aging process. Those who remain fit have better performance records, a slower aging process, less degenerative disease, and a greater life expectancy. And there's no question about it, a much better quality of life than the general sedentary population.

Fitness is the prescription for a fuller and healthier life. In the past, only the fittest survived. In the modern world, only the fit are able to enjoy the true pleasure of living.

By being physically active you will be returning to your physical heritage. You will also be assuming responsibility for your health and your physical and mental well-being. The big muscle work will permit you to work closer to your potential. You were given a body with a 70 to 120 year warranty. How long your body lasts depends on how you keep up the warranty. There is no other way. With regular, vigorous activity you will move closer to your potential. It is your job to learn to work at peak efficiency for you to get the best out of your body physically, intellectually, spiritually, and emotionally.

CHAPTER

7

Doing It For The Head!

Q: *What's the best reason for exercising?*
A: For me, it's that exercise helps my head. To be honest, I don't exercise to live longer or be healthier. I exercise because my head calls for it. Sure I'm happy to get the benefits derived from looking better and being healthier. But as far as I'm concerned they are only side effects. The real reason is mental. Exercise adds life to my years.

The real value of exercise is its effect on life itself. Look at the people around you. How many of them *look* like they enjoy life? How many times have you heard reference to life as a rat race? Life is more than just existing, and exercise can give you that extra ingredient.

Most of the time people start exercising for physical reasons. They want to drop their weight or blood pressure. They have chest pain. Their waistline is no longer attractive. That gets them started. But they stay on a program because of the way they feel. It unwinds them and makes them feel a lot better.

People will say to me, "What keeps you running and exercising, Kuntzleman?" My answer is: The first ten minutes into a run I don't know. I have all kinds of excuses. "I should be back at the office," "My legs hurt," "I don't feel good," "It's cold." The next twenty minutes are for my body. I start to get into sync. I realize what's happening to me. I feel my muscles working, my heart beating faster, I like the physical challenge. I'm proud to be exercising. I'm proud that I'm doing something about my physical existence. About 30 minutes into the run my creative juices start to flow. I solve all kinds of administrative, writing, family, and personal problems in a very short period of time. Most of my book, program, and article ideas have come on the run. I agree with Dr. George Sheehan, "Never trust an idea that you have sitting down." (Atta boy George!) Near the end of the hour, it seems like my mind has been blown. I have a difficult time thinking about anything concrete. I become mesmerized by the run. I try to think about a problem, but I can't. I feel like I've blown all my circuits. I'm in a world of my own. I have the "runner's high." I have no problems, no anxiety—nothing. I feel good. Satisfied, elated, pleased with myself. Relaxed, happy. I like me and my world around me.

I'm not unique. Other exercisers, runners in particular, have experienced the same feelings I have had. Bob Rodale, whom I introduced to you in the Foreword, walks 3 miles to work and 3 miles from work every day. He started walking since it was the only way he could consistently get the exercise he felt he needed. But what surprised and pleased him most were the mental benefits. Before he started walking in 1968, he would drive home. When he arrived at 5:30 or so, he was still hyper from the pressures of the job—writing and overseeing a good sized publishing business. But the walk changed all that. The 45 minute walk home at night allowed him to relax—unwind. Put the day into perspective.

Q: *Do you think exercise does more for the body or for the mind?*
A: The body and mind are so intertwined it's difficult to say. You can't really have a healthy mental outlook without your body being in tune and vice versa. We live in a stress-filled world, with mental and emotional illness as severe a problem as physical ailments. Sometimes it's hard to separate the two because so many physical ailments are directly related to emotional stress. When I started my graduate programs at Temple University, the psychologists and physicians were saying 10% of all physical ailments were triggered by some mental condition. When I graduated, about 12 years later, it was 50-50. Today, some of

these same people are saying that anywhere from 60 to 80% of all our physical ailments have some type of mental involvement or trigger.

Few nervous conditions occur without accompanying physical problems (ulcers, colitis, etc.). Nervous tension can cause heart disease, cancer, backaches, muscle pain, arthritis and stiff necks. Tension or mental involvement can even make you more susceptible to colds by lowering your resistance.

Pills and medication only cover up the symptoms. They really don't get to the root of the problem, but only give us momentary relief. Therapy and analysis are often beneficial, but they are expensive and for some people may be unnecessary. In fact, one psychiatrist, Dr. Thaddeus Kostrabula of San Diego, California, has his patients run with him. He feels that exercise is one of the best forms of therapy for emotional problems and uses it extensively in treating his patients.

Exercise has a pervasive effect on life itself. When we feel generally better, we become more creative, productive, and imaginative, as well as active. Because we begin to look better, we start liking ourselves more. Our self-concept improves as we see that we *can* change our world. One of the greatest "highs" in life is the exhilaration of the shower after a hard workout. You're tired, you're beat, you might even be a little sore. But you've done it! To sweat felt good. The shower feels better. But the best feeling of all is the satisfaction of accomplishment. Such a feeling is crucial to a healthy mind, body, and soul. Exercise? A small price to pay for such wide-spread results.

Q: *Can exercise make me more creative?*
A: Certainly. There are a number of reasons why exercise can make you a more creative person. A lot of times, our busy schedules prevent us from periods of reflection necessary to the creative process. We get all wrapped up in our daily routine and tend to do things out of habit. We know we should spend some time alone, thinking, perhaps meditating, but we are filled with so much nervous energy we can't sit still. Here's where exercise helps. The calm solitude of running alone outdoors gives you a chance to work things out in your mind. New ideas to help you approach old problems are more likely to pop into your head

while running, cycling, or walking than if you spent that same time watching TV or worrying about that problem.

Dr. Paul Dudley White, former physician to President Eisenhower, had another theory. He suggested exercise improves circulation to all parts of the body, including the brain. He contended that this increased circulation prevents senility in older people, allowing them to lead a more creative and productive life.

Dr. Thaddeus Kostrabula, the running psychiatrist mentioned earlier, expands on this theory. Kostrabula has done extensive study on the effects of long distance running on the mind, and made some interesting observations. As the runner approaches the 30 minute mark, he feels depressed. Some subjects have even told him that at the 30 minute mark they feel like crying and occasionally do. Perhaps it's the pain, perhaps it's the desire for sympathy. But a short time after the 30 minute mark is reached, some people experience an "opening up" phenomenon. Their breathing becomes easier, their legs feel stronger, and they feel almost euphoric.

Now Kostrabula admits that this is a pretty amazing phenomenon. His explanation deals with the left and right sides of the brain. The left side controls the functional aspects of day to day living while the right side controls, among other things, creative functions. The only problem is that to break through to that right side takes some doing. In a sense we have to escape one level of consciousness to give the brain a clear slate from which to produce new ideas—to create. This level of consciousness is often approached through various forms of repetition. The "OM" of transcendental meditation is one example. Nearly all religions of both East and West utilize a form of repetition to reach a particular level of consciousness or communion with a higher being.

Kostrabula maintains that the repetitive nature of running along with whatever repetition you intone mentally with each step helps you to reach this level of consciousness. He suggests that after 30 or 40 minutes of slow long-distance repetitive running, the left side of the brain gets bored and lets the right side of the brain take over.

Q: *Is there any research to back this up?*
A: Unfortunately, we are dealing with concepts and terms that

are difficult to measure. Regardless of how convincing Kostrabula's theory is, we have to recognize that it is just a theory and not a medical or psychological fact. At least one study (conducted by Drs. A. Ismail and L. E. Tractman of Purdue University) found that volunteers in a program of regular physical activity became more self-sufficient, resolute, emotionally stable, and imaginative. So I guess you could say their mental alertness increased.

Q: *How does exercise improve productivity?*
A: Exercise increases your endurance for all activities, so you're able to work longer before feeling tired. When you are tired, you are unable to produce as much work in a given period of time as you can when you are alert and fresh. Once you begin to tire, your productivity decreases proportionately.

Q: *But won't exercise just make you more tired? If you work 8 hours a day, and then spend another 30 to 40 minutes in physical activity, won't you be just that much more tired?*
A: It might seem so, but actually exercise has the opposite effect. People really develop fatigue from inactivity. A common example is the desk-bound typist who comes home at the end of the day and feels very tired. Students often suffer from inactivity fatigue after sitting through long class periods and long hours of study. The natural tendency for both the office worker and the student is to sit down and watch TV and many times to also have an evening cocktail. The cocktail will probably dull the senses to the point that fatigue is no longer noticed at the conscious level. But the cocktail really does nothing to promote alertness or relieve fatigue. Surprisingly, neither does sitting or lying down. This just causes more inactivity. The best antidote for fatigue at the end of the day is doing some physical activity, whether it is your favorite sport, a walk, dance, or swim. Activity makes you feel more energetic and the sense of fatigue disappears.

A: *Why would I feel renewed energy after exercise?*
A: One explanation for this feeling of energy is that during inactivity the body accumulates adrenalin. The adrenalin products are stored in the brain and the heart. Exercise literally speeds up the metabolism and burns up the accumulated adrenalin stores. This

improves the function of the body cells and also affects the brain cell function.

Along these same lines, it is possible that people are fatigued simply because of the psychological drain of the job. The pressures of the day and added responsibilities take their psychic toll. Exercise can play a role here too. You may have mental fatigue from the job pressure or even boredom, but the exercise gives you a sense of accomplishment—I covered so many miles on my bicycle, exercised for so many minutes, or whatever. All of that is good and all of that is good for your psyche. It gives you a sense of personal fulfillment and also helps you achieve a meaningful goal.

By conditioning your body through exercise, your 8 hours on the job do not tax you as heavily as they did before you exercised. The explanation is that exercise makes you stronger physically. Because you are stronger you work more efficiently, getting the same amount done with less fatigue.

Q: *What type of hard evidence is there to suggest that exercise actually improves productivity?*
A: Most of the experiments that support this claim of higher productivity from exercise concern attendance. I did a simple experiment several years ago. Thirty women employed in a large corporation participated in a voluntary fitness program. The program consisted of 10 minutes of aerobic exercise twice a day, every working day. After two years, the participants' personnel records were checked and it was found that they had missed an average of 2.37 work days, compared to 4.28 work days of another random sampling of workers who didn't exercise. In other words, the ones who exercised missed fewer days than the ones who did not exercise. Perhaps more significant were the comments from the participants. "We feel better," "happier," and "more productive" were typical reactions from this group. Of course, it may be argued that our women were better motivated to begin with. So I checked their attendance records one year prior to initiation of the exercise program. There was no significant difference between my subjects and the random sampling of women.

A more impressive study was that of Dr. Victor Linden of

Norway. In a study of 203 men employed in a variety of occupations, Linden found that those with perfect attendance records for 5 years had all engaged in some kind of physical activity during off-the-job hours.

So exercise really improves productivity with a double-barreled approach. First, it keeps you healthy and on the job. Fewer absences mean greater possibility for improved productivity. Second, exercise helps you feel stronger, more alert, and less fatigued so that when you *are* on the job, you're working at near maximum efficiency level.

Q: *Why don't employers try to encourage their workers to get involved in fitness programs?*
A: That's a good question. In fact, some Japanese firms are doing just that. The Japanese industrial complex is highly competitive and they recognize the importance of getting a good day's work from their employees. That's why many companies in Japan begin each work day with organized calisthenics for the workers. I've even heard that one factory has a room with a punching bag. On the bag is a likeness of the company president's face. Employees are encouraged to drop in and take a few whacks whenever they feel like it. In addition, those same firms are building gymnasiums and athletic facilities next to the factories. The facilities are for the express use of employees and their families. Evidently they too have read the research showing reduced absenteeism among workers who exercise.

Q: *Are there any such programs in the United States?*
A: There's a new momentum gathering in industry to provide exercise programs for employees. For example, there is an American Association of Fitness Directors in Business and Industry with the express purpose of promoting physical fitness in industry. Some leading presidents of various corporations have given their reasons. R. H. Dobbs, Jr., President of the Life Insurance Company of Georgia says, "It's good business to keep our key personnel healthy—it means less time lost. I'm also convinced that if we can add a few years to our employees' lives, it will mean a tremendous financial saving. Our people feel better, stay in better humor, and handle people better because of their

participation in our fitness program. And they do participate—on company time. In fact, I insist on it. If they can't leave their job for at least one hour, two or three times a week, they're not organized and they shouldn't be in an executive position."

W. W. Keeler, chairman of the board of Phillips Petroleum Company, puts it this way: "For most of us, the benefits of a physical conditioning program will be under personal well-being. And those benefits accrue to our businesses. When our employees are gaining physical fitness through regular exercise, they become more productive and happier individuals. They live longer. When we consider the investment our companies have in people, and our reliance on their skills and experience, it is clear that the longevity of employees is a real benefit to our organization, as well as personal satisfaction to us."

Q: *How does exercise improve mental attitudes?*
A: Attitudes are a funny thing. Generally, attitudes are directed at other people, though psychiatrists tell us that attitudes begin with the feelings we have about ourselves. Dr. Edward Greenwood, M.D., states that "among adults who exercise regularly, there also seems to be a feeling of greater self-confidence, stability, and calmness." In other words, the more physically fit we are, the more we like ourselves.

Q: *Why do you think the unfit don't like themselves?*
A: There are a number of reasons. They don't like the way they look. They are fat, their muscles sag, their posture is poor. When they dress up for an evening on the town, they are embarrassed because their clothes don't look right on them. They don't like the way they feel. They fatigue easily. They don't sleep right. Their food is not digested properly. The slightest activity makes breathing difficult. They are plagued with hurts that bother and worry them. And they don't like the way they act. They are frustrated because they can't do the things they used to do. They don't like to admit to themselves the real reason they don't take the kids to the beach is because they would have to be seen in a bathing suit. They don't like the fact that they have become spectators rather than participants.

What especially bothers them is that they become dishonest

and say, "I don't want to" instead of "I can't" when their friends ask them to spend a weekend with them canoeing, skiing, or backpacking. All this leads to a very poor self-image, which in turn leads to a poor mental attitude. It's very difficult to like others when you don't like yourself. Something is drastically needed.

If you'll look back at those reasons I just mentioned, you'll find that exercise plays an important part in helping solve some of those problems. No, I'm not saying that exercise is the only answer to an improved self-image. It's not that simple. But it's a start, and often spurs an interest in other areas that leads to a sounder picture of your mental health. The work of Dr. A. H. Ishmail and R. John Young, Purdue University, tends to substantiate this claim that physical fitness is related to some highly desirable self-images. For example, their research showed that physical fitness is associated with emotional stability, composure, youthfulness, confidence, and sophistication.

Dr. Frederick D. Harper, of Howard University, has said that people who exercise regularly have "positive feelings about their bodies." They also have greater sexual appreciation, better feelings about their health, and less anxiety.

Q: *The areas of creativity, productivity, and attitude seem to be closely related to stress. Have any studies been done to show that exercise reduces stress?*
A: Yes there have. Some doctors report that exercise helps people who are uptight, people who have all the symptoms of nervous behavior. Dr. Herbert deVries and Gene Adams of the University of Southern California did a study which I think illustrates this point. They solicited volunteers who ranged in age from 52 to 70. All these volunteers had symptoms of nervous tension; that is, sleeplessness, irritability, and continual worry. The research design included giving the subjects 400 mg. of meprobamate (a widely-used tranquilizer). On some days they gave the subjects an identical looking placebo. Finally, they gave the subjects 15 minutes of exercise. The exercise was found to be the most effective measure of reducing tension.

Other studies produced similar findings. Fred Heinzleman, Ph.D., and Richard Bagley, in work supported by the U.S. Heart

Disease and Stroke Control Program, conducted an 18 month study of 239 men aged 45 to 59 years, many of whom suffered from high blood pressure and elevated cholesterol levels. They participated in a program of supervised physical activity—one hour a day, 3 times a week. A control group of 142 men did not exercise. Of those in the exercise group, 43% said they experienced reduced stress versus 18% in the control group. Eighty-five percent said they felt their health was improved, while only 19% of the control group expressed a similar feeling. And in that same study, 37% of those who exercised, versus 4% of the control group, said they slept better.

In another study at the University of Illinois, Dorothy I. Popejoy, Ph.D., worked with 33 normally sedentary women. After placing the women on an exercise program four days a week for 20 weeks, she found that 22 of the 33 women showed improvement in both psychological and physiological measures of anxiety. Their health also improved. In other words, whether the stress was produced by physiological or psychological problems, the exercise program improved their ability to handle such stress.

I think Dr. Alan Clark of St. Joseph's Infirmary in Atlanta, Georgia, summarized it best: "It is well known that exercise is the best tranquilizer. I refuse to medicate patients with simple neurotic anxiety until they have given aerobic exercise an adequate trial."

Q: *Can exercise do anything to reduce anxiety?*
A: Dr. Richard Driscoll, a psychologist at Eastern State Psychiatric Hospital in Knoxville, Tennessee, thinks so. He found that running in place and thinking pleasant thoughts makes people less anxious.

One psychiatrist from the University of Wisconsin, Dr. John Greist, felt that running may be effective in helping depressed people. In one study he assigned a group of abnormally depressed people to a 10-week running program. He assigned another group to traditional psychotherapy. He found the running to be as effective as the psychotherapy.

Q: *Why does running seem to work so well in reducing anxiety?*
A: Marjorie H. Klein, associate professor of psychiatry at the

University of Wisconsin, has a plausible explanation. "Running may well be an antagonist to depression . . . since the way we feel in our minds can make us feel bad physically, it may work the other way too. . . . Depression is usually accompanied by feelings of not being able to accomplish anything. By running, participants *are* accomplishing something—running a certain distance and improving their health."

Of course, not all of the evidence is in. But there's a striking similarity in all of the research surrounding exercise and stress. The factors causing stress may not be easily minimized or eradicated. By exercising we can improve our ability to cope with the stress we must necessarily face in order to live in our pressure-packed society. It would be nice if society would change, but I don't think that's possible or realistic. But we do have control over our own behavior.

Q: *Can exercise actually change behavior?*
A: I would hesitate to say that exercise alone changes behavior. Exercising for 30 minutes or longer a day in itself will not change behavior. Behavior is much more complex than that. However, much of what we have been talking about in this chapter is closely related to behavior. Improved creativity and productivity as well as an improved self-image contribute toward your making positive changes in your behavior. I have said before that exercise improves not only your physical health but your mental health as well. I've also said that the two are closely related. It is true if you feel better and feel better about yourself, you will become a different person. You have a greater zest for living and a better outlook on life. You now have hope where before you felt there was no better way than to continue in the doldrums of inactivity. Behavioral change or modification is a relatively new field, and I'm not about to advance new theories in that area.

I am not alone, however, when I contend that exercise can be an element useful in changing behavior. Several psychiatrists are prescribing exercise along with other activities to change behavior. Dr. Klein, the University of Wisconsin psychologist, has said that running and psychotherapy are probably necessary for these people. "Running gets the patient over his bad feelings, but he still has to talk with someone and get at the heart of the problem."

Q: *Can exercise be used as therapy for neurotics and psychotics?*
A: I've already mentioned Dr. Thaddeus Kostrabula, the psychiatrist who feels that slow long-distance aerobic running followed by a group therapy session can and has produced observable, positive changes in behavior and life style. He has found that this is especially helpful among those people addicted to drugs, alcohol, or depression. Emma McCloy Layman, Ph.D., suggests that exercise is a potential aid in the rehabilitation of psychiatric patients. She is careful to point out that even superior physical fitness will not make us immune from the effects of other types of traumatic experiences of home, school, or community. But she does list several possible uses of exercise in treating those in psychiatric care:

1. Exercise may help improve the behavior of certain psychiatric patients who do not respond well to traditional therapy.
2. Exercise may help patients profit more from the other types of therapy.
3. Exercise may reduce the need for physical restraints and sedation.
4. Exercise may help children with psychiatric problems improve their behavior.

Q: *Why isn't exercise used more often as therapy?*
A: One reason is that it is new, and anything new takes some time before it receives wide-spread approval. Another reason is simply the fact that each case of neurotic or psychotic behavior must be treated differently. Psychotic conditions are much like heart conditions in that they may advance to a stage where exercise may not be the best possible solution for that particular time. That is why it is important to think of exercise as a preventive measure rather than a cure or treatment, though it works in both areas.

Q: *Would I need less sleep if I exercise?*
A: In most cases, yes, and I don't know if the reason is psychological or physiological. It may be a combination of the two. Dr. Thaddeus Kostrabula has a theory. He says that a runner gets a runner's sleep. According to him, the runner's sleep pattern will

change. "He will sleep more lightly, dream more, and awaken more refreshed in the morning." He goes on to explain that, "one probable reason for this particular shift in sleep pattern has to do with the function of dreams. Each night the soul attempts to repair itself in sleep. If, however, the person is deeply troubled, either within himself or due to external circumstances, his dreams will be repressed. The ego sees the dream as another meddlesome intrusion upon an already rocking boat. Thus, the first step most people take is to try to override the dream aspect. They will complain bitterly of the insomnia and may use sleeping medication, or drugs such as alcohol to help them through the night. They blame their fatigue on their insomnia. In fact, all they're doing is getting more out of touch with themselves.

"The running reverses this process. The dreams do surface and can be brought into therapy. It's really fun to hear a patient who used to complain bitterly of insomnia report one day, 'I didn't sleep last night, but it didn't bother me at all, and I feel just fine. In fact, I'm full of energy.' This phenomenon is directly related to running."

Quite frankly, doctors don't know why this happens. It's a fertile field for investigation. I'll relate my own experience to you. I need 7 hours of sleep when I train and around 8 to 8½ when I don't. Call it the power of suggestion, call it whatever you want. But there's one thing I know. I fall asleep faster. I sleep better and sounder when I'm in good physical shape than when my fitness level slips. I think you'll find the same thing too!

Q: *Why is it that the more I sleep, the more sleep I need?*
A: It may be related to the depression we talked about earlier or it could also have to do with your aerobic capacity. The less active you become, the lower your fitness level becomes. Because your fitness level becomes lower, you demand more and more sleep. The more sleep you get, the lower your fitness level drops. It's a vicious cycle and is only reversed via good aerobic-type exercise.

Q: *What is the physiological reason for the change in sleep patterns with exercise?*
A: That is the $64,000 question. I don't think there is a com-

pletely definitive answer. Let me tell you a couple theories. I'm sure that because your physical fitness level improves, you start to feel better, but there may be something more direct. The actual exercise may affect the brain. Here are some illustrations.

When clinical psychologists at the Veterans Administration Hospital in Buffalo, New York, administered pure oxygen to senile patients placed in a pressurized chamber, the patients' mental alertness improved. After being treated with the oxygen twice a day for 15 days, these elderly people took a standard memory test and scored as much as 25% better than they had before the oxygen therapy.

The late Dr. Paul Dudley White, dean of American Cardiologists, said, "The brain . . . needs to be well-fed with oxygen and other chemicals and its waste products removed. Only the blood can do that. For its optimal function, therefore, the brain must have a good fresh supply which is delivered by a good heart and *good blood vessels* (my italics) which should be kept in good condition." He also goes on to note that vigorous leg exercise helps prevent or retard the atherosclerosis or rusting process in our arteries. And those arteries may be in either the brain or in the heart itself.

Furthermore, Dr. Ismail at Purdue University whose study I mentioned, said that some of the changes they saw occurring in their subjects were due to this general theory: Any alteration in personality brought about by exercise is due to salutary physiological and biochemical changes such as improved circulation, which brings more oxygen to the brain. Better circulation also means that the brain is getting greater amounts of glucose, a substance vital to its nutrition.

I guess you might say that if one accepts the concept of personality as a manifestation of "mind," and that the mind is located in the brain, then what affects the brain—in this particular case exercise providing a greater supply of oxygen—may also affect the personality. It would certainly seem so.

The National Institute on Mental Health is currently conducting a study to investigate the biochemical changes in the brain that occur when a person is exercising. Experiments have demonstrated that depressed people placed on a regular exercise program have mood elevations. Further investigations have revealed that norepinephrine, a neuro-transmitter, is produced in the brain of depressed persons during short-term exercise. Interestingly, severely depressed persons are deficient in this particular hormone.

Q: *Are the chances of developing such problems as depression, anxiety, and "the blues" reduced with exercise?*
A: I think so. Let's say it's the one area where you have a little more control than other areas. You can't change society, or at least not right this minute. You can't reduce the pressures of a job, finances, marriage, and home. What you can do is gird yourself with as many defenses as possible to fight off the negative effects of such pressures. Getting enough sleep is one way. Adequate relaxation is another. Good nutrition is still another way to give you the edge against neurosis. But exercise just may be the most important defense of all.

PART II

GETTING MORE OUT OF YOUR EXERCISE

"Health is not what you know, it is what you do."

ANONYMOUS

CHAPTER

8

How Much Exercise Do You Need?

Q: *How hard should I exercise to get the benefits from the exercise I do?*
A: Your own body provides the answer. Experts have found that the best guidelines are your pulse rate and personal feelings.

Q: *How can I measure my personal feelings about the benefits of exercise?*
A: If you're exercising and you find you're having a difficult time holding a conversation with somebody next to you, you're probably going too hard. (Don't hold a conversation if no one's there or the men in white jackets will pick you up.) Even if you're alone, you can use your imagination. Do you feel like talking? If not, you probably can conclude the exercise level is too hard. This is called the Talk Test and it is especially useful during the early stages of exercising. Also, while you're exercising you should slow down and stop if you experience any chest, jaw, or neck pain. Then check with your doctor. If after exercising you seem excessively tired for an hour or so, it was probably too hard for you. No matter how good an athlete you used to be, you must learn to "listen" to your body. It will tell you a great deal about your proper amount of exercise.

Q: *But what about the person who says, "Everytime I get the urge to exercise I lie down"?*
A: He is just kidding himself. It's a cop out. So a second technique is used. When you exercise you can also listen to your body by checking your pulse rate. Exercises that produce a pulse rate that is 70 to 85% of your maximum heart or pulse rate are best.

Q: *How can I determine my maximum heart rate?*
A: The ideal way to determine your maximum heart rate would be to put yourself on a treadmill and run till exhaustion. At the end of the run your heart rate would be at its highest point. Its maximum.

Q: *How high can a heart rate go?*
A: That takes a little explanation. Physiologists have calculated that if a young child is placed on a treadmill and run to exhaustion, his maximum heart rate would be around 220 beats per minute, give or take a few beats.

Physiologists also know that as you grow older, your maximum heart rate drops about a beat a year. So if you are 40 years of age, your maximum heart rate would be 180. That is, 220 minus your age. Therefore, a 20-year-old would have a maximum heart rate of 200, a 30-year-old a maximum heart rate of 190, a 40-year-old a maximum heart rate of 180, a 50-year-old a maximum heart rate of 170, and so on. The whole process is really quite easy. Once you know what your maximum heart rate is, you simply take 70 to 85% of your maximum heart rate and you are able to determine your desirable heart rate for your particular age. The 70 to 85% range gives you what doctors call your target heart rate range. The chart below does this for you. It also tells you the heart rate best for your age group.

Age	Target Heart Rate
10–19	145 to 180 beats per minute
20–29	140 to 170 beats per minute
30–39	130 to 160 beats per minute
40–49	125 to 150 beats per minute

50–59	115 to 140 beats per minute
60–69	105 to 130 beats per minute

Q. *What's the best way to take your pulse rate?*
A: The easiest places to count your pulse or heart rate are the radial artery on the wrist and the temporal artery on your forehead. Use the second, third, and fourth fingers of the hand to feel for the pulse along the thumb side of your wrist or use those same three fingers along your forehead. You should take your pulse rate for 10 seconds in this pattern. Right before you actually start counting, count the beats by going zero, zero, zero. As soon as the sweep second hand reaches the twelve, you start counting. But the first number you count is zero and from there on it's one, two, three, four, and stop counting when the sweep second hand reaches the two or ten seconds. The count should then be multiplied by 6 to find out how many times your heart beats per minutes. It's best to practice taking your pulse rate while at rest. Once you feel comfortable, you can then take it on a regular basis either before, during, or immediately after exercise.

Q: *Should you take your pulse at your neck?*
A: Today, more and more physicians and exercise physiologists frown upon it. There are two reasons: When people place their fingers at their neck, they may develop heart arrhythmias. That is, their heart throws some irregular heart beats. The second problem is that their pulse rates may actually slow down. Consequently, you will get a false reading. While it is easy to find the pulse at the neck, there is a tendency for some error. So the best places are your wrist and temporal area.

Q: *Why is pulse rate so important?*
A: Your "ideal" exercise level is determined by measuring your "maximum aerobic power." As I stated before, there is a point where, despite your best efforts, the heart and circulatory system cannot deliver enough oxygen to those tissues that by now are screaming for help. When this occurs, you have reached your maximum aerobic power level. But this is a very difficult measurement to obtain, for it requires a great deal of sophisticated equipment, a medical doctor, or exercise physiologist. It will also

require a healthy portion of your time and money. But you needn't despair. Further research has shown a close relationship between maximum aerobic power and maximum heart rate. Therefore, since everyone can find his pulse rate it becomes a valuable tool for measuring how hard you are exercising.

Q: *How long should I exercise?*
A: Though there are a number of factors to take into consideration (intensity of exercise, your weight and physical condition, etc.), most experts agree that anything less than 15 minutes probably does you little good. If you are exercising aerobically and spend the entire session getting the job done rather than sitting around and thinking about it, 15 to 30 minutes will be sufficient for most people.

Q: *What's the best way to "warm up" to my target heart rate?*
A: You should spend about 5 to 10 minutes on warm-up exercises before reaching your target zone. A proper warm-up increases the elasticity of the muscles and tendons and helps to prevent strains. It also raises the temperature of the muscles and helps to facilitate biochemical reactions that supply energy to the muscle tissues. Drs. Fred Kasch and John Boyer of San Diego State University found that a good warm-up readies the joints for further action by increasing the synovial fluid that lubricates them, and by thickening the joint tissue itself. They prefer to call the warm-up "joint readiness."

Dr. Thomas Cureton, the retired professor from the University of Illinois whom we talked about in Chapter 2, feels that a warm-up is necessary for the circulatory systems of sedentary people, especially middle-aged people whose blood vessels have become less flexible.

A recent study by Dr. James Barnard in California also demonstrated the importance of the warm-up. Dr. Barnard and his associates tested healthy police officers and firefighters, focusing on their responses to sudden activity. When subjected to the sudden hard exercise of running on a treadmill, the subjects showed striking electrocardiographic changes that indicated their hearts were not getting sufficient oxygen to perform the work.

A warm-up also improves performance during the first 10 minutes of exercise. This is especially true in games like tennis, handball, squash, and basketball.

Along with the physical value, a good warm-up can be a psychological boost to you as you face your exercise routine. When I'm running, for example, I find the first few minutes are a drag. I'm wondering why I'm here when I should be back at my work. My muscles are just a little stiff, perhaps, and my mind is still on my work. But after I get through the first 5 or 10 minutes, I find that I'm breezing along quite nicely. A warm-up eases you into the session. After a few minutes of relaxing, comfortable stretching exercises, and easy running, you really feel like doing something more strenuous.

Q: *Is five to ten minutes of warm-up sufficient?*
A: Exactly how much of a warm-up is necessary depends on the individual, but a good rule of thumb is to spend the 5 to 10 minutes. A person who is very unfit or considerably older should err on the side of providing extra minutes for warm-up. I know one gentleman who is 78 and spends 20 minutes warming up prior to his exercise.

Q: *What kind of warm-up exercises are best?*
A: If you intend to run, allow some time for stretching, slow walking, fast walking, then jogging. For handball, it's advisable to do some running, side stepping, and actual volleying before the game starts. Some specific warm-up exercises are given in Appendix A. The actual jogging, handball, or keeping the heart rate at the target heart rate range is called the peak period. That should last 15 to 30 minutes or so. After that, 5 to 10 minutes are to be devoted to a cool-down. So a workout should last 25 to 50 minutes—5 to 10 minutes for a warm-up; 15 to 30 minutes for peak work; and 5 to 10 minutes for a cool-down.

There is one more thing. The warm-up and cool-down can be used to work on flexibility (good range of motion) to prevent muscle, tendon, and joint injuries. It can also be used to work on muscle strength and endurance.

Q: *What is a "cool-down"?*
A: The cool-down is the same as the warm-up, only in reverse.

Some people call it tapering-off. To taper-off, simply exercise at a slower pace than you did during the peak period for 2–3 minutes and do exercises listed in Appendix B.

Q: *Why is a cool-down necessary?*
A: Your body has been exercising at a pretty high level for about 15 to 30 minutes or longer. Now it's suddenly time to stop. When you are exercising, the capillary beds in your muscles are wide open. When you stop, there's a tendency for the blood to pool in the legs. As a result, not enough blood gets back up to the heart and you feel light-headed. But if you keep your legs moving, there is a better return of blood to your heart. Your leg muscles act as your second and third hearts of your body.

Q: *How can the legs act as a second and third heart for the body?*
A: When you are exercising, the heart is pumping blood at a faster than normal rate. That way the active muscles are supplied with oxygen and life-sustaining nutrients. The blood is pumped into the muscles by the forceful contractions of the heart. But there is no similar force to remove the blood from the muscles to the heart via the veins. The blood, therefore, is pushed back to the heart by means of the "milking action" of the veins. The veins are not as heavily muscled as the arteries and are easily compressed. When the veins are filled with blood, the exercising muscles literally massage or milk the vessels and push the blood back toward the heart. To aid in this process, the veins have valves to help trap the blood and to push it back to your heart.

When you immediately stop exercising, the heart continues to pump blood at a vigorous rate to the muscles. But since the muscles are no longer active, there's no action to send the blood back to the heart. The blood then has a tendency to pool in the muscles and the veins. By tapering-off gradually, you avoid the delay in the return of the blood to the heart and aid in helping the body adjust to the new situation of less activity.

Q: *Is taking a cold shower a good way of tapering-off?*
A: The key in tapering-off is to allow your muscles to cool down gradually. To supplement the lessening of activity, you may find it beneficial to take a shower or bath to help taper-off. It is preferred

that the shower or bath be warm and gradually reduced to a more tepid temperature. This aids in the cooling-down process because the tepid water forces the more superficial blood vessels to constrict and force the blood back into the larger vessels. That process makes more blood available to circulate throughout the body via the large vessels to such critical organs of the body as the brain and kidneys.

Of course, the shower is not necessary. It's just an additional thing that you may want to do.

Q: *Is it beneficial to put on a sweater or jacket after exercise?*
A: No. The sweater is not necessary. After sweaty exercise, allow your body to return to its original state by leaving it off. When you are no longer sweating, you may then put your sweater on to keep you from chilling. If you "listen" to your body, you'll know when it is time to put extra garments on.

Q: *How long should I taper-off?*
A: Again, the rule of thumb is to take 5 to 10 minutes to get your heart rate back down to 110 beats or less. It's when you feel comfortable.

Q: *How many times a week should I exercise?*
A: Exercise is just like eating and sleeping. Your body requires uniform amounts regularly and steadily. To be effective, your exercise program should be performed on a regular basis at a minimum recommended rate of 3 days per week. Alternate days are best. Laying off for more than 2½ days between workouts will nullify the gains you were just starting to make. Of course, 5 times or even 6 times a week is best, but many people are unable to maintain this level. You will still be able to improve the way you look and feel if you exercise at least 3 days a week. That's your prescription.

Q: *Should I exercise 7 days a week?*
A: I don't advocate doing the same exercise 7 days a week. But that's a personal preference. I think it's a good idea to take one day off a week. That doesn't mean you don't have to exercise. Just do something different. It's a great way to keep you

motivated. Let's say that you have been bicycling for 40 minutes a day. On your seventh day you may decide to take a walk, swim, or go back packing. Even Roger Bannister, the world's first sub-4 minute miler took time off when training. A few weeks before he broke the 4 minute barrier, he went rock climbing. If a finely conditioned athlete can do it, so can a fitness enthusiast.

Q: *Will exercising 3 times a week for 25 to 50 minutes really improve my fitness level?*
A: Absolutely. Improving your fitness level isn't something that is achieved through a magical exercise that gives instant fitness. If so, such an exercise would be patented and sold with a very high price tag. Many people would like to believe that a magical exercise exists. I hate to disappoint you. It just ain't there.

To improve your fitness level you must exercise at target heart rate levels. That's the trick. In addition, you need to pay attention to what your body is trying to tell you. Get into the habit of checking your pulse rate during your exercise program. This will enable you to discover if and when that program needs to be stepped up a bit if you want to improve your fitness level. For example, you may find that after 2 or 3 weeks of playing doubles tennis your target heart rate (70 to 85% of your maximum heart rate) is not being reached. You may need to switch to singles tennis or play with someone better to keep that heart rate in the target zone. As your body becomes more accustomed to exercise, you will find you can increase the intensity of your activities and still enjoy it as much. At the same time, your fitness level increases.

Listen to your body. That is, if you find when you are exercising you seem excessively fatigued, pull back. You don't have to be full of macho in this kind of contest. You're not in it for proving your ability in athletic competition. You're trying to follow an exercise program for life. Joe Henderson of *Runner's World* tells us that you should be a lifer in exercise.

Q: *Is there a best kind of exercise?*
A: Yes, there is. Exercises which are continuous and non-stop are best. These are the kinds of exercise which permit you to keep your heart in the 70 to 85% range. They also burn the most calories. Many times people involved in stop-and-go exercises

find that their pulse rate and burned calories fluctuate. The exercise you want is non-stop.

Q: *What are the best kinds of non-stop exercises?*
A: Walking, bicycling, swimming, and jogging are best. These will be discussed in Chapter #9. Such exercises as cross-country skiing, tennis, handball, and badminton can be used but they have their own set of problems. I'll discuss those sports and problems in Chapter #10.

Q: *Is exercising at 70 to 85% of maximum, for 15 to 30 minutes, three times a week all the exercise I need to prevent a heart attack?*
A: Exercise will not prevent a heart attack. It will, however, reduce your chances of having one. Exercising at 70 to 85% of maximum will also reduce many of the coronary heart disease risk factors. Most physicians feel that the 70 to 85% of maximum, three times a week for 15 to 30 minutes is sufficient. But I would be remiss in not mentioning that there are other scientists who recommend greater amounts of exercise. Two in particular are Dr. Thomas K. Cureton, from the University of Illinois, and Dr. Thomas Bassler, the pathologist in Inglewood, California.

Dr. Cureton, who has done a tremendous amount of research in the area of exercise physiology, has recommended for years that exercising for 60 minutes, 6 times a week is the correct level. He has also said that it takes this much exercise to reduce your chances of heart disease. Only in a pinch will he permit 30 minutes of exercise.

Dr. Bassler advocates something similar. He says to prevent (notice I said prevent) a heart attack you must:

1. Run 6 miles a day, 6 days a week.
2. Cover 1,000 miles a year in this manner.
3. Be able to complete a marathon.
4. Be a non-smoker.

Only when you adopt this life style (the life style of a marathon runner) do you have assurance that you will not have a fatal heart attack. He feels that these four steps will bring immunity to heart disease. Few experts agree with Bassler, but many adopt this life style hoping that he's right.

Doctors still don't know if exercise can actually prevent heart attacks, but if I had to speculate, I would surmise that the longer you exercise the better it is in reducing coronary heart disease risk factors. It would also seem that your chances for developing a heart attack would be greatly reduced.

Dr. A. Tooshi conducted a study a few years ago which supports my belief. He found that middle-aged men who exercised 15 minutes a day, five days a week, showed an improvement in physical fitness. Those who exercised 30 minutes a day, five times a week, reduced body fat as well. But those who exercised 45 minutes, five days a week, showed these changes *plus* a significant reduction in blood fats. In other words, the longer they exercised, the greater the reduction in coronary heart disease risk factors.

More recently, Dr. Ralph Paffenbarger, Jr., professor of epidemiology at Stanford School of Medicine, arrived at the same conclusion. Paffenbarger looked at almost 17,000 men over 10 years. His conclusions: as the level of activity goes up, the incidence of heart attack goes down. In fact, if you expend 2,000 extra calories a week your chances of a heart attack are reduced by 64 percent! The study that Dr. Ken Cooper did at his Aerobics Center in Dallas, Texas on risk factors and exercise showed similar results: the more fit you are, the lower your risk factors.

Q: *How much exercise is necessary to stop someone from getting too fat?*
A: Again, it depends upon each person. Remember the importance of calories in versus calories out discussed in Chapter #3? The thing you must remember is how many calories you are out of balance. The more you are out of whack, the more exercise you will need. A general rule of thumb for you is this: for every 100 calories you are out of balance, you will need to engage in target heart rate exercise for 10 to 15 minutes of exercise a day. Ten to 15 minutes of exercise with your pulse rate at 70 to 85% of your maximum will burn about 100 calories.

There is one more important thing to remember about controlling obesity through exercise: the longer the better. At rest, most of your energy comes from the carbohydrate stores in your body. Furthermore, in short bursts of effort such as sprinting, practically all of your energy comes from glycogen. During such exercises as jogging, swimming, and bicycling, about 50% comes from the glycogen and 50% from the body's fat stores. If the exercise lasts for an hour or more, there is a significant increase in the amount of fat used. And if the exercise lasts even longer, the fat stores of the body supply almost 90% of the energy.

Q: *How long do you have to exercise before the body begins to burn 90 percent of its energy from its fat stores?*
A: It will be an individual thing depending upon how intensely a person exercises. But as a rough rule of thumb, it might be about an hour and 40 minutes for a well-trained athlete and 2½ to three hours for the average fitness enthusiast.

Q: *Why would this time period be shorter for the well-trained person?*
A: That has to do with the amount of work accomplished. I can explain this with reference to marathon runners. In about an hour and 40 minutes, a world-class distance runner will run about 20 miles. At this point, he "hits the wall." The glycogen in his body is virtually depleted. On the other hand, the fitness enthusiast will cover 20 miles in 2½, 3 hours, or longer. At this point, he too will be depleted of glycogen. Most of his energy will be coming from fat stores.

So the best rule of thumb for the average exerciser trying to lose weight is to exercise at about 70 to 85% of maximum four times a week for 30 minute. That's your minimum goal.

Q: *Does exercise reduce blood pressure?*
A: The research is contradictory. Anyone who has a normal blood pressure will find that exercise will not reduce his blood pressure. In those people who have elevated blood pressures, however, exercise may play a role, but not in the way you would expect. Exercise seems to affect what is called dynamic blood pressure. Dynamic blood pressure is not the blood pressure that's measured in the doctor's office. It's the blood pressure you have throughout the day—when the boss yells at you, when you and your spouse argue, or when the freeway is tied up. It's those times when things aren't going right that your blood pressure skyrockets.

You say, "Boy, I've got to get my blood pressure under control." Or your spouse says, "Keep your cool. Don't let your blood pressure get out of hand." Your blood pressure fluctuates throughout the day. It is dynamic. Apparently, aerobic-type exercise helps keep your dynamic blood pressure from peaking too much. You might not see the change in the doctor's office, but you reap the benefits throughout the day.

Q: *How much exercise is necessary to reduce blood pressure?*
A: We don't know. If anyone has elevated blood pressure, he should check with his doctor before exercising. Furthermore, I would recommend that he participate in low intensity exercise and exercise for longer periods of time. Do not worry so much about target heart rate. The problem is that many people with high blood pressure adopt a "guts-buster, clenched-fist" attitude. They're headed for trouble. Go easy, go long. That's my advice.

Q: *How do you adjust your exercise program as you become more fit?*
A: Let your pulse be your guide. If you are really serious about exercise, it is important that you begin with a low-key program that is not too difficult. This is especially true if you have been inactive. Remember, at no time should you exceed your target heart rate (70 to 85% of your maximum range). If you find that your exercise program does this, then next time you'll have to work at a little lower intensity. On the other hand, when you find that those sessions produce a lower pulse rate, your body is not getting as much benefit from it and the activity level needs to be increased.

Don't forget: listen to your body. If you find that you are excessively fatigued, experience any chest pain, or your pulse rate is over 110, ten minutes after exercise, you're probably working too hard. Next time slow down a bit.

Q: *You seem to have different recommendations on how much exercise is needed for different people. Would you please summarize how much exercise is enough?*
A: Most of the recommendations listed in the chart below are based on current research, and contain the best advice of many experts available at this time. Remember that the times listed do

not include 5 to 10 minutes for warm-up and 5 to 10 minutes for cool-down.

How Much Exercise Do You Need

1.   **To improve fitness:** work at 70 to 85% of maximum heart rate for a minimum of 15 minutes, 3 times a week. By the way, 20 to 30 minutes is the preferred length of time.

2.   **To drop weight and body fat:** work at 70 to 85% of maximum heart rate for 30 minutes or longer, 4 times a week.

3.   **To reduce coronary heart disease risk factors like cholesterols and triglycerides:** work at 70 to 85% of maximum heart rate for 30 to 45 minutes, 4 or more times a week.

4.   **To help yourself mentally (i.e., reduce depression and anxiety) the best advice seems to be:** work at 70 to 85% of maximum for 45 minutes to an hour, 3 or more times a week.

5.   **To reduce blood pressure the answer is ambiguous. My advice is:** don't worry about target heart rates unless you can exercise at that level comfortably. Exercise slowly for at least 30 minutes, 5 or more times a week.

Q: *Can a beginning exerciser start at these levels right now?*
A: No. First, follow my Starter Walking Program. In addition to the Starter Walking Program, you should adhere to the guidelines set forth in the next few chapters. That way you will reduce the chances of over exercising. Physicians know that most sedentary people develop orthopedic problems by trying to do too much, too soon. Dr. Kenneth Cooper also found that most people who have heart attacks while exercising do so in the first few weeks. Again, too much, too soon. My personal experience supports this point of view. Dr. Fred Kasch of San Diego State University has said that you should spend one month reconditioning yourself for every year you have been sedentary. Excellent advice. The point is: "make haste slowly." Don't overdo. It's a natural human tendency. Believe me. Go slow, the rewards are well worth it.

Q: *What is your starter program?*
A: The charts summarize the starter program. You are to walk a minimum of 4 days a week. I really prefer that you do it 6 days a

week. Unfortunately, most men will think the starter program is too easy. Men recall their high school and college days and want something hard—something that will really make them sweat. Bull! Look, you've abused your body for years with easy living. Go slow—trust me. Time is in your favor if you follow my advice. What good is high intensity exercise if you quit after 2 to 4 weeks? Life is filled with good intentions. Remember, I want you to be a lifer in exercise, not a quitter. Quit is an ugly word. You should remove it from your vocabulary. So ends my sermon. Here's the starter program.

Starter Program A

Level 1: Walk 20 minutes a day 4 times a week or walk 15 minutes a day 6 times a week.

Level 2: Walk 25 minutes a day 4 times a week or walk 17 minutes a day 6 times a week.

Level 3: Walk 30 minutes a day 4 times a week or walk 20 minutes a day 6 times a week.

Level 4: Walk 35 minutes a day 4 times a week or walk 23 minutes a day 6 times a week.

Level 5: Walk 40 minutes a day 4 times a week or walk 26 minutes a day 6 times a week.

Level 6: Walk 45 minutes a day 4 times a week or walk 30 minutes a day 6 times a week.

Starter Program B

Level 1: Walk 10 minutes a day 3 to 4 times a week.

Level 2: Walk 12 minutes a day 3 to 4 times a week.

Level 3: Walk 14 minutes a day 3 to 4 times a week.

Level 4: Walk 16 minutes a day 3 to 4 times a week.

Level 5: Walk 18 minutes a day 3 to 4 times a week.

Level 6: Walk 20 minutes a day 3 to 4 times a week.

Q: *Why do you use two starter plans?*
A: Plan A is for those who don't get their heart rate up into the

target heart rate zone while walking. That will be most people. Plan B is for those who find that walking puts their heart rates into their target heart rate zones.

Q: *How long should I spend at each level?*
A: It depends upon you. Most people spend about a week, so their starter program lasts 6 weeks. Others may spend two weeks or more at each level. It's even possible to start out spending one week at each level and then find as you move up the chart that you have to progress to two weeks or more. It's an individual thing. Let your body be your guide.

Q: *How fast should I walk on this starter program?*
A: Don't worry about the speed. Just walk for time. As you walk, you should be able to hold a conversation with somebody next to you. You may also want to take your pulse rate. If it's below your target heart rate zone, that's ok. If it exceeds your target range, slow down.

Q: *How many miles will I cover?*
A: You really shouldn't worry about that. But most people will cover a mile in 20 minutes. Some slower, some faster. Mileage is not important. Time is important.

Q: *How should I warm-up when doing the starter program?*
A: Here's a good time to get used to including your warm-up and cool-down in your exercise routine. Do the warm-up as outlined in Appendix A. Follow this with the Starter Walking Program. The workout is then to be concluded with a cool-down period. A cool-down in this instance may be just walking at a slower pace and then the exercises listed in Appendix B.

Q: *Do I follow the starter program regardless of the activity I select, i.e., walking, jogging, swimming, bicycling?*
A: Yes. The starter program is exactly what its name implies. It is to get your body ready for target heart rate exercise.

Q: *Do I need a physical exam before starting the starter program?*
A: If you have any questions about your health, see your physician. If you are in apparently good health, free from high blood

pressure, dizziness and the like, it's probably safe for you to start exercising. In fact, it's probably safer for you to start exercising than it is for you to be sitting around all the time, watching TV, and tossing down beer. Remember, go slowly, listen to your body. If you suspect anything is wrong, check with your doctor.

If you've digested everything so far, I think you're ready to exercise. Now all you have to do is select the exercise which is best for you, learn its strengths and weaknesses, follow the guidelines, and get going.

CHAPTER

9

The Big Four—Plus

Q: *Why are walking, jogging, bicycling, and swimming considered to be the best exercises?*
A: They are the simplest exercises to use to improve your aerobic fitness. There are other reasons:

   1.   They are non-stop exercises—they don't give you a chance to sit down and rest.
   2.   These exercises use major muscle groups of the body.
   3.   Your heart rate is kept up where it should be when performing these types of exercises.
   4.   They burn calories.
   5.   This kind of exercise is best for the heart.
   6.   These activities accrue all the benefits we've talked about so far in this book.
   7.   You can quantify the exercise load.

Q: *What is quantifying the exercise load?*
A: Quantifying your exercise load involves measuring how far, how fast, and how long you exercise. Let's say you're going to start walking. You've been quite inactive and you don't want to try too much too soon because that's not good. So you decide you're going to walk 10 minutes a day for several days. As you leave your yard, take a look at your watch. Let's say it's half past

9. Continue on your walk for 5 minutes (9:35), turn around, and come back. Now look at your watch and check your time. How long did it take you? It should have been around 10 minutes (9:40). How far did you walk? Four blocks or five? Let's assume you went four blocks away from your house and four blocks back. Now you have established a distance. When you walk tomorrow, again refer to that 10 minute mark. Did you walk further in that 10 minute period this day or not? The time and distance will give you a very definite picture of the amount of work you are doing. You can measure distance covered and time elapsed.

With sports it's difficult to do that. Dancing, handball, squash, and tennis are good activities, but tend to be difficult to duplicate day in and day out. It's difficult to measure how hard you danced, how fast you ran playing tennis, and how difficult your opponent happened to be. From day to day there is little consistency. With walking, jogging, swimming, or bicycling, time and distance can be measured easily. You can see how much work has been done. Physiologists say one advantage of walking, running, cycling, and swimming is that you can quantify the amount of exercise.

Q: *Are there any other activities which can be quantified?*
A: I guess you could say running in place and rope skipping would be examples. But again the question becomes: how hard did you play, how fast, etc.

Q: *Why is walking such a good exercise?*
A: Practically anyone can do it! I have found that many women 35 years and older are turned off to exercise. That is not a sexist statement, it's a cultural phenomenon in the U.S. Of course, times have changed, which is good. More and more women are jogging, bicycling, playing tennis, walking, and swimming. But the cultural bias still exists. Because of this, walking is a great exercise for women over age 35. It burns a lot of calories: about 80 per mile for a 125 pound woman and about 100 for a 150 pound woman.

Q: *Will walking get my heart rate up to target levels?*
A: Walking certainly allows your heart rate to get up to that

target level. Of course, you must walk faster to do that. You can't just shuffle along and expect it to reach 70 to 85% of your maximum. Dr. Mike Pollock, when he was at Wake Forest University, found that middle-aged men could get their pulse rates up to 70 to 96% of their heart rate range. That was simply because he had them walk faster and faster until they reached that rate. Some of his men were walking 5 mph. But even if you can't walk that fast, you can go longer at a lower pulse rate. This is especially beneficial to the person who is just beginning walking or for the heart patient who is just beginning a program of activity.

As a rough rule of thumb you might do this: If you find that walking, or any exercise, does not permit you to work at a target level, double the exercise. For example, if you want to do 30 minutes of target heart rate exercise and find that you can't get your heart rate up that high, go for 60 minutes or more. It's a fair compromise.

Q: *Why do you recommend walking if, through walking, it's difficult to reach the target heart rate?*
A: As I said, many people don't like jogging, swimming, or bicycling for fitness. So I recommend walking. In fact, in the town of Spring Arbor, Michigan, where I live, at any hour of the day you will see people walking, particularly women. They often walk in groups of 2's, 3's, or 4's. I've seen as many as 14 at one time. In the summertime around 8 o'clock in the morning, you can expect a whole host of them at my wife's door with their walking shoes on and ready to go. And these are not college-age people. They're women in their 20's, 30's, 40's, 50's, 60's, and 70's.

In my fitness classes, women are asked to walk 20 to 60 minutes a day. Some are avid walkers: 45 minutes in the morning and 45 minutes in the evening. They call themselves Charlie's Street Walkers!

Q: *What is a good walking program?*
A: The primary requirement is that walking be done regularly. The first time out, most people can walk 10 to 20 minutes safely. They will also find that if they walk that distance they won't overdo. Here's my advice:

Walking Program A

If your heart rate is not in the target heart rate range,

Levels 1–6:	See Starter Program A on page 134.
Level 7:	Walk 50 minutes 4 times a week or 33 minutes 6 times a week.
Level 8:	Walk 55 minutes 4 times a week or 36 minutes 6 times a week.
Level 9:	Walk 60 minutes 4 times a week or 40 minutes 6 times a week.
Level 10:	Walk 65 minutes 4 times a week or 43 minutes 6 times a week.
Level 11:	Walk 70 minutes 4 times a week or 47 minutes 6 times a week.
Level 12:	Walk 75 minutes 4 times a week or 50 minutes 6 times a week.
Level 13:	Walk 80 minutes 4 times a week or 53 minutes 6 times a week.
Level 14:	Walk 85 minutes 4 times a week or 57 minutes 6 times a week.
Level 15:	Walk 90 minutes 4 times a week or 60 minutes 6 times a week.

Walking Program B

If you find your walking puts your heart rate in target heart rate range,

Levels 1–6:	See Starter Program B on page 134.
Level 7:	Walk 22 minutes 3 to 4 times a week.
Level 8:	Walk 24 minutes 3 to 4 times a week.
Level 9:	Walk 26 minutes 3 to 4 times a week.
Level 10:	Walk 28 minutes 3 to 4 times a week.
Level 11:	Walk 30 minutes 3 to 4 times a week.
Level 12:	Walk 33 minutes 3 to 4 times a week.
Level 13:	Walk 36 minutes 3 to 4 times a week.

Level 14:   Walk 39 minutes 3 to 4 times a week.
Level 15:   Walk 42 minutes 3 to 4 times a week.
Level 16:   Walk 45 minutes 3 to 4 times a week.

The selection of Program A or B depends upon whether you get to your target heart rate or not. Walking Program A is for those who find that the walk does not elicit a target heart rate and Program B is for those who find that the walking puts their heart rate up to target range.

Q: *Should everyone try to progress to the last level?*
A: It depends upon your fitness objective. Remember page 133. If your goal is minimum fitness, somewhere between level 6 and 11 is your end goal. If your goal is weight control, then level 11 is your minimum. If your goals are reduction of coronary heart disease risk factors, such as triglycerides, etc., and also deriving psychological benefits discussed in Chapter 7, level 15 or 16 is best. These recommendations apply to these and all the charts which follow.

Q: *Are there any disadvantages to walking as an exercise?*
A: One of the big disadvantages of walking is that it take a lot of time. But it is still considered a "best" exercise because many people can do it safely with a minimum of problems. In the long run, it may not be that long since you may not have to change clothes (other than shoes) and not shower or go to a special facility.

Q: *What are some problems people should watch out for when they walk for exercise?*
A: The biggest danger is foot ailments. But these can be corrected by wearing good shoes. Any good running shoe will do. Also make sure you wear a pair of clean socks to prevent blisters.

Q: *How do I select a good shoe?*
A: Again the answer is not simple. *Runner's World* says choosing a good shoe is like ordering a fine steak. "The quality of what you choose may depend on your personal taste, preference, and

needs. The final analysis is made according to your individual peculiarities.

"No one can tell you what shoe to buy nor why to buy it. Many shoes have better qualities than others, but then who's to say which qualities are best? This means the final choice involves deciding which features are important to you."

Dr. Harry Hlavac, chief podiatrist at the Sports Clinic in San Francisco, California, has said that "A proper shoe should provide support and cupping of the heel, firm arch support, protection of the ball of the foot, and flexibility of the front sole for easy push off."

Shoes are for protection, support, traction, cushioning from the ground, balance of foot deformities, and accommodation of foot injuries.

Runner's World also notes that you really don't have to worry too much about your shoes unless you get in a significant amount of mileage each week. And then they focus primarily on runners.

I can't agree. At the present time my wife and I have hundreds of men and women involved in walking programs. We found the same kinds of problems that runners encounter with respect to feet. If they use tennis or basketball shoes, they're headed for trouble. I've found that once a person starts to go past level 6 on a regular basis, he needs a shoe that gives good support. Some people encounter problems even at lower levels. My advice is if you are serious about fitness and are going to use a starter program, get a good pair of running shoes. I would also suggest that you get the annual October issue of *Runner's World*. It only costs $2.00. In it you will find a complete guide to good shoe selection.

Q: *How does walking compare to jogging in the number of calories burned per hour?*

A: If you compare jogging and walking, you'll find that if you walk for 20 minutes you'll burn about 100 calories, but if you jog for 20 minutes you'll burn 200 calories. However, if you compare the mileage covered, it's pretty much the same. One mile of jogging will burn about 100 calories while one mile of walking will burn about 100 calories also. Give or take 5 to 10 calories.

To understand, think in terms of a long line. If you run a mile in 10 minutes or walk a mile in 20 minutes, you'll notice that each minute you burned 10 calories while running and 5 calories while walking.

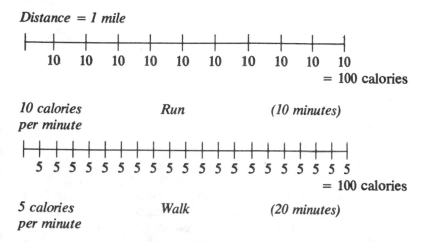

Distance = 1 mile

10   10   10   10   10   10   10   10   10   10

= 100 calories

10 calories   *Run*   *(10 minutes)*
per minute

5 5 5 5 5 5 5 5 5 5 5 5 5 5 5 5 5 5 5 5

= 100 calories

5 calories   *Walk*   *(20 minutes)*
per minute

It's like two guys digging a ditch. One guy digs a 10-foot trench in two hours. Another guy digs a 10 foot trench in four hours. Both did the same amount of work except that one took twice the time. Of course, in 20 minutes the runner can cover 2 miles; the walker about one.

Q: *Does that mean you don't ever have to jog to keep in shape?*
A: Remember, this discussion referred to weight control only. To improve your cardiovascular fitness, you should walk at a rate that elicits a target heart rate for 15 to 30 minutes. If you can't walk that fast, then you have to walk longer, say around 1 to 1½ hours. So at a certain point in your fitness program, running becomes more efficient. While walking may be a "best" exercise, it is time consuming. So jogging may be a better alternative, especially if you have a busy schedule and cannot afford to spend the time that walking requires. But again, it's an individual matter. Either one is good in terms of weight control and aerobic fitness.

Q: *Are there any reasons why a person shouldn't jog?*
A: There has been quite a bit of controversy surrounding jog-

ging. Criticism has come from both the medical profession and the public press. Some of the criticism is legitimate and focuses our attention on areas of prevention that should be considered. Much of the criticism is unfounded and sensationalized, though it attracts a great deal of attention. Basically, the criticism falls into three categories: orthopedic, cardiovascular, and psychological. The first area has to do with our bones and tendons. Because a jogger's foot hits the ground 600 to 750 times during each mile covered, care should be taken to protect the feet, legs, and lower back from injury.

Q: *How can I protect my feet from injury when I jog?*
A: One big problem can be solved if joggers have the right shoes. If they think old loafers or canvas shoes will do, they'll have problems. Most of these shoes do not have adequate arch support nor do they provide enough padding on the heel to absorb the abuse of repeated impact. Therefore, it's little wonder that such things as shin splints, bad knees, achilles' tendons, and heel aches and pains are common complaints of joggers. It is the current consensus among experts in sports medicine who run or jog that most of the injuries are due to overwork, faulty shoes, weakness and lack of flexibility, and improper running techniques.

Q: *Is there a proper way to run?*
A: Yes, and it's not as hard as you might think. A lot of people see a track meet and see a sprinter racing down the track and think that's the way they should look when they run. They try to imitate the sprinter and stiffen up, get up on their toes, and work at it too hard. The best advice for proper running form is simply to relax. A jogger and even a long distance racer does not run on his toes the entire time. You should land comfortably on your heels and roll across on the ball of your foot and push off. Even more flat-footed is ok. You should try not to let your foot flop down hard on the pavement. Do not let your feet slap the ground. Your arms should lean just slightly forward to take the strain off the lower back. The length of your stride (measured from the point where your right foot touches the ground to the point where it touches again) should equal your height.

Q: *Can jogging be dangerous for the heart?*
A: There have been some physicians who say jogging is too vigorous and will cause or precipitate heart attacks. One of the most strongly worded examples of this point of view was the 1976 *Playboy* magazine article "Jogging Can Kill You." In this article, E. G. Schmidt, a physician, claimed that jogging can cause heart attacks, all sorts of leg and back problems, sagging breasts, and displaced ovaries. But if you read the article carefully, you'll see it's an opinion piece. No facts are given, only some doctor's ideas with no data to back it up. The article was an example of irresponsible journalism by a doctor who was using his degree to impress people, to make extra money, and give himself notoriety—a pretty poor example of the Hippocratic oath.

Dr. Larry Lamb, the syndicated columnist and former professor of medicine at Baylor College of Medicine, agrees with me. He said, "The article contains no documented factual information and is filled with much misinformation. In general I find it a totally unreliable presentation. . . . I tried hard to find one redeeming fact in the article that had merit and couldn't find it. Fun is fun . . . but when you are kidding around about important health matters, the joke isn't funny. It's sick."

Q: *Does jogging waste heart beats?*
A: Peter Steinchron, M.D., holds that position, which I think is a myth. He believes you only have a limited supply of energy. He says you are given somewhere between 2 and 2.5 billion heart beats in your "bank" when you are born. And you can't afford to throw away and waste heart beats by overexertion. He claims, "You can't get back a wasted heart beat."

The idea that you can't get back a wasted heart beat is ridiculous. First, there's no evidence that a person has a "bank" of only 2 to 2.5 billion heart beats in a lifetime. But even if this were true, the statement reveals ignorance of an important principle of exercise physiology.

As you train, your resting heart rate drops; consequently, you save heart beats. For example, let's assume that you have a resting heart rate of 80 beats. Let's also assume that you get your heart rate up to 150 beats for ½ hour every day. That's an extra

70 heart beats per minute for ½ hour, which comes out to 2,100 extra heart beats a day. However, because of the training, your resting heart rate will probably drop 10 to 20 beats (to 60 or 70 beats per minute). If it drops only 10 beats per minute, the lower rate over the remaining 23½ hours would amount to 14,100 fewer beats per day than before training. It's like Keynesian economics. You spend money to earn it. And in this case spending an extra 2,100 or so beats a day will save you 14,100. That's a net gain of 12,000 heart beats, each day!

So don't worry about the old ticker when it comes to jogging. More and more physicians are speaking out in favor of jogging as an excellent method of improving overall cardiovascular health.

Q: *What is a good jogging regimen? How should I start?*
A: First, forget how fast you're going to jog. Many people make the mistake of thinking they're training for the Olympic trials.

A friend decided to run with me a few summers ago. All he wanted to do was keep an eye on the stop watch and see how fast he could run the mile or two. He was all vim and vigor for about 2 months. I cautioned him that he shouldn't worry about the time and just go out and enjoy the run. But he kept thinking about his competitive basketball days. I told him that running will take care of itself if he approached it in a relaxed manner. All to no avail. The constant pressure of trying to compete against the clock, himself, and me, finally got to him. He quit.

When you run, go at a pace you think and feel is comfortable. In fact, precede your jogging with the Walking Starter Program. It's the only fair way for your body. Another personal experience illustrates what I'm trying to explain. My friend Darrell Dunckel approached jogging sanely. At first he walked. He interspersed the walking with jogging after a few weeks. But for the first 2 months he mostly walked. Mileage or speed was not foremost for him, but time was. As a result, near the end of the summer we ran a ten-miler together. He's been running for over a year and he gets somewhere between 20 and 30 miles a week. His goal is half a marathon, and maybe a full marathon eventually.

His routine, interspersing walking and jogging, is generally good. That is, jog a telephone pole, walk a telephone pole. (I don't mean the width of the pole either. I mean the distance between the poles.) Repeat this cycle for as many telephone poles as you feel you can handle comfortably. Go at your own rate. Let your body and heart be your guide. That way you will be able to progress without getting too tired. You have to get away from the idea that running is a form of punishment. It's not. You are rewarding your body. If you find that you are fatigued, just walk. Enjoy the scenery, and once you catch your breath, start jogging again. Learn to listen to your body. Are you breathing too hard? Would you be able to hold a conversation with someone? Do you have chest or abdominal pain? If you answered yes to any or all of the above, slow down or stop.

Q: *Does speed really matter in jogging?*
A: No. You may want to check your pulse and see if it's at the proper rate (and it probably will be). If not, you'll have to increase or decrease your pace depending on what your pulse tells you.

Q: *Where should I run?*
A: At first you may be attracted to a track. I caution against this. You'll get bored. Run the roads, paths, and woods. It's more enjoyable. You'll get to see a lot more and you'll find it more relaxing.

Q: *How often should I run?*
A: Three to 4 times a week would be fine.

Q: *How far should I run?*
A: Distance is not important; time is. Your goal is to jog 15 to 30 minutes or more depending on your fitness objective.

Q: *What's the difference between running and jogging?*
A: Probably the spelling and nothing more. Some experts say a jog is considered anything less than an 8 minute mile, while running is anything faster than an 8 minute mile. It's a matter of individuality. A 70 year old may find that an 8 or 9 minute mile is a run, whereas long distance runners such as Frank Shorter and Bill Rogers may find a 6 or 7 minute pace a jog.

Q: *What is a good jogging/running routine?*
A: The chart summarizes it best.

Jogging/Running Routine

(All these levels imply that the routine includes a pace of walking, jogging, walking, jogging, etc. Under no circumstances are you to cover the entire distance non-stop until your body is ready. Then you may jog or run without interspersing the walking.)

Levels 1–6:   See Starter Program on page 134.
Level 7:   Walk/jog 20 minutes 3 to 4 times a week.
Level 8:   Walk/jog 23 minutes 3 to 4 times a week.
Level 9:   Walk/jog 25 minutes 3 to 4 times a week.
Level 10:   Walk/jog 27 minutes 3 to 4 times a week.
Level 11:   Walk/jog 30 minutes 3 to 4 times a week.
Level 12:   Walk/jog 33 minutes 3 to 4 times a week.
Level 13:   Walk/jog 36 minutes 3 to 4 times a week.
Level 14:   Walk/jog 39 minutes 3 to 4 times a week.
Level 15:   Walk/jog 42 minutes 3 to 4 times a week.
Level 16:   Walk/jog 45 minutes 3 to 4 times a week.

The level you want to achieve depends upon your specific fitness objective. (See page 133.)

Q: *Is swimming a better exercise than walking, jogging, or bicycling?*
A: Actually, swimming is neither better nor worse than running or walking for good exercise. Remember we're talking about the Big 4. Each is good but each has its drawbacks.

Q: *What are some of the drawbacks of swimming?*
A: First, you need a pool, and it's not always possible to find one available. Second, not everyone can swim. I certainly wouldn't advise swimming for people who can't swim. That certainly wouldn't be good for your health. Another drawback is climate. If you can't find a pool, a local lake, pond, or stream suffice only if the weather is right.

Q: *Are there any other drawbacks to swimming?*
A: Yes. For example, swimming puts you in a horizontal position where it is more difficult to get your heart up to the target rate. People tend to think that when they are in the pool they are getting exercise. You have to do more than just be in the pool. It's awfully easy to hold on to the edge of the pool, let your feet float up to the surface, and just lay there letting the waves gently rock you. But that isn't exercise. You have to be in the pool really swimming your laps and going at a pace that will keep your heart at target heart rate.

Q: *What are the advantages of swimming as an exercise?*
A: Swimming is great for the obese and those with orthopedic problems. They can swim without fear of trauma to their joints. Also, there is little stress because you are in a relatively cool environment for the entire time.

If an obese person came to me and wanted my choice of exercises of the Big 4, I would recommend swimming until he had reduced his weight and fat. When used properly, swimming is aerobic in nature and an excellent exercise. For the person who finds jogging boring, swimming may be the answer.

Q: *What is a good swimming regimen?*
A: The chart gives a good summary. But when you use this chart, you may use a target heart rate of 60 to 85 percent of maximum, rather than 70 to 85 percent of maximum.

Q: *Why don't I have to get my pulse rate to 70 percent when I swim?*
A: There are several reasons. First, you are horizontal in the water, which makes it more difficult to get your heart rate up, than if you were walking or jogging.

Second, you are buoyant in the water. Consequently there is less resistance.

Third, you are not exposed to a heat stress. When you walk or run, the warm air, humidity, and clothing raise your body temperature and heart rate. But when you swim, the water acts as a coolant so your temperature and heart rate don't go as high.

Fourth, some swimmers become so efficient with their strokes that it's very difficult to get their pulse rate all the way to 70 percent or higher.

Quite frankly, the research is not definitive here. But my personal experience and observation of fitness enthusiasts seems to attest to this modification.

Levels 1–6:	See Starter Program on page 134.
Level 7:	Swim 20 minutes 3 to 4 times a week.
Level 8:	Swim 23 minutes 3 to 4 times a week.
Level 9:	Swim 25 minutes 3 to 4 times a week.
Level 10:	Swim 27 minutes 3 to 4 times a week.
Level 11:	Swim 30 minutes 3 to 4 times a week.
Level 12:	Swim 33 minutes 3 to 4 times a week.
Level 13:	Swim 36 minutes 3 to 4 times a week.
Level 14:	Swim 39 minutes 3 to 4 times a week.
Level 15:	Swim 42 minutes 3 to 4 times a week.
Level 16:	Swim 45 minutes 3 to 4 times a week.

The level you want to achieve depends upon your specific fitness objective. (See page 133.)

Q: *Must other adjustments be made for swimming?*
A: Swimming is unique and the training is specific. Some people may find it difficult going from a walking program to swimming, so I suggest the following: swim a length; walk a length (in the water); swim a length; walk a length, etc. Gradually increase the length of the swim and decrease the length of the walk.

Q: *What if the pool is too deep to walk?*
A: Simply swim your length, then get out and walk a length. Gradually increase the swimming time.

Q: *Would it be possible for a person to swim right away and forget the walking program?*
A: I guess it would be ok if you followed the principle of alter-

nating swimming and walking. But I still prefer the starter program.

Q: *Does it matter which stroke I use in swimming?*
A: It sure does. The butterfly is too intense for most people, especially older people, and should be avoided. Most people will find that the target heart rate is exceeded with this stroke. People who have cardiac problems should be careful about the excessive arm movement. The chart refers to people swimming the crawl, breast stroke, backstroke, or sidestroke. Again, the two programs have to do with getting your heart up to target heart rate.

Q: *What are the advantages of bicycling as an exercise?*
A: Bicycling is a good exercise that has several advantages. If you maintain a steady speed and don't cheat by coasting, you will stay in the target heart range. You will also burn a lot of calories. The bicycle itself provides body support so there is less trauma to the ankles and knees. Bicycling is also enjoyable exercise that can be used as a family type of fitness program.

Q: *What are some of the disadvantages of bicycling?*
A: You need a bike. Not only do you need to have a bike, you need to know how to ride it. If you can't, as a compromise you can use a large tricycle.

Climate, too, may be a factor. While you can jog in snowy weather, it can be much more hazardous on a bike. Ice, blowing winds, and the speed of the bike really complicate bicycling in the dead of winter. Another possible danger is that you have to cycle rather hard to get your target heart rate up, and this can produce local muscle fatigue in the upper legs. Many people feel a 10 minute spin on a bicycle is all they need. To use bicycling as a primary means of exercise, you have to get up to the target heart rate level and stay there.

Q: *What is a good exercise program for bicycling?*
A: The following two charts summarize a good bicycling program for you.

Bicycling Program A

(To be used if your heart rate is not in the target heart rate range)

Levels 1–6: See Starter Program A on page 134.

Level 7:   Bicycle 50 minutes 4 times a week or 33 minutes 6 times a week.

Level 8:   Bicycle 55 minutes 4 times a week or 36 minutes 6 times a week.

Level 9:   Bicycle 60 minutes 4 times a week or 40 minutes 6 times a week.

Level 10:   Bicycle 65 minutes 4 times a week or 43 minutes 6 times a week.

Level 11:   Bicycle 70 minutes 4 times a week or 47 minutes 6 times a week.

Level 12:   Bicycle 75 minutes 4 times a week or 50 minutes 6 times a week.

Level 13:   Bicycle 80 minutes 4 times a week or 53 minutes 6 times a week.

Level 14:   Bicycle 85 minutes 4 times a week or 57 minutes 6 times a week.

Level 15:   Bicycle 90 minutes 4 times a week or 60 minutes 6 times a week.

The level you want to achieve depends upon your specific fitness objective. (See page 133.)

Q: *Are there any problems involved with bike riding?*
A: I've found that many people who ride at target heart rate develop leg pains while pedaling at this rate. For them the exercise is just too difficult. My suggestion is to pedal hard for 2 to 3 minutes; then pedal easier for 2 to 3 minutes; pedal hard for 2 to 3 minutes; pedal easy for 2 to 3 minutes, etc. Gradually increase the time spent pedaling hard and decrease the time spent pedaling easy.

Q: *Are stationary bicycles effective?*
A: They are a good compromise in inclement weather, for

Bicycling Program B

(To be used if you find swimming puts your heart rate in the target heart rate range)

Levels 1–6:	See Starter Program on page 134.
Level 7:	Bicycle 20 minutes 3 to 4 times a week.
Level 8:	Bicycle 23 minutes 3 to 4 times a week.
Level 9:	Bicycle 25 minutes 3 to 4 times a week.
Level 10:	Bicycle 27 minutes 3 to 4 times a week.
Level 11:	Bicycle 30 minutes 3 to 4 times a week.
Level 12:	Bicycle 33 minutes 3 to 4 times a week.
Level 13:	Bicycle 36 minutes 3 to 4 times a week.
Level 14:	Bicycle 39 minutes 3 to 4 times a week.
Level 15:	Bicycle 42 minutes 3 to 4 times a week.
Level 16:	Bicycle 45 minutes 3 to 4 times a week.

people who can't ride a bicycle, or who have a difficult time getting outside. One of my wife's and my prize pupils is Pearl Logan. She selected a stationary bicycle for her exercise, because she had a difficult time getting out of the house in the evening and early morning. She pedals about 140 miles a week! She has over 10,000 miles on her bicycle—she even had to have the bike repairman come to fix it. She is 70 years old. She has dropped her weight from 160 to 121 pounds.

Don't forget that when you use the indoor bicycle, you should pedal at target heart rate. If you can't, then you will have to use Program A. If you have a difficult time keeping to your target heart rate, you will have to put more resistance on the bike wheel or pedal faster.

Q: *Are motorized bicycles effective?*
A: Don't waste your money. You get the same benefit from a regular bicycle or the typical stationary bicycle. Besides, they are dangerous to the unskilled or uninitiated. I don't recommend them.

Q: *Are rope skipping and running in place considered good exercises?*

A: These are my plus activities. Rope skipping and running in place can be used in target heart rate exercise. One of the big problems with both of these activities is leg ailments. The repetitive hopping and jumping in one place can aggravate your legs. Many people who rely on these activities complain that their calf muscles hurt them. But there is no question about it, they can be used for healthier living.

I personally feel that the real advantage of these two activities is the fact that some people can do them while listening to music, watching TV, or listening to the radio. They claim that it keeps them from getting bored and helps them keep the rhythm.

As a personal preference, I prefer rope skipping to running in place because it provides more variety.

Q: *How much rope skipping and running in place are necessary?*

A: The same amount as with other activities. Fifteen to 30 minutes of target heart rate exercise, 3 to 4 times a week. The following chart summarizes a possible program for these activities.

Rope Skipping/Running In Place Program

Levels 1–6:	See Starter Program on page 134.
Level 7:	Skip rope or run in place 20 minutes 3 to 4 times a week.
Level 8:	Skip rope or run in place 23 minutes 3 to 4 times a week.
Level 9:	Skip rope or run in place 25 minutes 3 to 4 times a week.
Level 10:	Skip rope or run in place 27 minutes 3 to 4 times a week.
Level 11:	Skip rope or run in place 30 minutes 3 to 4 times a week.
Level 12:	Skip rope or run in place 33 minutes 3 to 4 times a week.
Level 13:	Skip rope or run in place 36 minutes 3 to 4 times a week.

Level 14:   Skip rope or run in place 39 minutes 3 to 4 times a week.

Level 15:   Skip rope or run in place 42 minutes 3 to 4 times a week.

Level 16:   Skip rope or run in place 45 minutes 3 to 4 times a week.

The level you want to achieve depends upon your specific fitness objective. (See page 133.)

At the beginning do not do the exercise continuously. Jump or run in place for 2 to 3 minutes. Then walk in place or move around the house for 2 to 3 minutes. Keep moving though. Then return and jump or run in place for 2 to 3 minutes; then walk for 2 to 3 minutes, etc. Gradually increase the time spent jumping rope or running in place and decrease the time spent walking. Only jump rope or run in place on a soft surface and wear a good running shoe.

Q: *How many steps should I take per minute when running or skipping in place?*
A: The question is not how many steps per minute, but did you keep at target heart rate? I think that should be your suggested goal.

Q: *Is it true that 10 minutes of rope skipping is the equivalent of 30 minutes of jogging?*
A: No. Rope skipping does not possess some magical power. Target heart rate exercise is target heart rate exercise. Your heart provides the key.

Remember that the times on the previous charts don't include time for a warm-up and cool-down. You should take about 5 to 10 minutes for the warm-up; then spend your allotted time at target heart rate; and then another 5 to 10 minutes for cool-down. The warm-up will prepare the body for more vigorous activity. The joints will be ready, there will be less likelihood of muscle or tendon tears, and the circulatory system will be better prepared for the activity.

The cool-down is essential to allow the body to return to normal levels. The cool-down should consist of easy exercise for a few minutes and then some stretching exercises found in Appendix B.

CHAPTER

10

Being A Sport For Fitness

Q: *Can all types of recreational sports keep you fit?*
A: Although it's a popular notion that sports are a good way to become fit, it usually doesn't work out that way. For example, you rarely see athletes getting into shape by playing their sport. They do additional conditioning such as running, calisthenics, and weight training.

A sport may be a great way to become fit or it may be troublesome. How well the sport can be used for getting you into shape depends on: 1) How you play the game; 2) Your skill level; 3) Your fitness level; and 4) Your approach to competition. These four factors are important and must be considered. The way you play a sport is vital. I've seen many people who play tennis with little vigor. They just sort of stand around while the other person chases the ball. That type of activity is not going to improve anyone's fitness level. To add to the problem, most sport play is intermittent. You stop to serve, retrieve a ball, or correct your equipment. The activity is stop, go, stop, go. Your pulse rate goes up, down, up. . . . So you lose the conditioning effect. You must play continuously to derive cardiovascular benefit. Most players—even the good ones—don't play that way.

Furthermore, when you play a sport there is no plan for progression in how hard you exercise, how you measure, and how much harder you must exercise the next week to improve in fitness. With running, bicycling, walking, or swimming you are able to adjust your program by going faster or longer. It depends upon your inclination and your fitness level. The problem with sports is that it is difficult to plan progression and people tend to play casually and intermittently—especially when just getting started.

The second problem is your skill level. If you have a good skill level and the person you're playing with or against does not, you're in trouble. Besides not being much fun, you're not getting much exercise. Your buddy is, but you're not. In fact he may be getting too much. If you're going to use sports as a means of getting into shape, you must play with someone who has a similar skill level. That way you will have continuous play—a crucial factor in cardiovascular fitness—and you will probably not over extend yourself.

The third consideration is your current fitness level. You really should get in shape to play your sport rather than play your sport to get into shape. Most of the time people play sports just once or twice a week. Consequently, there is little physiological change. If you play the sport 3 or 4 times a week and do it continuously with people of similar ability, then fine. That way it would be possible for you to get into shape. Unfortunately, 99% of the people don't and then they assume that because they play basketball once or twice a week at the Y they're in great shape.

You should also remember that in Chapter 8, I gave you a starter program for exercises like walking, bicycling, jogging, and swimming. If they need a starter program, certainly sports do also.

The fourth consideration is your competitive nature. Competition may be great to keep you motivated to the program, but it can also be disastrous. Competitiveness can cause you to overextend yourself on the handball, tennis, or basketball court. You might feel tired but just because you want to win, you push yourself just a little bit more. You're no longer pushing against yourself, you're pushing against your opponent. And that can be traumatic. When you exercise at too-high a level, your heart may rebel.

Q: *If I want to use sports to become fit, how can I do it?*
A: Combine your sport with walking, jogging, swimming, or bicycling. That way you will see some measurable progress. For three months before engaging in your favorite sport, walk, cycle, swim, or jog for 20 to 30 minutes at your target heart rate. Use the techniques I outlined in Chapters 8 and 9. Continue to jog, cycle, swim, and walk 3 times a week and engage in your sport one or more times a week over and above that. You'll find that your game will be better and you'll have more stamina. You'll soon notice that you don't tire as easily. You may even have the winning edge.

Also, it's only a game. That may be hard to understand if you are highly competitive. But remember, in terms of the big picture of your life, a single basketball game or handball match is not the main feature. That statement may offend you, but one of the most important purposes of sport is to let you relax. Enjoy. That's what sport is really about.

To make sure you are not overdoing, check your pulse rate to see if you are in the target range. You should also listen to your body. If it is rebelling and telling you to slow down, for goodness sake, slow down.

Q: *What should I do to improve fitness if I'm already playing a sport once or twice a week?*
A: Add running, walking, cycling, or swimming to your sport program. Do the additional activity a minimum of 3 times a week for 3 months. Follow the charts in Chapter 9. At the end of the three months, you can cut back to twice a week if you wish, provided you continue to play your sport at least once a week. Doug Hansen, a friend, who is the marketing manager for Monsanto, is a perfect example. He's a class A handballer. For years he played handball only. He thought it was a great way of staying in shape. When he reached 35, he noticed that he tired in the third game. Then one day some of his friends encouraged him to go for a jog. After some prodding, he agreed. He covered only half a mile at the boy scout pace. Slowly he increased his time running. Now he runs 2 to 3 miles, 3 times a week. He says the running gives him the stamina he needs to hold up in his third

game. Now he's not only a class A handballer in the first and second games, but in the third game as well. By the way, he recently entered a 1 mile run and finished first in the 40 and over group. Now he has two sports to enjoy.

The same thing appears to have happened to Billie Jean King. Playing tennis was not enough for her personal physical fitness. Quite frankly, her play was not continuous enough. Furthermore, she was not at her target heart rate for 15 minutes or more when playing. Her pulse went up, down, up, down, etc.

To keep on top of her game Billie Jean King, one of the world's top tennis players, bicycles 20 minutes (at target heart rate) 3 days a week, performs selected calisthenics and yoga stretches, and does weight training. Billie Jean thinks the weight training has made her shots smoother and the bike riding has given her greater endurance on the court. Take a lesson from the pros—get fit to play and enjoy your favorite sport.

In summary: if you enjoy competition, have a favorite sport, have a good skill and fitness level, play against someone who is of equal ability, don't overextend yourself, play continuously, play 3 or more times a week consistently, and keep your heart rate at target levels, you can sport to achieve fitness. But that's a pretty big order—almost impossible. My way is far safer and saner. That is, add walking, cycling, swimming, and/or jogging to your sports program.

Q: *What can I do if I find jogging bores me?*
A: If your skill level improves with your greater stamina and less fatigue, jogging won't be a bore. You'll be impressed by its importance.

Q: *Which sports are best for fitness?*
A: Casey Conrad, executive director of the President's Council on Physical Fitness and Sports, asked the same question of several experts. The chart on pages 162–163 is a summary of their opinion.

Q: *What's the contribution of basketball to physical fitness?*
A: Most experts feel that participation in basketball can make a

significant contribution to cardiovascular fitness. Leg strength and leg endurance will probably increase if you play regularly, that is, 3 or more times a week.

The big danger of basketball is that people tend to be overly competitive. So they overextend themselves. Their heart rate exceeds 85% of their maximum. Most people find that it's better to get into shape to play basketball than to use basketball to get into shape.

Q: *What shape should I be in to play basketball?*
A: My suggestion would be to include walking, jogging, jumping rope, or running in place. These activities will improve your cardiovascular fitness. Once you are able to run comfortably for 15 to 30 minutes at your target heart rate, you are in good enough shape to play recreational basketball.

It would also be advisable to do some other kinds of stop-and-go running so your leg muscles are finely conditioned and won't be subjected to pulls or tears.

Some weight training exercises are also a good idea. These will strengthen your leg muscles. A few exercises are: toe raise, sitting leg raise, and one-half squat. These exercises are described at the end of this chapter. If your upper body is weak, you may want to do some weight training exercises for your arms and shoulders also.

Q: *Can golf contribute to my fitness level?*
A: Don't expect a significant increase in your muscular strength, power, or endurance through golf. Quite frankly, the contribution of golf to fitness is marginal. To make golf a "fitness" activity, you must play in pairs or singly, and carry your own clubs. Walk from the tee to the hole at a brisk pace. Most people don't walk briskly on the course. The average golfer walks about 1 mph on the course.

At the risk of being attacked by all the serious golfers of the world, I should mention that Dr. Thomas K. Cureton, whom I introduced to you earlier, has said that "golf is a good way to spoil a walk." Furthermore, its contribution to burning calories is not very significant. Housework burns as much, if not more.

Twelve Sports: Their Contribution to Fitness

Seven experts were polled by the President's Council on Physical Fitness and Sports. The following sports were ranked on a 0 (no benefit) to 3 (maximum benefit) scale by each of the seven experts. Thus 21 would be a perfect score (3 points × 7 experts). The sports were ranked according to their contribution to physical fitness including: cardio-respiratory endurance, muscular endurance, muscular strength, flexibility, balance, weight control, muscle definition, digestion, and sleep.

Physical Fitness	Jogging	Bicycling	Swimming	Skating (Ice or Rolling)	Handball & Squash	Skiing (Nordic)	Skiing (Alpine)	Basketball	Tennis	Golf	Softball	Bowling
Cardio-respiratory endurance	21	19	21	18	19	19	16	19	16	8	6	5
Muscular endurance	20	18	20	17	18	19	18	17	16	8	8	5
Muscular strength	17	16	14	15	15	15	15	15	14	9	7	5
Flexibility	9	9	15	13	16	14	14	13	14	8	9	7
Balance	17	18	12	20	17	16	21	16	16	8	7	6

General
Well-being

Weight control	21	20	15	17	19	17	15	19	16	6	7	5
Muscle definition	14	15	14	14	11	12	14	13	13	6	5	5
Digestion	13	12	13	11	13	12	9	10	12	7	8	7
Sleep	16	15	16	15	12	15	12	12	11	6	7	6
Total	148	142	140	140	140	139	134	134	128	66	64	51

Q: *Do I have to be in good shape to play golf?*
A: If you want to be a good golfer and remain one, you should expect to increase significantly your endurance, muscle strength, and flexibility. If you don't work on these particular aspects of fitness, you're going to find your golf game going downhill. Many modern-day professional golfers have a specific exercise routine to get and keep them in shape for their season. Many run, walk, and lift weights. Gary Player is such a golfer. He has a rigorous fitness routine that helps keep his golf game in shape. He feels that his fitness regimen has enhanced his longevity and earning power in the game of golf.

Q: *What must I do to get in shape for golf?*
A: Anyone who's going to play golf seriously should be able to walk 1 hour non-stop at a pretty good clip. That means your legs, heart, and lungs will be able to tolerate walking around the golf course. It will also help prevent your game falling apart at the 14th or 15th hole.

If your drives are a little short, you may consider some weight training exercises. A few of the better exercises for golf would be the arm press, upright rowing, supine pullover, barbell curl, wrist curl, and supinator-pronator.

One more thing. Many people are hoodwinked into thinking golf makes them active. It does not. I consider golf to be a pleasurable activity which many people can enjoy. Its contribution to physical fitness is low. It must be supplemented.

Q: *Is handball a good sport for improving fitness?*
A: Handball ranks high in developing cardiovascular fitness because it involves the entire body; your arms deliver force to the ball, your legs move you rapidly across the court, and your back and abdominal muscles bend and stretch in retrieving the ball. While excessive strength is not essential, strong arms and shoulder muscles do help you enjoy the game more.

Q: *What's the best way to get in shape for handball?*
A: Since handball involves the use of the total body, you should select a conditioning program that will involve most of your mus-

cle groups. You should give special attention to developing the non-dominant side of your body.

Anyone who takes up handball seriously and wants to play at peak efficiency should be able to engage in target rate exercise 20 to 30 minutes non-stop. Consistently. So, 2 to 3 months may be necessary to reach that level. That will give you sufficient cardiovascular fitness to enjoy the sport. I've known too many people who simply tried to play the sport for fitness, only to tire in the third game. In 1973 a friend and I took up the game together. Steve was a better player than I, yet I consistently beat him two out of three games. I usually lost the first game, but I tried to keep the game as close as possible. My strategy was to tax his stamina. If I did that, his game started to falter midway in the second game. The third game was a piece of cake for me. The difference was that I ran and he didn't. My stamina prevailed.

Naturally, some flexibility exercises are desirable and these can be done in the warm-up. If you find that your strength is not what it should be, I would suggest that you do the following: arm presses, upright rowing, supine pullover, barbell curls, wrist curls, and supinator-pronators. If you find that your leg strength is not up to par, the one-half squat and toe raise will be helpful.

Q: *Is racquetball a good sport for improving fitness?*
A: One of the reasons racquetball has gained in popularity is that it doesn't require you be ambidextrous, as does handball. It's relatively easy to master, especially for tennis players. Another advantage is that it is often a co-ed activity, while handball tends to be played more by males.

If played regularly, racquetball is good for muscle strength and endurance, hand-eye coordination, and flexibility. It can also be used for developing cardiovascular fitness.

Just as with handball, there's a certain amount of satisfaction in playing a hard game of racquetball. Whacking a ball hard releases a lot of tension and frustration in a socially accepted way.

To get the most out of your play I would suggest doing the same kind of conditioning program as recommended for handball. Fifteen to 30 minutes of running should be the standard for conditioning your body to withstand the cardiovascular demands of racquetball. Furthermore, the weight training exercises suggested are also desirable.

Q: *How does downhill skiing increase fitness?*
A: Skiing is a vigorous sport that's a lot of fun. Unfortunately, many people ski without being properly conditioned. Consequently, they get fatigued easily. And when you tire easily, your muscles don't respond and you're ripe for an accident.

You should try to develop cardiovascular fitness to permit you to ski for at least an hour. Fifteen to 30 minutes of nonstop target rate heart exercise should do it. Naturally, you can ski with a lesser level of fitness but this is the kind of exercise which is needed to reduce incidence of injury.

Q: *What other exercises do you recommend to prepare for skiing?*
A: I think you should do the toe raise, sitting leg raise, and one-half squat weight training exercises described at the end of this chapter. If you find your upper body needs work, you might try the arm presses, upright rowing, and supine pullover exercises.

Finally, if weight training or running isn't your cup of tea, then look at the calisthenic programs outlined in Chapter #11. You should be able to work up to the moderate or high intensity workout charts.

Q: *Is cross-country skiing different from downhill skiing in terms of increasing fitness level?*
A: Cross-country skiing is unique. You can use it as a conditioning program much like walking, bicycling, jogging, or swimming. You can measure the length of time you exercise and the distance covered. Consequently, cross-country skiing can be classified as an excellent activity for improving cardiovascular fitness. I was tempted to include cross-country skiing as one of the Big 4 and make it the Big 5. I didn't only because most people do not live where the climate makes cross-country skiing possible.

But there's no question that cross-country skiing is an excellent cardiovascular fitness exercise. The problems are the equipment, the necessity for snow, and the fact that in most of the country people can't use cross-country skiing as a regular exercise program. But anyway, here are two charts for all you avid cross-country skiers. If you find that you can't get your heart rate up to the target zone and keep it there, follow Program A. If you ski fast enough for target heart rate exercise, then use Program B.

Cross-Country Skiing Program A

(To be used if your heart rate is not in the target heart rate range)

Levels 1–6:	See Starter Program A on page 134.
Level 7:	Ski 50 minutes 4 times a week or 33 minutes 6 times a week.
Level 8:	Ski 55 minutes 4 times a week or 36 minutes 6 times a week.
Level 9:	Ski 60 minutes 4 times a week or 40 minutes 6 times a week.
Level 10:	Ski 65 minutes 4 times a week or 43 minutes 6 times a week.
Level 11:	Ski 70 minutes 4 times a week or 47 minutes 6 times a week.
Level 12:	Ski 75 minutes 4 times a week or 50 minutes 6 times a week.
Level 13:	Ski 80 minutes 4 times a week or 53 minutes 6 times a week.
Level 14:	Ski 85 minutes 4 times a week or 57 minutes 6 times a week.
Level 15:	Ski 90 minutes 4 times a week or 60 minutes 6 times a week.

Cross-Country Skiing Program B

(To be used if you find skiing puts your heart rate in the target heart rate range)

Levels 1–6:	See Starter Program B on page 134.
Level 7:	Ski 20 minutes 3 to 4 times a week.
Level 8:	Ski 23 minutes 3 to 4 times a week.

Level 9:	Ski 25 minutes 3 to 4 times a week.
Level 10:	Ski 27 minutes 3 to 4 times a week.
Level 11:	Ski 30 minutes 3 to 4 times a week.
Level 12:	Ski 33 minutes 3 to 4 times a week.
Level 13:	Ski 36 minutes 3 to 4 times a week.
Level 14:	Ski 39 minutes 3 to 4 times a week.
Level 15:	Ski 42 minutes 3 to 4 times a week.
Level 16:	Ski 45 minutes 3 to 4 times a week.

The level you want to achieve depends upon your specific fitness objective. (See page 133.)

Q: *Is squash a good sport for improving fitness?*
A: The comments I made for handball and racquetball apply also to squash, so there is no reason to repeat them. Simply go back and re-read that section and the target heart rate comments. The weight training exercises apply here also.

Q: *How does tennis rate as a sport for improving fitness?*
A: Tennis will not greatly increase your muscle strength. But a certain amount of strength is necessary in the legs, racquet arm, shoulders, and chest, and strength will certainly contribute to better play.

Muscular endurance in certain body areas is improved through tennis. Endurance of the legs will gradually increase the more you play. The main muscles used in the serve and the ground strokes will certainly need muscle endurance in order to carry out given movements as many times as necessary during competition or recreational play.

Q: *What strengthening exercises do you recommend for tennis?*
A: I recommend the barbell curls, wrist curls, supinator-pronator, and supine pullovers. They are described at the end of this chapter.

Q: *Can tennis improve your cardiovascular fitness?*
A: Quite frankly, the degree to which cardiovascular fitness will be improved depends on the manner in which you compete. Car-

diovascular fitness can be improved if you are a well-skilled, competitive player. Since most people do not play tennis in that manner, its contribution to cardiovascular fitness is marginal.

To play the sport well, it is necessary that you have a good degree of cardiovascular fitness. That way you will be able to have extended volleys and rallys without becoming excessively tired.

Again, I would recommend that you be able to run, walk, swim, or bike for 20 minutes at target heart rate on a regular basis to get optimum play out of tennis. If you're an older person, you may want to try walking. You should be able to walk for 30 minutes to an hour non-stop at a rather vigorous pace. If you're able to do that, you're probably ready for a pretty good game of tennis.

Q: *Can target heart rates be applied to sports?*
A: Everything I've said so far about target heart rates applies also to sports. If you want to derive any cardiovascular benefit from the sports mentioned, you have to be able to get your heart rate up to target rate and hold it there for the specified period of time. Fifteen to 30 minutes for minimum fitness, 30+ minutes for weight control, and 30 to 45 minutes for reducing coronary heart disease risk factors such as triglycerides.

Q: *Do the principles of warm-up and cool-down apply to sports as well as jogging, bicycling, etc.?*
A: Yes. It is vitally important, when playing any sport, to prepare your body with a warm-up and to finish with a cool-down period.

Q: *What is the difference between weight lifting and weight training?*
A: Weight lifting is a competitive sport, the object of which is to lift a greater total poundage than your competitors in three basic lifts. Weight training, on the other hand, refers to the process of developing muscular strength and/or endurance by exercising with weights or resistive devices. The whole concept of weight training is based on the principle that the body is capable of adapting to the stresses placed on it. This is called overload.

Under no circumstances is weight training to be thought of as a complete fitness program. Weight training may help you improve in sports but it does absolutely nothing for the most important muscle of your body, your heart. Because of this, more and more weight trainers are now involved in running programs or some other type of aerobic exercise which will help the heart muscle.

Generally, weight training is unsurpassed as a method of developing and maintaining muscular strength.

Q: *Do people who lift weights or train with weights become muscle-bound?*
A: The term muscle-bound is really a misnomer. In the early days, weight lifters tended to be people who had little flexibility to begin with. Consequently, when they lifted weights, they appeared to be muscle-bound.

If you lift or train with weights correctly, you will not become muscle-bound. By correctly, I mean that the muscles must be exercised through their full range of motion. As long as you extend your muscles completely and then contract them fully, your chances of inflexibility or "muscle-boundness" are reduced.

Q: *How does weight lifting and weight training affect my heart rate?*
A: To develop cardiovascular endurance or fitness, increased pulse rate is only one part of the equation. It must be kept there for a period of time. Relatively short bursts of activity as generally practiced in weight training will raise your pulse rate, but since the activity is of short duration—30 to 90 seconds—cardiovascular fitness is not improved. Weight training is stop and go exercise so your pulse rate shoots up and then drops down, shoots up and then drops down. Another problem is that there is so much local muscle fatigue that you cannot keep your whole body moving for extended periods of time.

Q: *How should I begin a weight training program?*
A: I think one of the best ways is to follow the "set system." Here, I'm talking about the muscle strength of the average fitness enthusiast. Not college, professional, or high school athletes.

The idea of the set system is to do somewhere between 4 and 8 repetitions of each exercise. The 4 to 8 repetitions are to be done 3 times. For example: you do 8 repetitions of barbell curls, rest for 1 to 2 minutes, do a second set of 8 repetitions, rest for 1 to 2 minutes, and then do your third set of 8 repetitions. After the third set of repetitions, you go to the next exercise, arm presses for example, and repeat the cycle.

Q: *How heavy should the weights be when I start a weight training program?*
A: That's an individual matter. One technique is to select enough weight so that on the first set you can do only 8 repetitions. Rest. Then start to do your second set. You'll find that you are only able to do 6 repetitions because of muscle fatigue. Rest. On the third set, maybe you'll only be able to do 4 repetitions of that exercise. Over the next couple of weeks you stay at that weight until you are able to do 3 complete sets of 8 repetitions. Once you're able to do that, you can add more weight and start the cycle again.

Q: *How many times a week should I train with weights?*
A: It seems as though 3 times a week is best. Every other day will be fine.

Q: *Is weight training alone enough exercise to build muscle strength and endurance?*
A: What I've given you here is a program for building muscle *strength.* If you want to improve muscle *endurance,* it's necessary to do lower resistance exercise and higher repetitions. So instead of doing 8 repetitions (which is strength development), you will want to do 15 repetitions. But again, the same cycle is repeated. Select a weight that permits you to do only 15 repetitions the first time. That means the next time you'll probably do around 13 repetitions and finally 10. Remain at that level until you are able to do 3 complete sets of 15 repetitions.

Q: *What are some good weight training exercises?*
A: There are thousands. I've selected 9 lifts which I think are appropriate for most people. If you're interested in overall body strength, then you might do all nine. Otherwise, just do those I

have marked for your particular sport. You will see that I did not include exercises for the abdomen, stomach, or waist, because I think you get enough abdominal strength by doing the exercises described in Chapter #11. If you find that those exercises aren't hard enough, you might hold a 2½ pound plate behind your head or across your chest as you do sit-ups. If you don't like the weights, you can use a book. Here are the exercises:

1.   Arm Press—Assume a standing position with a barbell in front of the chest, palms forward. Extend the barbell over the head with your arms straight; return. The press develops shoulder, upper back, upper chest, and back of upper arm muscles.

2.   Upright Rowing—Stand with your feet spread apart, holding your body upright. The knees in back are straight. Grasp a barbell right in the middle with hands touching and palms down. Raise the bar up to the chest, by bending the elbows and bringing the bar up to the chest. This exercise develops the muscles on the top of the shoulders (deltoids) and the muscles under the arm pits (latissimus dorsi). It also involves the chest muscles.

3.   Supine Pull-Over (on back)—Assume a supine position; extend your arms above the head with palms facing up. Raise the arms to a 90° angle, and then return to the original position. The arms must be kept straight through the entire movement. The pull-over develops muscles of the front of the chest, back of the upper arms and sides of the chest.

4.   Barbell Curls—Stand with arms extended downward, the barbell against your thighs and your palms up. Flex your forearms to bring the bar to the shoulders. Return until your arms are fully extended. This develops the muscles of the front of the upper arms and forearms.

5.   Wrist Curl—Sit on a bench with your forearms resting on your thighs, and wrists extended beyond your knees. Hold the barbell with palms facing up. Extend your hands at the wrists, lowering the bar as far as possible. Then flex the wrists bringing the bar upward as far as possible. The curl develops the flexor muscle of the forearm and hand.

6.   Supinator-Pronator—Sit on a bench with your forearm on the table and only the wrist and hand extended over the support. Grasp a dumbbell bar with a weight on only one end and in an upright position. Lower the weight to the one side so that the

palm is facing upward, then return to an upright position, and lower it to the other side so that the palm is facing downward. The exercise develops the supinator and pronators of the forearms.

7. One-Half Squat—Stand with feet comfortably spread. Hold a barbell on your shoulders behind the neck. Bend your knees to perform a one-half squat (90°). Then return to a standing position. The squat develops muscles of the front thigh and lower leg.

8. Sitting Leg Raise—Sit on the edge of a table with your legs hanging over the edge. With a weighted boot, raise your lower leg to a horizontal position, return slowly. This exercise develops the extensors of the leg.

9. Toe Raise—Assume a standing position with a barbell resting on your shoulders behind the neck. The balls of your feet should rest on a 1 to 2 inch block of wood, with your heels on the floor. Raise up on the toes as far as possible, then return to original position. The raise develops muscles of the back of the lower leg.

The following chart summarizes which exercises are best for various sports.

Lift	All-Around Fitness	Basketball	Golf	Handball	Racquetball	Skiing	Squash	Tennis
Arm Press	X	X	X	X	X	X	X	
Upright Rowing	X		X	X	X		X	
Supine Pull-Over	X	X	X	X	X		X	X
Barbell Curl	X		X	X	X	X	X	X
Wrist Curl	X		X	X	X		X	X
Supinator-Pronator	X	X	X	X	X		X	X
One-Half Squat	X	X		X	X	X	X	
Sitting Leg Raise	X	X				X		
Toe Raise	X	X		X	X	X	X	

Q: *What are isometrics?*
A: Isometrics are special exercises that exert a muscle or group of muscles against an immovable object. The object you work against could be a wall, a steel bar, a taut rope, towel, or even another set of muscles.

Q: *Do isometrics give quick results in increasing strength?*
A: Isometrics do increase strength fairly rapidly, anywhere from 2 to 5% per week. But there's nothing easy about isometrics if you're interested in the muscles of your entire body, and it's not quick either. Let me explain.

Isometrics is very specific; you exercise one muscle at a time. Your body has many muscle areas. If you want them all to increase in strength, which is wise, you're going to have to give equal time to all those muscle areas. Besides, the only way to make isometrics work is to perform each exercise at ⅔ of your maximum exertion level, assuming your know how to measure your level of exertion. Any activity that requires that level of exertion is tough and requires discipline, so you should not base your entire fitness hopes on isometrics alone.

Q: *How can you incorporate isometrics into a regular exercise program?*
A: For the person interested in increasing strength isometrics are a simple supplement to your regular program of aerobic activity. If you decide to incorporate a few isometric exercises into your routine, compensate by adding some stretching and flexibility exercises and by all means don't neglect good aerobic activity. You should keep moving through your entire session. Do your chest pulls and presses while you're walking.

Q: *Can isometrics be dangerous?*
A: It could be if you suffer from heart disease or high blood pressure. Isometrics demand great exertion. Even though it is for a short period of time, it may be too much for your cardiovascular system, especially if you hold your breath when exerting. So if you have had trouble with blood pressure or heart problems, stay away from isometrics entirely.

Q: *Is yoga a good way to stay in shape?*
A: With over 300 books on yoga, I'm afraid I can't really tackle the subject properly. Yoga itself is a philosophy or a way of life—a religion. One particular type of yoga, Hatha Yoga, is concerned with body posture and breathing exercises. Many of the yoga exercises are ideal for certain aspects of fitness, but yoga itself cannot maintain good cardiovascular fitness. For those of you who are truly interested in this form of activity, I would recommend it as part of a warm-up or preparation for more vigorous aerobic activity. The two greatest values of yoga for fitness are flexibility and relaxation. Some claim that assuming a few basic postures prior to jogging or cycling puts them in a proper frame of mind while preparing their bodies for the more vigorous activity. When used in this manner, I think yoga exercises can be one beneficial aspect of a total fitness program.

Q: *Does yoga have any harmful aspects?*
A: Not really, though I would caution against trying some of the more elaborate and difficult postures. No beginner should attempt a particular position that places a great amount of strain on various parts of the body. A class or session with an experienced yoga instructor might be helpful it you want to incorporate yoga into your exercise program. The instructor will show you the easier exercises to begin with and demonstrate the methods of assuming those postures without placing undue strain on your knees, legs, back, neck, etc. The danger comes when a novice picks up a book, finds an interesting posture, and on his own tries to imitate that posture. But otherwise, there are no inherent harms in yoga, though you might be cautious about some of the claims made about yoga. Yoga is a great activity for relaxing, improving flexibility, reducing muscle tension, and making a more flexible spine. All the other claims are generally wishful thinking or carefully-worded misconceptions. Yoga is NOT a total fitness program. It does not improve heart/lung function or control body weight.

CHAPTER

11

Exercises For The Hips And Thighs

Q: *What can calisthenics do to improve my fitness level?*
A: Most of the time calisthenics are done to improve your figure or to increase the size of your muscles. And that's not all bad. But the problem is, most people do not do their calisthenics properly, so they're not satisfied with the results.

Q: *Can calisthenics help to firm up or take flab off specific areas of the body?*
A: No. This is not true—there is no such thing as spot reducing. If spot reducing worked, people who chewed gum would have thin faces. And there is research to back up my claim. Drs. Grant Gwinup, R. Chelvan, and T. Steinberg at the University of California did a study which illustrates this point. They studied the arms of tennis players who'd been playing tennis at least six hours a week for two years or more. The doctors measured the circumference and the thickness of the fat as specific sites on the players' arms and took comparative measurements of a control group of people who did not play the game.

Obviously, the right and left arms of the tennis players had been subjected to significantly different amounts and kinds of exercise. But as it turned out, in all cases the circumference of the arm used to swing the racket was *larger* than the less active arm: Exercise had not reduced but had increased the size of the arm instead. The difference in size, of course, was due to greater muscle development.

The most significant finding of the study, however, was that the tennis players as a group had less subcutaneous fat (fat stored directly under the skin) on *both* arms than did the control group. The conclusion of this study was that exercise, regardless of type, reduces fat from the entire body and not merely from specific areas.

The simple fact is that it takes complicated biochemical mechanisms to get the fat into the fat cells. To get it out requires the same type of thing. For example, let's say you consume 3,000 calories a day and burn off only 2,500. Because you are taking in 500 extra calories a day, you'll be gaining about a pound a week.

Since you probably have more fat cells on your waist, the fat tends to get deposited there, and your waist will begin to expand. Assuming you're out of caloric balance and your waistline is expanding, you might decide that the best way to trim your waistline is to do sit-ups. Let's say you decide to do 30 sit-ups. Before you begin you measure your waist and it is 38 inches. Now you do the sit-ups faithfully for a month. At the end of the month you measure your waist again. Lo and behold, it's no longer 38 inches but 38½ inches. At this point you conclude that you are probably not doing the sit-ups correctly. So now you bend your knees. And the number of sit-ups is increased to 50. Again, you do the exercises without fail for a month. At the end of the month you measure your waist. It's now 39 inches. Disgusted, you give up. Exercise doesn't work.

The real problem was that you were out of caloric balance. The sit-ups had nothing to do with it. The sit-ups that you did—maybe even the 50—burned only an extra 10 calories. You were still out of caloric balance by 490 calories, so your weight and waist continued to increase. If you got involved in an exercise program that burned a lot of calories, you would find that your waistline would be reduced. Because you would be burning off more calories than you would be eating. It is that simple.

Q: *Are exercises such as sit-ups and push-ups not good?*
A: It's not that these types of "spot-reduction" exercises aren't good for you, it's that they're inefficient in burning off calories.

Such exercises are effective in firming and strengthening the muscles, but they're not likely to make you lose inches in a specific area. Spot reducing is physiological hogwash. Research indicates that you're either born with a certain number of fat cells, or their actual number is determined during the first few years of life. After that, the number of fat cells you have remains constant throughout life. When you are young and physically active, the cells are depleted of fat. As you grow older, and become more sedentary, and burn off fewer calories than you eat, your cells act like fuel storage tanks and fill up with fat. These fat cells are located all over your body, and their location is usually determined by heredity.

Fat is stored in case of an emergency such as a period of famine and your fat cells swell up for later energy use. Then when you go into a calorie deficit, the nervous, endocrine, and circulatory systems act together to release fat for energy. Fat is released from all over your body.

Vigorous movement of a group of muscles—the stomach muscles, for instance, cannot reduce or decrease the number of fat cells that lie immediately around those muscles. There is no physiological pathway for such a direct outlet. Instead, when you exercise, your nervous system triggers the release of small quantities of fat from the cells all over the body. The circulatory system then picks up the fat and takes it to the liver where it is converted into energy which is used by the muscles.

The calisthenics are done simply for the purpose of firming up the musculature. To remove fat, you need big muscle activity.

Q: *What's the best way to combine calisthenics with an aerobic exercise program?*
A: The rule of thumb is this: if there's too much flab, then you have to go into calorie deficit with a big muscle activity such as walking, cycling, swimming, or jogging. If you find that the abdomen, for example, is weak, then sit-ups, etc., will be effective in helping to flatten that particular area of the body. My own feeling is that there should be a combination of the two. Many times when people have excessive flab around their abdomen they also have weak tummy muscles. So if they are engaged in a jogging, swimming, bicycling, or walking program, they should be doing specific exercises to firm up a problem area.

Q: *Which calisthenic exercises are best for firming my bust?*
A: Regardless of what those magazine advertisements tell you, no exercise (and/or piece of exercise equipment) can make your breasts larger. Most advertisements are 1% truth and 100% bust. What you were born with, you will keep unless you submit to dangerous silicone injections or hormones. What you can do, however, is to restore that youthful look to your bustline by developing the pectoral muscles that lie underneath your breasts. Some exercises allow the muscles to hold your breasts high, thus giving them a youthful appearance.

The first four exercises use books or weights—whatever you prefer. You should be able to do only 8 of each exercise at one time. If you do more, add weight—if you do less, remove some weight. Your sessions should include 3 sets of 8 repetitions, though you will probably reach 8 repetitions only on your first set. When you can hit 3 complete sets of 8 repetitions each, then increase the weight. Do these exercises every other day. You may want to re-read the section on weight training. Remember that behind every curve, there is a muscle. Well-conditioned muscles give your body shape.

1. *Arms Over:* Hold a book in each hand (hands at sides) while lying on your back. Raise the books over your head, reaching as far back as possible, then return hands to sides. Perform 3 sets of 8 repetitions.

2. *Right Angles:* Lie on your back with your arms at right angles to your body and a book in each hand. Raise your arms so that they come together (arms straight) above your chest, and in your abdomen at the same time. Again, perform 3 sets of 8 repetitions.

3. *Barrel Roll:* Lie on your back with a pillow under your shoulders. Raise your arms above your chest as though you were holding a barrel. Holding books in both hands, open your curved arms as far as possible and return slowly.

4. *Arm Arc:* Lie on your back with your arms extended toward your knees. Holding a book in each hand, sweep your arms out to the sides as though you were making an arc to at least shoulder height. Return.

5. *Pectoral Push:* While standing or sitting, grasp the left elbow with the right hand and your right elbow with your left

hand. Push your arms together as hard as possible and then relax. Perform 3 sets of 8 repetitions.

6. *Hand Push:* Clasp your hands at various heights in front of your body: waist, chest, and forehead. Push your hands together for 6 seconds then relax. Repeat three times in each position in the morning, at noon, and in the evening.

Q: *Which exercises are best for my facial features?*
A: Yes, your face has muscles, many of them, and by exercising them they will begin to tighten up, thus reducing wrinkles and sagging. You need to be a little careful where you do these. If it is in public, people may think you're crazy. If it's in front of a mirror, you may become exhausted from laughing too hard.

7. *Nose Wrinkler:* This exercise fills in the furrows between the nose and cheeks. Slightly open the mouth and flair the nostrils as you wrinkle your nose, causing the upper lip to draw up. Now concentrate on forcing the upper lip down which will also lower the nose. Repeat the exercise 5 times.

8. *Cheek Thinner:* To reduce overly full cheeks, close your mouth and part your teeth slightly. Suck the cheeks between your teeth. Relax and repeat at least 5 times.

9. *Crow's Feet Exercise:* To erase crows feet and strengthen muscles behind the eyes, open your eyes as widely as possible, look up, down, to the left and to the right. Hold each position for a slow count of 6.

Q: *What exercises are good for firming the thigh muscles?*
A: The thigh muscles are sometimes called the "second heart," so these exercises are important to promote better blood flow back to the heart.

10. *Sitting Single Leg Raise:* Starting Position: Sit erect, hands on side of chair seat for balance, feet on the floor. Raise left leg waist high. Return to starting position. Repeat with opposite leg.

11. *Standing Leg Swing:* Stand erect, feet together, one hand on a chair. Swing the right leg forward and up then back and up. Return to starting position. Repeat with the left leg. This exercise is good for firming up the thigh, hips, and buttocks area.

12. *One-Half Knee Bend:*   Stand erect, with the feet close together and hands on hips. Bend the knees to a 90° angle (the heels are allowed to come off the floor). Return to the starting position. This exercise strengthens the thigh muscles.

13. *Skier's Exercise:*   The skier's exercise is identical to the previous exercise except that as the knees are bent to a 90° angle, they are turned alternately to the left and right. When the knees are bent to the left, move both arms to the left. When the knees are bent to the right, both arms go to the right. This exercise strengthens the thigh muscles and stretches the calves.

14. *Side Stretch:*   Stand erect with your hands on your hips, and your feet spread wider than shoulder-width. Lunge to the right, bending the right leg, keeping the left leg extended. Return to the starting position and repeat to the opposite side. This exercise firms the thighs, hips, and buttocks.

Q: *What are the best "derriere exercises" for someone who sits for most of the day?*

A: Though it may not feel like it, your posterior is (or should be) all muscle. It's called the gluteus maximus and is one of the largest muscles you have. These exercises will firm up that muscle so that it will both look and feel less pudgy.

15. *Standing Leg Swing:*   Stand erect, feet together, left hand on a chair. Swing the right leg forward and up and then back and up. *Do not arch your back.* Return to the starting position and repeat on the other side.

16. *Two Way Stretch:*   Kneel on all fours. Bring your left knee up under your chest and bend your head toward your chest. Then return your head to the starting position, simultaneously extending the left leg back and upward. *Do not arch your back.* Return to the starting position and repeat with the right leg.

17. *Leg Raise:*   Standing, Place your hands on top of your desk. Try to keep your upper body as straight as possible. Your feet should be approximately 12 to 18 inches from the desk. Now slowly raise one leg backward and upward as high as possible. *Do not arch your back.* Return to the starting position. Alternate. This exercise helps to firm the derriere.

18. *Bench Stepping:*   Locate a step or a stack of securely

tied newspapers 12 to 18 inches high. Standing tall with your feet together, step up with your left leg, follow with your right, and stand erect. Now step down with your right leg followed with your left. Do this with a steady rhythm. Alternate legs periodically. You should step at a rate of about 20-30 steps a minute (counting the left leg only). This exercise firms up the leg muscles, derriere, and improves circulo-respiratory fitness.

19. *Mountain Climber:* Assume a push-up position. Bring the right leg up underneath the chest with the knee bent. The left leg is extended backward. The exercise action is to switch the legs and continue alternating fairly rapidly. Each time a leg is brought up under the chin, count one repetition. This exercise firms the buttocks, legs, and hips.

Q: *Are there any exercises that will firm up the hips?*
A: Actually, the exercises for the thighs may also help the hips, for the most common hip complaint is actually the condition of "saddle bags" at the top and side of the thigh area. Hip size is determined mostly by bone structure, though a sedentary life style can soften the muscles surrounding the hips, giving them a baggy appearance. When that occurs, these four exercises will help.

20. *Standing Side Leg Raise:* Stand erect, hands on hips, feet together. Raise your left leg sideways and up as high as possible. Return to the starting position. Repeat with right leg.

21. *Side Leg Double Leg Raise:* Lie on your right side, legs extended, head supported by the right arm. Raise both legs together as high as possible, then lower to the starting position. Do a few times and then repeat on the opposite side. This exercise helps to firm the lateral muscles of the trunk and hips.

22. *Leg Cross-Over:* Lie on your back, legs together, arms extended sideward for balance. Raise your left leg to a vertical position. Keeping the leg straight, lower the leg to the floor on your right side. Return to the starting position. Repeat with the right leg. This exercise firms the hip muscles.

23. *Fire Hydrant:* Assume a kneeling position with your hands on the floor. Keeping your knee bent, raise your right leg parallel to the floor. That is count one. Then straighten and extend the leg to the side perpendicular to your body on count two.

Return to bent knee on count three. Place your knee on the floor on count four. Repeat with the left leg. That is one repetition. This exercise firms the hips and buttock area.

Q: *Which exercises are best for my waist?*
A: When the tape measure tells you your waist needs some work, remember it may also be the fault of sagging abdominal muscles, so read the next question too. There are five especially good exercises for the waist.

24. *Side Bend Up:* Lying on your side with your legs held down by a partner or a piece of furniture, raise your body sideways from the waist as high as you can. Repeat on both sides.

25. *Body Twist:* Step forward with the left foot, twist the upper torso to the left as far as possible and swing both arms to the left. Then step forward with the right foot, and twist the upper torso to the right as far as possible and swing both arms to the right. Exhale as the body twists to the side. Inhale as the body returns to the forward position. This exercise is good for helping stretch the muscles of the abdominals and lower back region.

26. *Side Trunk Bending:* Stand erect with your feet spread shoulder-width apart, left hand on hip, and right arm extended at shoulder height. Bend your trunk to the left, reaching over beyond the head with the right arm. Return to the starting position and repeat on the opposite side. Motion to left and right is one repetition This helps to exercise the lateral muscles of the trunk.

27. *Single Leg Raise:* Lie on your right side, legs extended, right hand supporting the head. Raise the left leg as high as possible. Lower to the starting position. Do on the right side and then on the left side.

28. *Trunk Twister:* Stand with your hands clasped behind your neck and elbows drawn back. As you walk in place, raise your knee as high as possible and turn the body to the left, having your right elbow touch your left knee. The touching of the right elbow to your left knee is one repetition. Repeat to the other side. This exercise conditions the waist and improves the hip flexors.

Q: *What can I do to get rid of that saggy look in the abdomen?*
A: Perhaps the most unsightly and yet common problem area of

both men and women is the sagging or protruding abdomen. Given such colorful names as bay window, pot belly, and spare tire, this problem plagues many people. Incorporating the following exercises into your daily routine will help strengthen the muscles that should be holding that area firm and flat.

29. *Look Up:* Lie on your back, knees slightly bent, and arms at your side. Raise your head and shoulders from the floor until you can see your feet. Lower your head to the floor. The look up and return constitutes one repetition.

30. *Curl Down:* Start from a sitting position with the knees bent and hands across the chest. Lower the upper body slightly until you feel a pull on your tummy. Hold that position and return. The lowering and return is one repetition.

31. *Abdominal Curl:* Lie flat on your back with the lower back touching the floor; knees bent. Curl the head and upper part of the body upward and forward to about a 45° angle. At the same time, contract your abdominal muscles. Return slowly to the starting position. The curl up and return is one repetition.

32. *Curl Down—45° Angle:* Start from a sitting position with your knees bent and hands placed behind your head. Lower the upper body to a 45° angle. Hold that position and return. That is one repetition.

33. *Sit-Up:* Lie flat on your back with knees bent and arms across your chest or at the side. Curl the body up into a sitting position by first placing the chin on the chest and then lifting the upper body off the floor. Keep your back rounded. Sit up as far as possible then return to the starting position. That is one repetition. I should note that you can place your hands above the head or across the chest if you like.

34. *Bicycle Pump:* Sit with your legs extended and hands resting on the floor on or beside your hips. In this inverted position, simulate a bicycle riding or pedaling action. Each time the right leg is extended, count one repetition. This exercise strengthens your abdominal muscles.

Q: *Which exercises are best for firming the arms and shoulders?*
A: Two hundred years ago this would not have been a problem, as men chopped wood and women used scrub boards. But with the advent of convenience devices, our upper bodies have had to

do less and less work. As we approach middle age, the shoulders appear stooped and the arms become flabby and formless. Try these exercises to firm up those arms and straighten your shoulders.

35. *Arm Circles:* Stand erect, arms extended sideward at shoulder height with palms up. Make small circles backward with your hands. Keep head erect. Helps keep the shoulder joint flexible and strengthens muscles of the shoulders.

36. *Alternate Arm Swing and Bounce:* Stand with the feet parallel shoulder-width apart and knees bent at a 45° angle. The body should lean forward and the arms hang relaxed. Swing one arm forward as the opposite swings back. Continue by reversing the position of the arms with an easy swinging motion. As the motion is continued, bend the knees more than the 45° angle and then straighten them. Try to coordinate them together. This exercise firms the leg muscles and improves shoulder flexibility.

37. *Punching Bag:* Simulate punching a punching bag by beginning with the arms extended, and alternately drawing them back in front of the body. A drawing in toward the body and returning to an extended position constitutes one repetition. This exercise helps tone both the triceps and biceps muscles.

38. *Wall Push-Up:* Stand about 3 to 4 feet away from the corner or wall of a room. Place one hand on each wall at shoulder height. Keeping your body rigid, slowly bend the arms and touch the chin to the wall or corner. Take three seconds to go into the wall, and three seconds to return. This helps to strengthen the arm and shoulder muscles.

39. *Modified Push-Up:* Start in a lying position, hands outside the shoulders, fingers pointed forward, and knees bent. Lift your body (from the knees up) off the floor by straightening your arms and keeping your back straight. Return to the starting position. This exercise firms the muscles on the back of the arm.

40. *Regular Push-Up:* Assume a prone position on the floor, feet together, hands beneath the shoulders. Keeping your body straight, extend your arms fully, then return to the starting position. That is one repetition. This develops the shoulders, chest, and arms. Modified push-ups may be substituted for regular push-ups. Women should not automatically substitute modified for regular push-ups. Women can do regular push-ups as

well as modified. You just have to understand your limitations. My 8th grade daughter Debbie was able to do 164 regular push-ups. Non-stop!

Q: *How many repetitions of each exercise should I do?*
A: I didn't put down specific repetitions because everyone's different. If you are going to follow an exercise regime for a certain body part, it is best to take the first exercise I list. The exercises are listed in order of increasing difficulty. Do five to seven repetitions and build up to 20 repetitions. When you are able to do 20 repetitions, it's time to move to the next exercise. You may want to attempt 2 or 3 exercises for a particular area at a time. Again, your own body is your best judge. If you find it extremely difficult, then back off.

Q: *How can I be sure I'm doing the exercises properly?*
A: All the exercises given will help you burn calories. Sit-ups will burn calories as well as push-ups, V-seats, or jumping jacks. Putting them into a sequence of continuous exercise makes the exercises more efficient.

Q: *How does developing a sequence of continuous exercise make exercises more efficient?*
A: Push-ups will burn about 6 to 7 calories in a minute and sit-ups around 4 to 5 calories a minute. Unfortunately, most people just do a certain number of sit-ups, a certain number of push-ups, and then rest between the exercises. Result: few calories are burned. They watch Jack LaLanne talk to his dog or an advertisement on TV. The resting is the problem. To burn calories you must get your metabolism up and keep it there.

When you rest you burn about one calorie or so a minute (60 an hour). When you sit on the floor and start to do sit-ups, your metabolism increases during the next minute, so that near the end of the sit-ups you burn 4 to 5 calories a minute. If you stop and rest, waiting for the next exercise, your metabolism starts to drop back to one calorie a minute. After you are refreshed you do your push-ups. Your metabolism is stepped up again and after a minute of exercise you might approach 6 to 7 calories a minute. You rest, and again your metabolism slows to approach 2 to 3 calories a minute. Next jumping jacks are performed, etc., etc. Your metabolism is up, down, up, down, up, down, and therefore few calories are burned.

If you keep moving from one exercise to another, or intersperse the movement between exercises, even if you simply move from one part of the room to another, you will burn more calories. For example: start by walking in place. Your metabolism increases, and after one minute it's up to 3 calories a minute. Immediately sit on the floor, perform your sit-ups, and during the entire exercise you are burning 4 calories. As soon as the exercise is over, get up and walk in place; again your metabolism stays between 3 and 4 calories a minute. Then move into push-ups; at about 30 seconds into the exercise you are burning 6 to 7 calories a minute. After the push-ups, get up immediately and walk in place for one minute. At the conclusion of walking, move into jumping jacks.

This pattern is more efficient because it will help you burn about twice as many calories in the same period of time as you would if you took rest periods. If you are on a current calisthenics program that lasts 20 minutes, you probably exercise 10 minutes and rest 10 minutes. Furthermore, you are probably burning 80 to 100 calories in that 20 minute period of time. If you intersperse your exercise with walking, jogging, or running in place, you would double your calories burned—160 to 200 calories.

Q: *Do exercises have to be done vigorously to be effective?*
A: Not necessarily. For calisthenics to be effective, you must keep moving from one exercise to another, smoothly and without pause for station identification.

Q: *Can I use target heart rate with calisthenics?*
A: Absolutely. That way you'll derive the benefit of firming body parts and working on cardiovascular fitness and weight control. It also helps you guard against over exertion. In fact, all my group exercise sessions are done in this manner. It doesn't matter whether I'm working with adults or children. I don't believe in traditional stationary calisthenics. You've got to move between specific exercises or calisthenics to help your heart and to burn calories. We do calisthenics, but they are non-stop in nature.

Q: *Could you give a specific recommendation on using calisthenics for improving your heart/lung function and burning calories?*
A: On the next few pages are charts for a low intensity workout, a moderate intensity workout, and a high intensity workout. Begin with the program outlined under Step 1 Low Intensity Workout. The exercises listed in the left hand column are described on the preceding pages for a particular area of the body. Spend at least one day at each step. If at any time you find the step too difficult, stay at that step for several days and then proceed accordingly. Most people will find that they can move up one step every second day.

I tried to take into account individual differences. If you find that after the first day the exercise is ridiculously easy, then move to Step 8. You may also find that you progress faster on one particular exercise than another. That's no big deal. Simply do a higher number of repetitions on one step and a lower number on another. For example, let's say that you're at Step 14 on the Low Intensity Workout. You can easily do 30 arm circles but you find that you have difficulty doing 20 wall push-ups. No sweat. Do your 30 arm circles and maybe only 16 wall push-ups if that makes you feel more comfortable. Remember, the purpose of these calisthenics is to show you how you can use calisthenics as a means of conditioning your heart and lungs.

Q: *How fast should I do the exercises?*
A: Try to do them at a pace that will elicit a target heart rate.

Q: *How often should I do the exercises?*
A: Do them 3 or 4 times a week.

Q: *Has the program been tested?*
A: Yes. It is a modification of the workouts I do with my YMCA adult program. To make the exercise session more fun, turn on some good upbeat music (about 128 to 132 beats per minute) and MOVE!

Q: *How long will it take to complete these exercises?*
A: I like to let people progress at their own rate and find their own most comfortable rate of exercising. However, you can gen-

erally figure that the workouts, including the warm-up and tapering-off, will take: 20 to 25 minutes (Low); 28 to 33 minutes (Moderate); and 35 to 40 minutes (High).

By the way, this program is so flexible you could put any of the 40 exercises in place of another one. Pick an exercise for an area of the body you would like to work on. For starters, use the repetitions listed for the exercise replaced. Just don't skip the running in place, walking in place, or bench stepping. Good luck!

Low Intensity Workout

STEPS

	1	2	3	4	5	6	7	8	9	10	11	12	13	14
Warm-up (Outlined in Appendix A)	5–10 minutes													
Walk in place	10 seconds						15 seconds							
Arm circles #35	17	18	19	20	21	22	23	24	25	26	27	28	29	30
Walk in place	10 seconds						15 seconds							
Wall push-up #38	7	8	9	10	11	12	13	14	15	16	17	18	19	20
Walk in place	10 seconds						15 seconds							
Look up #29	7	8	9	10	11	12	13	14	15	16	17	18	19	20
Walk in place	10 seconds						15 seconds							
Curl down #30	7	8	9	10	11	12	13	14	15	16	17	18	19	20
Walk in place	10 seconds						15 seconds							
Walk stairs	30 seconds						60 seconds							
Walk in place	10 seconds						15 seconds							
Side trunk bending #26	7	8	9	10	11	12	13	14	15	16	17	18	19	20
Walk in place	10 seconds						15 seconds							
Single leg raise #27	7	8	9	10	11	12	13	14	15	16	17	18	19	20
Walk in place	10 seconds						15 seconds							
½ Knee bends #12	17	18	19	20	21	22	23	24	25	26	27	28	29	30
Walk in place	10 seconds						15 seconds							
Walk	2 minutes													
Cool down (Outlined in Appendix B)	Do 5 minutes of stretching													
Take 10-second pulse rate; multiply by 6 and record														

MODERATE INTENSITY WORKOUT

STEPS

	15	16	17	18	19	20	21	22	23	24	25	26	27	28
Warm-up (Outlined in Appendix A)	5–10 minutes													
Run in place	10 seconds							15 seconds						
Punching bag #37	20	20	20	25	25	25	30	30	30	35	35	35	40	40
Run in place	10 seconds							15 seconds						
Modified push-ups #39	7	8	9	10	11	12	13	14	15	16	17	18	19	20
Run in place	10 seconds							15 seconds						
Abdominal curls #31	7	8	9	10	11	12	13	14	15	16	17	18	19	20
Run in place	10 seconds							15 seconds						
Curl down—45° angle #32	7	8	9	10	11	12	13	14	15	16	17	18	19	20
Run in place	10 seconds							15 seconds						
Bench stepping #18	1½ minutes			2 minutes				2½ minutes			3 minutes			
Run in place	10 seconds							15 seconds						
Trunk twister #28	7	8	9	10	11	12	13	14	15	16	17	18	19	20
Run in place	10 seconds							15 seconds						
Leg cross-over #22	7	8	9	10	11	12	13	14	15	16	17	18	19	20
Run in place	10 seconds							15 seconds						
Side stretch #14	20	20	20	25	25	25	30	30	30	35	35	35	40	40
Run in place	10 seconds							15 seconds						
Walk	2 minutes													
Cool down (Outlined in Appendix B)	Do 5 minutes of stretching													
Take 10-second pulse rate; multiply by 6 and record														

HIGH INTENSITY WORKOUT

STEPS

	29	30	31	32	33	34	35	36	37	38	39	40	41	42
Warm-up (Outlined in Appendix A)	5–10 minutes													
Run in place	20 seconds							30 seconds						
Alternate arm swing and bounce #36	20	20	20	25	25	25	30	30	30	35	35	35	40	40
Run in place	20 seconds							30 seconds						
Push-ups #40	7	8	9	10	11	12	13	14	15	16	17	18	19	20
Run in place	20 seconds							30 seconds						
Sit-ups #33	14	16	18	20	22	24	26	28	30	32	34	36	38	40
Run in place	20 seconds							30 seconds						
Bicycle pump #34	20	20	20	25	25	25	30	30	30	35	35	35	40	40
Run in place	20 seconds							30 seconds						
Bench stepping #18	3 minutes			4 minutes				4 minutes			5 minutes			
Run in place	20 seconds							30 seconds						
Trunk twister #28	20	20	20	25	25	25	30	30	30	35	35	35	40	40
Run in place	20 seconds							30 seconds						
Fire hydrant #23	7	8	9	10	11	12	13	14	15	16	17	18	19	20
Run in place	20 seconds							30 seconds						
Mountain climber #19	20	20	20	25	25	25	30	30	30	35	35	35	40	40
Run in place	20 seconds							30 seconds						
Walk	2 minutes													
Cool down (Outlined in Appendix B)	Do 5 minutes of stretching													
Take 10-second pulse rate; multiply by 6 and record														

CHAPTER
12

Fitness Is Ageless And Sexless

Q: *Should people exercise differently as they get older?*
A: If you have been physically active during your younger and middle years, you probably know how to "listen" to your body and make proper adjustments for breathlessness, excessive fatigue, and so on. Consequently, almost no adjustments will be necessary. You will find that you can probably exercise vigorously at a relatively old age.

John A. Kelly, aged 70, is a prime example. A legend in Boston, John Kelly has been running for over 50 years. He ran his first Boston Marathon in 1928 when he was 21. For some unknown reason he skipped the race until 1932. He has run every year since then. John still runs 50 miles a week and he averages 15 to 17 races a year. Most are 10 miles in length. At age 70 he still looks like 60 and will probably continue running for many more years.

If, on the other hand, you have been sedentary, you must proceed with caution. Remember, it took you 10, 20, or more years of easy living to get out of shape. You won't get back in shape in a week or two. Your re-entry into exercise must be gradual. I said earlier you need to spend one month exercising for every year you have been sedentary in order to regain fitness. That's about 2 or 3 years if you've been sitting around for 20 or 30 years.

When exercising, give yourself some recovery time between

exercises and include lots of easier stretching exercises with the harder aerobic drills. Precede your sessions with a good, long warm-up and allow plenty of time at the end of your sessions for cool-down or gradual tapering-off of activity.

Above all, pay attention to your body. If you "listen" you will know when to cut back. If your session leaves you extremely fatigued past the 10 to 15 minutes that are normal after exercising, cut back the next day. If at any time you are dizzy, suffer chest pains, exceptional fatigue or pain—STOP! The same goes for staggering, mental confusion, loss of facial color, or nausea.

Sure, there may be some adjustments to make as you get older, but you should never consider yourself too old to exercise. Exercise is healthful and beneficial to the older, mature citizen.

Q: *How crucial is a warm-up if you're older in years?*
A: Very crucial. In fact, some experts recommend a longer warm-up for older people. Dr. T. K. Cureton, the world famous exercise physiologist, has had remarkable success with an extended warm-up. During the years 1944 to 1969, Cureton led many fitness classes at the University of Illinois. He also conducted thousands of fitness clinics around the world. During his clinics he encouraged people to jump right in and participate. And there was no screening! Yet none of the participants had heart attacks. The reason, according to Cureton: "adequate warm-up." A warm-up, by the way, that may have lasted 20 minutes or more.

Q: *Are cool-down's also important for the older exerciser?*
A: A cool-down is absolutely necessary, especially for older people. Many people who die when on exercise programs do so when they sit in the car after the run, or sit in the locker room after a swim in the pool. If these people had cooled-down properly, their chances of having a heart attack would have been reduced substantially.

Q: *What type of exercise is best for an older person?*
A: Any exercise that stresses total body movement. At first, exercises which rely on local muscle power, like sit-ups and push-ups, should be avoided by mature adults. The trouble with these exercises is that they are very fatiguing. That's because one

particular muscle group is emphasized. So the exerciser has to stop and rest before he can go on to another. It would be far better for him to engage in exercise which is non-stop and does not emphasize a local muscle group. Naturally, some strenuous exercises can be incorporated into a routine, but not so many that the exerciser becomes exhausted. Exercises such as push-ups, weight lifting, or isometrics are not recommended because of the possibility of overexertion. Perhaps more importantly, they do not aid in overall cardiovascular fitness.

Q: *Are there any precautions an older person should take with regard to exercise?*
A: Because most Americans have, by the time they are 65, been conditioned to having everything from automatic can openers to sit-down lawn mowers, some care must be taken so as not to overload your body's ability to accept a more vigorous level of stress. All evidence points to the fact that your re-entry into an active life must be gradual. It is also a good idea to have a complete physical exam before you begin and, if possible, some form of stress test (see Chapter 4) so that you have a good idea of your fitness level. If you can't take the stress test, it's a good idea to get a second medical opinion. Even so, the most important thing is to employ the talk test when exercising. Furthermore, you should be free of pain when exercising. That means you don't want to have any chest, arm, neck, or abdominal pain. These pains may be a sign that your heart is overtaxed.

Finally, you should be especially diligent with a warm-up and a cool-down. Your body may find it quite a shock to jump right into and out of an exercise session. By following these simple precautions, any older person will be able to enjoy a regular program of exercise.

Q: *What exercise would you select for mature adults?*
A: Walking. The Starter Program is the way to go. If you have been totally sedentary, you may not want to start out with 20 minutes. Five to ten minutes may be fine. I know one elderly lady who started to walk to her mailbox and back, about 50 feet. Over the next five months she progressed to about 20 to 25 minutes of walking. She was 81 at the time. She had had several heart at-

tacks between her 77th and 80th years and had really become an invalid, refusing to leave her home and dress herself. Progress for her was slow but she did start to improve and, I might add, she felt a heck of a lot better. Now she dresses herself, gets her own meals, and even takes the wash off the line.

Of course, other people her age have made even more remarkable progress. Eula Weaver is a prime example. Eula was 77 years old when she suffered a heart attack. Tests showed that she was in very bad shape. Her doctor told her she should go home, take her pills, and let everyone wait on her hand and foot. She would probably live a few more years but she would be a total invalid. The doctor also offered her one other choice. She could go home and walk. Poor Eula could barely feed herself. The thought of being an invalid was distasteful, but she couldn't conceive of the other choice. How could she walk, when just raising her arm was an exhausting task? She went home and tried to walk, but it was difficult.

Besides a bad heart, she had high blood pressure and hardening of the arteries. Her heavy medication made her uncomfortable. She was not making much progress and finally could take it no longer. Eula Weaver was a fighter. She told her doctor she'd rather be "dead than down" so she tossed her pills away and began walking longer distances. Simply put, she rededicated herself to life. She affirmed the fact that she would rather live one day being alive and active than 10 years confined like some sick house pet.

Eula is now 88 years old and holds the age group records in the half mile and mile runs. She gets up around 5:30 every morning, trots to the local high school, jogs a mile, then trots back home. Her latest goal is to run with her grandson when she is 100 years old. Her greatest asset, of course, is her outlook on life. While most people her age (those fortunate enough to make it to 88) are keeping rest homes in business, Eula approaches each day as an adventure.

Q: *What activities can older people do?*
A: Practically any kind. I've known joggers, walkers, swimmers, and bicyclers in their 70's and even 80's. Larry Lewis, aged 106, ran about 6 miles a day in Golden Gate Park in San Francisco until he died of cancer. Pearl Logan, whom I told you about in

Chapter 10, is 70 and bicycles 20 miles a day. I've met scores of people at YMCAs across the country who are very vigorous. And who would put many younger people to shame in terms of their ability to withstand rigorous, hard exercise. Lloyd Morgan, a retired YMCA director, leads a group of retired auto workers in Detroit through an exercise routine that would make the average high school student plead for mercy.

It's quite clear fitness is ageless. You are never too old.

Q: *Are there any people who are unable to exercise at all?*
A: Very, very few people fall into this category. Some people do, however, due to severe heart or lung conditions. Some people with rheumatoid arthritis also fall into this category. For people with these conditions, exercise may do more harm than good and it should be avoided entirely at least until they have recovered fully. Naturally, these people would be under a physician's care and should follow his recommendations regarding exercise. If you are in doubt, check with your personal physician. But keep in mind, you're never too old, too fat, too out of shape, or too busy to exercise. Remember, if you decide NOT to exercise, you had better get a physical to see whether you can withstand it.

And when you check with your doctor, don't let him frighten you with old doctor's tales such as "Remember if you walk a mile, you have to walk a mile back." It's time he started practicing medicine and avoided putdowns. He should be happy that you have taken on your responsibility to exercise for better heatlh.

One more thing about older people. They do have a pretty good idea of how much exercise they need. In their younger days they didn't have all the modern gadgets we have. So they adapt surprisingly well to walking and other vigorous exercise. It's almost as though they had such a good beginning that it carried over into later life.

Q: *When should children start to exercise vigorously?*
A: Just as it is never too late to begin exercising, it is never too early. Young children (preschool age) make excellent "students" of exercise. They are active, flexible, and receptive to learning new things. They certainly can handle vigorous activity, perhaps better than adults. Parents who start their children exercising at

an early age are doing them a big favor. Research has shown that more active children learn more because they experience more objects, body positions, and movements. Their brains and nervous systems are stimulated, which enhances their learning experiences. Along with encouraging children to develop such good health habits as proper diet, dental care, adequate rest, and personal hygiene, parents should encourage their young children to keep physically fit.

But above all, do not make fitness a chore. Exercise should be fun and enjoyable for the child.

Q: *Are there any precautions a parent should take when starting his children exercising?*
A: Yes, though they are on the psychological/emotional level rather than the physical. Unfortunately, the few activity programs that exist for children are generally competitive and, therefore, selective. To compound the problem, team sports rather than life-time activities are emphasized. Parents need to watch closely the little league programs and avoid those that regard physical exercise as a lot of work, stress, and pressure. Early age fitness MUST stress fun. When your child is chewed out because he didn't slide into second, the program has missed the boat as far as fitness and life-long activity is concerned.

Q: *How do I get my young child started in an exercise program?*
A: The biggest problem may be your own concept of exercise. As I've mentioned so many times before, don't be narrow-minded about exercise. Young children may not get too excited about regimented sessions and calisthenics. They may not even get too thrilled about jogging or walking, especially if you stand on the side lines and give directions. Sell the program as a family project with *everyone* participating. Be creative in devising activities that are fun. Remember, you are competing with TV, comic books, and toys that do it all, so you've *got* to be good.

The key word should be FUN. Attention spans waiver at early ages so keep each session loaded with fun-filled activities. Avoid doing the same thing day in and day out. Instead try different activities on different days, and even try to do many different activities during the session itself. Learning a new sport together as a family can be an enjoyable experience. Or, equipping the back yard with simple apparatus for chin-ups, rope climbing, or high jumping may help "induce labor." Why not set up a make-shift obstacle course and time everyone once a week, then chart everyone's improvement. There are endless possibilities here including old tires to run through, a two-by-four tightrope, bales of straw to hurdle, a rope stretched between two trees to hand walk.

Some families have tried a "No Car Day" once a week where the car is locked in the garage and everyone relies on leg power rather than horse-power. Others have found that children enjoy jogging or calisthenics when everyone (Mom and Dad included) participates. Some competition may help here in the form of relay races, establishing goals for sit-ups, of miles run, push-ups done, or weights lifted. Or record your family's mileage with a felt pen on a world map. Jogging becomes more attractive when you are passing through Manila or Istanbul.

Extremely young children may enjoy simple games of talk, skipping rope, or wheelbarrow. Another fun activity for the little ones is imitating the walks of animals (kangaroo, crab, inch worm, bunny, etc.). Also, supervised wrestling in its various forms (arm, leg, thumb, Indian, etc.) are excellent strength and endurance builders for children.

Finally, a local Y, fitness club, or gymnasium offers a wide variety of activities that seem more attractive simply because they involve a special trip to a special place. In addition, these places offer instruction in activities that you may not be equipped for at home.

Now you should have some ideas, but don't stop there! Create your own activities for fun and fitness. If you keep the fun element in mind, you will find that soon your children would rather spend a half hour or an hour in an activity program with the entire family, than spend that same time sitting in front of the television set.

Q: *What do you think about television and fitness?*
A: Next to the automobile, the television set is probably the biggest cause for sedentary living in America. And with children it is particularly disastrous. They are encouraged from a very early age to be entertained or babysat via television. They learn to

be passive people. As parents, you could do your children a big favor physically by moving the television out of the house or just having it on during selected times of the day.

For the last three years we have not permitted television in our house. We have 5 children, the oldest is now 15 and the youngest is 7. You say how can you deprive your children of that kind of stimulation? My answer is how can you deprive your children of the physical stimulation that they need. It's amazing how creative children are and how much additional time is spent with each other and with the family, simply because the television is removed. I think one of the best feelings I had about television was last Christmas when I decided to let the children watch a Charlie Brown special. So I hooked up the television and told them that at 7:30 they could watch it. I went outside at about 6:45 and started to shovel snow. The kids were sledding. At 7:25 I yelled that it was time to watch Charlie Brown's Christmas. Tommy, my 9-year old said, "Oh Dad, do we have to? We're having so much fun out here." All of them decided to play in the snow. It's a matter of attitude, and the example you set is vital. William Ruffer did a study in 1968 which showed that parents who were active had children who were active. That makes sense. If a son or daughter sees Dad and Mom watching TV day in and day out, they'll think that's what adults do. But if they see Mom and Dad out working in the yard, jogging, riding a bicycle, playing tennis, or whatever, they'll assume that that's what adults are supposed to do. They'll mimic their parents. Whether we like to admit it or not, our children reflect our attitudes, morals, and ideas.

Q: *Can you really get kids interested in walking?*
A: Yes. But you may have to play a few games with them. For example, if you're doing a family walking session, they may find that enjoyable at first. But after a while it may be old hat. So you've got to come up with a new twist by making it a game. Perhaps as you're walking you can ask them to write down or tell you how many different sights they see. Or how many different smells they smell. Or how many different sounds they hear, or how many different people they are. They can count the number of fire hydrants, or the number of blue automobiles; you name it. The kids will soon come up with their own ideas and you will find

that once they're hooked they no longer have to do that. They simply become aware of the world around them.

Many times on a holiday, we'll take the whole family backpacking for a day or so. We always make special treats of granola, dried fruit, and fruit juice. When our 8-year old, Lisa, was 5 or 6, she called it "snackpacking." Not bad.

Q: *What types of injuries are most common with active children?*
A: One reason why active children learn more is that they see more things and places. And one of those places they may see is the hospital, for it is not entirely uncommon for active kids to break an arm or finger or sprain an ankle. Generally, a broken bone is the most severe injury you can expect from a child who is active. Fortunately, a broken bone is relatively minor these days. Other types of injuries that are common to active children are abrasions, bruises, and simple cuts. These are easily cared for in the home with bandaids, ice packs, and a mild antiseptic. Now before all the mothers of the world unite and call me a "hardhearted male" hold on. This is all a part of growing up actively. Plopping your child down on a soft pillow in front of a TV set with a can of pop on one side and a bowl of potato chips on the other may keep him from getting a skinned knee or turned ankle, but it may also keep him from enjoying a healthful, happy childhood and adulthood. In fact, the TV, pop, sedentary living, and potato chips are setting the stage and planting the seeds for a far more serious disease—heart attack. Making life overly comfortable is not showing love.

Q: *Are there other specific, more serious injuries that children are susceptible to?*
A: Another injury, or rather disorder, that activity children may develop is Osgood Schlotters disease. This is a disorder which involves the bone and tissue just below the knee. Young girls from the ages of 8 to 13 and young boys ages 10 to 15 are most susceptible. Young boys are affected about 3 times as often as young girls. The symptoms are local pain in the area just below the knee and a swelling over that area. Kneeling, a direct blow, running, and climbing aggravate this pain. Also, by extending that knee against resistance, the pains can be reproduced. There are

several different explanations of what occurs. But there is no real agreement as to whether it is from a direct injury, a result of an infection, or just plain growing pains. The condition is not particularly serious and responds readily to very conservative measures aimed at lessening the stress placed on that particular leg.

The first step in treating this disease is to simply have the youngster stay off that leg as much as possible, either through staying in bed during the day or by using crutches. Occasionally, a cast may be placed around the knee to limit the activity and flexibility of the knee. Only under very rare circumstances is surgery used to correct the condition. If your young son or daughter complains of pain in the area just below the knee and the complaints persist, it would be a good idea to see your family doctor. If he or she does indeed have Osgood Schlotters disease, don't be alarmed. If your child follows the doctor's directions religiously, he will be back on his feet and active in a very short period of time.

Another childhood malady is Little League Elbow.

Little League Elbow can be a real problem with young children. The human body is not completely developed until a person is around 21. As the body develops, the long part of the bone (shaft) and its short end form separately. A type of pre-bone tissue (cartilage) separates the shaft and the ends of the bone. As a child grows older, the pre-bone tissue gets smaller. So at full growth (21 years or so) the long and short ends of the bone are completely fused.

Because of this growth pattern, two things can happen:

1. The repeated throwing action places a tremendous amount of stress on the tendons, ligaments, and muscles of the child's arm. Because these parts of the body are fastened to both the long and short parts of the bone, a repeated, unnatural movement such as throwing may cause a separation of the long end from the short end. One tendon may pull on the long part of the bone while another tugs on the short part.

2. The pre-bone tissue may become inflamed. This is called osteochondritis or "Little League Elbow."

Throwing an occasional baseball is not going to cause problems or hurt anyone. The condition occurs because of exaggerated actions—throwing hard, or pitching a curve in baseball for a long period of time. Osteochondritis usually occurs in children about 10 to 13 years of age. If untreated or not rested properly, it may cause a loss of arm movement and a chronic sore arm or odd bone growth.

Q: *Does that mean that children should not participate in baseball or other forms of athletic competition?*
A: No. But it does mean that you should not expect too much from growing bodies. Unfortunately, in our sports oriented society many parents, coaches, and friends pressure a child to keep playing even though he may feel tired. Parents should realize that this may be unnatural—and in many cases dangerous. I'd say 3 innings of pitching is plenty for the average child. And throwing curves should be discouraged until the child is older.

Q: *Does pre-conditioning help prevent injuries for active children?*
A: Absolutely. Children, anyone for that matter, playing sports should spend a minimum of 4 to 6 weeks getting into shape before the season begins. They should not expect to get into shape just by playing baseball, basketball, or football.

Even during the season of play, time should be spent on strength, flexibility, and circulatiory development.

Q: *Should women exercise differently from men?*
A: Men aren't the only people who should be healthy and good looking! Exercise is for everyone, including women. "But," you say, "I don't want all those huge muscles bursting the seams of my blouses." Of course you don't, and I sure don't want to see America's women looking like Mr. Universe. But exercise doesn't necessarily mean bulky muscles. You see, exercise is quite versatile. It can help you lose weight. It can firm up problem areas of your body. It can decrease your chance of heart disease, reduce stress and tension, and help overcome boredom. It can increase your ability to enjoy an active life. Women will find that exercise is not confined to either sex. It's an equal opportunity "implorer" and does not discriminate according to race, color, creed, or sex.

Q: *Are there any special exercises women should do?*
A: Not really. They respond to exercise just as men do. There-

fore, they can engage in the same exercises as men. If they like to walk, they can walk; if they like to cycle, they can cycle; if they like to swim, they can swim; and if they like to jog, they can jog. There's no difference between men and women when it comes to exercise. They can participate in weight training if they like. It's all a matter of attitude and preference.

Of course, if a woman is concerned about special problem areas (sagging breasts, protruding midriff, or flabby arms), she can check out the specific exercises in Chapter 11 which will firm up her muscles and give her a better shape. These will concentrate on special areas as well as contribute to overall fitness. Everything that I have said so far in this book—that is, trying to be healthy and looking better—you'll find applies to men, women, and children. You may have to modify for age or fitness level, but the objectives are the same. Choose activities that you enjoy doing and be diligent.

Q: *Don't women get enough exercise with housework?*
A: They do not. Although it is true that most housewives get a great deal of physical activity around the house, they still do not get enough to be of benefit in controlling body weight, improving heart-lung function, and keeping the body toned. To do this they are going to have to do something specific. It doesn't matter whether the woman is a doctor, lawyer, teacher, farmer's wife, urban housewife, mother, or nurse. She needs a separate program of activity to sustain both her physical and emotional health.

Q: *Why do women seem to complain about fatigue during their housework?*
A: It's because of low fitness levels. That does not mean women aren't active when they perform household work, it's just that housework doesn't involve aerobic activity. If a woman doesn't have heart/lung endurance, then vacuuming the rug, doing dishes, etc., *will* wear her out. Her low aerobic capacity forces her to rest between jobs. The rest produces a lower fitness level. The lower fitness level, the less physical work, the lower. . . . It's an extremely vicious cycle. To build energy, you must expend energy. There's no other way. You have to improve your aerobic capacity to reduce your fatigue. And you can't get enough exercise with day-to-day chores. Perhaps 100 or 200 years ago you could, but not in modern-day America.

Q: *Are there any special problems that women can avoid if they exercise?*
A: Yes. One of them is in the area of dysmenorrhea. Some women experience levels of pain during menstruation that range from a few slight twinges in the abdominal and low back regions to violent cramps, nausea, and headaches. This is known as dysmenorrhea or painful flow.

Q: *Can exercise do anything to alleviate menstrual cramping?*
A: In most cases, exercise can greatly reduce discomfort of painful flow. Gynecologists estimate that 20 to 30% of dysmenorrhea cases are caused by such organic problems as infection, cysts, or endocrine imbalance. In such cases, exercise will not solve the problem directly. However, 70 to 80% of the cases of dysmenorrhea are caused by poor posture, insufficient exercise, fatigue, weak abdominal muscles, and improper diet. In these cases, exercise can directly or indirectly relieve the discomfort.

Q: *How does exercise work to relieve menstrual discomfort?*
A: If you will look again at the causes of dysmenorrhea in the 70 to 80% category, you will see how exercise fits in. Poor posture is often the result of weakened muscles in the shoulders, stomach, and back. Naturally, a woman who is physically fit will have strengthened those muscles and improved her posture. Weak abdominal muscles simply need strengthening and there's no better way to do that than through exercise. Fatigue occurs when your physical activity exceeds your level of fitness. Women who are physically unfit experience fatigue more readily than women who exercise regularly. Again, it's the old cycle of low aerobic capacity producing more fatigue, less activity, lower aerobic capacity. . . .
Exercise provides the body with several mechanisms to defend against painful flow.

Q: *What kinds of exercises should you do to help prevent menstrual discomfort?*
A: Here are a series of exercises that can be effective in reducing dysmenorrhea. They are used for relieving the congestion in the abdominal area caused by poor posture, poor circulation, or poor muscle tone, and for relieving back and leg pain.

1.   Mosher Exercise—Lie on your back with your knees bent, feet flat on the floor, and right or left hand resting lightly on the lower abdomen. Slowly force your abdominal wall up against the hand as far as possible. Slowly contract the abdominal wall and relax. Repeat 10 times. Breathe normally throughout the movement.

2.   Cat Exercise—Kneel on your hands and knees. Raise your back as high as possible while tucking your pelvic girdle under and contracting the abdomen. Relax completely and allow the back to sag. Repeat 8 to 10 times, maintaining rhythm throughout.

3.   Knee-Chest—Kneel with your knees approximately 12 inches apart, hips directly over the knees, and your chest as close to the floor as comfortable. Hold the position for 3 to 5 minutes. Slide into prone position.

4.   Thigh-Chest—Kneel with your knees about 12 inches apart. Rest your chest and abdomen on your thighs, and place your hands back by your heels. Take 3 or 4 deep breaths. Keeping in the same position, move your arms out in front of your head. Breathe 3 or 4 times and stretch your fingertips forward, pushing the hips backward with each inhalation. Release on each exhalation.

5.   Walk—It's a great tension reliever and great for circulation and weight control.

Q: *Does exercise hurt a woman's chances of pregnancy?*
A: This is a popular belief held by many lay people, educators, and even physicians. Fortunately, it is a misconception. A report made by the American Amateur Athletic Union revealed that fertility, pregnancy, and pelvic measurements were all found to be within the normal limits for women who engaged in vigorous athletics. Exercise and sports are lousy birth control measures.

I should mention, however, that it has been reported that irregular menstrual cycles are common among female athletes who train hard and long.

Doctors don't know why this occurs. Dr. Ken Foreman, of Seattle Pacific University, first became aware of the irregularity 10 years ago when he was coaching an internationally famous distance runner. The runner revealed to him that she had not menstruated for almost 6 months.

More recently, he has investigated other long-distance runners and cross-country skiers. Generally, he found that the average number of miles run per week by the women with irregular cycles was much higher than for those with regular cycles; 79.6 miles compared to 63.8. Dr. Foreman also said that once a very irregular person reduces her training, her cycle reverts back to normal.

Again, researchers don't know why this happens. It will just take more time for studies to be conducted.

The point is, however, that most people do not train this intensely (about 12 hours of exercise each week). But I think you should be aware of it.

Q: *Does exercise make childbirth more difficult?*
A: On the contrary. Women who exercise have quicker and easier deliveries than the normal population. One study revealed the average duration of labor from rupture of membrane to delivery was 102 minutes in athletic women and 207 minutes in non-athletic women. Another study found that among women athletes there was a smaller incidence of complications and 50% fewer Caesarean sections. Active women generally have a shorter labor period because of an ability to relax, better breathing control, stronger abdominal muscles, and the ability to reduce useless contractions of the arms and legs. Indeed, most prenatal classes offer extensive training in exercises that help condition the prospective mother for her delivery. The value of exercise in pregnant women is immeasurable. Don't get caught in the pregnancy/sedentary trap.

Q: *What's the pregnancy/sedentary trap?*
A: Many times during pregnancy, especially during the last 3 months, a woman finds she is uncomfortable or has difficulty breathing, so she tends to become less active. Furthermore, once the child is born she sleeps when the baby sleeps so she can be ready for "action" once baby is awake. These situations beget a sedentary pattern of living. When a woman becomes caught in the sedentary trap, her weight starts to escalate, so she becomes less active, so she gains more weight. From that point on she is constantly fighting the battle of the bulge.

One final point. I have seen articles recently about women who have run and exercised right through pregnancy up until the last few days. Dr. Ken Cooper reported on a woman who jogged up to 3 hours before the birth of her child. As a postscript, Cooper noted that the child seemed to have a particular fondness for being bounced on the mother's knee. Who knows!

Q: *After a woman has had her baby, is her athletic performance affected?*
A: No. Studies have shown that childbirth does not have a harmful affect on an athlete's performance. In fact, a closer look at the careers of some of the world's top female athletes will show that having children does not slow them down at all.

Q: *How soon after childbirth can the mother start to exercise?*
A: If the pelvic examination reveals that everything is back to normal, most obstetricians recommend resumption of regular exercise from six weeks to three months after childbirth. I think the sooner the better. But then I've never been pregnant. Naturally, it is best to consult your physician before attempting something too strenuous. Once you receive the go-ahead from your physician, try beginning with these simple exercises to help regain your figure:

1.   Lying on your back, take 5 deep breaths. Breathe from the abdomen.

2.   Lying on your back with your arms out to the side at right angles to your body, lift your arms, keeping them straight, touch palms of hands, and return. Do five times.

3.   Lying on your back, raise your head off the floor so that your chin touches your chest. Do 10.

4.   Lying on your back, raise your left leg off the ground as high as possible. Keep the leg straight. Then lower the leg making full use of the abdominal muscles. Repeat with the right leg. Do 10 times.

5.   Lying on your back, raise your right knee, draw your thigh down on the abdomen and chest, and your lower leg against your thigh and buttocks. Straighten your leg and lower it to the floor. Alternate with both right and left legs. Do five of each.

6.   Starting gradually, walk 10 to 15 minutes a day. Gradu-

ally increase the distance walked. The Starter Walking Program is a good one to follow.

Q: *Will exercise masculinize a woman?*

A: Not any more than cooking feminizes men. Masculinity and femininity are determined by genetics and attitude, not by whether or not you exercise. Many Americans of both sexes still cling to the fallacious Old World beliefs about masculinity and femininity. In the "old days" men played at sports while women watched. Building one's body was a masculine activity designed to titillate young ladies who spent their free time preening and primping. Fortunately, times are changing. Women now enjoy the benefits of an active, healthful life. First, American beauties such as Linda Lee Mead, Miss American of 1960, announced that they enjoyed such pursuits as fencing, calisthenics, tennis, and basketball. Then Wilma Rudolph burst onto the scene in 1960. In 1969 Judy Ford was selected Miss America. She was a physical education major and a skilled trampolinist at the University of Illinois. Also, few people would call figure skaters, such as Peggy Fleming and Dorothy Hamill, unattractive or horsey.

CHAPTER

13

Fitness Is Weatherless

Q: *What adjustments do I have to make in my exercise program for weather?*

A: If you live in a four seasons climate like I do, you may find yourself faced with sub-zero weather in January and 90°+ weather in July. Fortunately, our bodies have amazing heating and cooling systems. But we need to know their capabilities and how they work.

First the cooling system. When your body starts to "heat up" your cooling system is turned on automatically; that is, you begin to sweat. Those beads of sweat will cool your body down only if they are allowed to evaporate. Wearing sweatsuits or nonporous clothing increases the sweat, but prohibits the cooling effect of evaporation, resulting in the body's temperature remaining dangerously high. So when exercising in hot weather, give your cooling system a break. Wear loose fitting shorts, a porous T-shirt, and don't be afraid to sip liquids slowly and frequently. All that water you are losing through sweat must be replaced or you will dehydrate.

When exercising in very cold weather, you rely on your heating system. By now, you know that activities burn calories and a calorie is a unit of heat. Generally, a cold environment poses no real problem because either we are sufficiently heated through our increased metabolism, or we can simply add clothing to retain what body heat we have generated. Anyone who has shoveled snow in sub-freezing weather knows that within just a few minutes you become warm and shed your heavy overcoat. When the job is finished, however, it isn't long before you get chilled, unless you put that jacket back on.

The same adjustments should be followed in exercise. Warm-up with some heavier outer wear such as a jacket or extra sweat shirt. When you have warmed up, shed the heavy clothing and continue with your more vigorous activity. When you're finished you can leave the jacket off until you feel your body is getting cooler. Or better yet, go back inside.

Q: *What kinds of clothes are best for cold-weather exercise?*
A: When I run in weather below 20° Fahrenheit, I wear a pair of running shorts, and two pairs of sweat pants. One pair of sweat pants is light and the other is heavy. On the upper body I wear a thin turtleneck with a muscle shirt pulled over it. On top of that I wear a sweat shirt. On my hands and feet I wear socks. I like socks on my hands since my hands seem more comfortable. I wear my running shoes and a ski cap to protect my head and ears. I prefer the ski cap so I can pull the mask down when running into the cold Michigan winds. I find that as I'm running I may have to shed my sweat shirt and on rare occasions my second pair of sweat pants. But I find it is most comfortable for the first mile to dress in that manner.

I have a friend, Dick Harris, who operates a good-sized health club in Pennsylvania. He runs in his shorts most of the time. Even when the weather is around 32°. I can't. It's probably an individual thing.

Of course, I don't worry so much about the cold as I do the wind-chill index.

Q: *What is the wind-chill index?*
A: This is a chart that combines temperature with wind speed to show how cold your skin "feels" it is. On some days, 10° below zero seems quite comfortable while on other days, 10° above zero seems unbearable. This is because on the 10° below day, the wind wasn't blowing, while on the 10° above day I was faced with 30 mph winds. Meteorologists tell us that increased wind velocity

directly affects the chilling effect of temperature. For example, at +10° Fahrenheit with a 30 mph wind, the wind-chill factor is −33°, while at −10° Fahrenheit with a 0 mph wind the wind-chill factor is −10°. *See the following chart.* If you are planning any outdoor activity in the winter, you should pay close attention to the wind-chill factor which is usually included in radio and TV weather reports. Also remember that your speed of running, bicycling, or cross-country skiing will also increase the chill factor substantially.

Wind-Chill Index

When windy, the cold becomes even colder. The chart, adapted from the U.S. Government, shows what happens to the air temperature as winds increase or decrease.

WIND SPEED

Temperature	10 MPH	20 MPH	30 MPH	40 MPH
+50°	40°	32°	28°	26°
+30°	18°	4°	−2°	−6°
+20°	4°	−10°	−18°	−21°
+10°	−9°	−25°	−33°	−37°
0°	−21°	−30°	−48°	−53°
−10°	−33°	−53°	−63°	−69°
−20°	−46°	−67°	−79°	−85°

Q: *Can your lungs freeze in cold weather?*
A: As long as you're alive, your lungs won't freeze. In fact, it's impossible. This is a common misconception used by many as an excuse to curtail their outdoor activity during the winter months. Even in the coldest weather, the air is warmed sufficiently by the time it reaches the lungs so that no danger of "freeze-up" is possible. I have run in −46° weather without a surgical mask and I have had no problems except with people offering me a ride.

Q: *Why do some people wear surgical masks when running in cold weather?*
A: A surgical mask has no great value to the average person. When exercising in a cold climate, the body is equipped to warm

the air as it passes down into the lungs. Some people, however, experience discomfort in the throat and chest while breathing hard in cold weather. As long as they are sure this discomfort is not related to a more serious health problem, a surgical mask or scarf may be worn over the mouth to prevent this problem.

If you are bothered with chest or lung pain during cold weather, I think the alternative suggested by Dr. Terrance Kavanaugh of the Toronto Rehabilitation Center in Canada is better. According to Dr. Kavanaugh you can attach a simple plastic disposable oxygen mask to 12 inches of flexible plastic tubing. The mask fits over the nose and mouth and is held firmly in place by an elastic headband. The tubing then extends beneath the person's T-shirt to the lower part of the chest. Over the shirt the jacket, sweater, or track suit is worn. This very simple device is great for letting angina patients exercise in cold weather.

Q: *Are there any other dangers from cold-weather exercise?*
A: The crucial thing is to keep exposed parts of the body well protected. The layer effect is best. A mask protecting the nose and ears, and proper coverage of the fingers seem to keep most people warm. I must tell you, however, there have been some male runners who have reported pineal frostbite. This is due to the fact that they did not wear enough clothing around their pelvic area. So they developed frostbite of the penis. While to some people this may be amusing, to the runner it's not. It is advisable that male joggers wear an extra layer of clothing around their pelvis. Many times an extra pair of jogging shorts will do. I stuff a handkerchief in my undershorts. It works fine.

Q: *What are the dangers of exercising in extreme heat?*
A: Heat presents an entirely different set of problems. When the temperature as well as the humidity start to climb, the exerciser experiences heat stress. Fortunately, the body can sweat. The sweating keeps your body cool. The sweat on your skin evaporates. So it cools the surface of the skin. This has important implications. As your blood is circulating around your body, it heats up at the core or the center part of your body. As the blood comes near the surface of the skin, the sweating, and the evaporation of the sweat, allows the blood to cool. Consequently, the

blood temperature drops a bit and the cooled blood is circulated back to the core of the body. Once at the core, it heats up again, only to be transported back to the skin again. So your body maintains the proper temperature in a hot environment. It's a beautiful thermostat mechanism. The thermostat malfunctions when the humidity gets too high or when your sweat can't evaporate.

Too much humidity presents a special problem for the exerciser. When you exercise in a hot, humid environment, your sweat doesn't evaporate because the moisture-laden air cannot absorb the additional water. Heat dissipation does not occur and your body temperature rises. If your temperature continues to rise (106–108°), death will occur. The rise in temperature and the excessive humidity brings on another condition: dehydration, or loss of water. It is not too unusual for some people to lose several pounds of water when exercising vigorously in a humid environment. I've known people to lose 10 or more pounds of water when exercising is a hot, humid environment. If you do not replace the water by drinking during your workout, your system will dehydrate.

Finally, this loss of water through sweating removes valuable minerals from your body, particularly salt and potassium. If you are not in good physical condition or are unaccustomed to high humidity, you may lose as much as 5 grams of salt in the first quart of sweat from your body. After prolonged training or repeated exposure to high humidity, the loss of salt and potassium drops substantially. But if you are unfit, a special set of circumstances arises. And you may have to take some measures to replace it.

Q: *What's the best way to replace salt and potassium lost through sweat?*
A: At one time it was believed that salt tablets were good for people who sweated a great deal. Now, salt tablets are frowned upon. Each tablet usually contains ½ gram of salt. It's too concentrated and causes problems. When exercising in a hot, humid environment a greater concentration of body fluid is lost than is salt. So sweating causes an increase in the salt concentration in the body (since more water is lost). Additional salt will only

widen the gap. Salt tablets are probably only necessary for those people who exercise in an extremely hot environment over a long period of time (a week or more). It is more important that you replace your water. You can probably make up your salt demands by eating foods which contain more salt.

Q: *Which types of food contain salt?*
A: Your largest supply of natural salt in food will come from pork, chiefly ham and bacon. One serving of ham provides you with as much as 2 grams of salt, so you can see that replacing salt naturally is not all that difficult. Most cheeses also have a high level of salt and are good natural ways of replacing salt. Fruits generally do not have high salt content, but the banana stands above all others with a good supply of salt. Most vegetables do not have a great deal of natural salt in them either, but endive, greens, lettuce, potatoes and spinach offer higher degrees of salt than most vegetables. In addition, there are many foods that are little else but carriers of salt. These include olives, pickles, relishes, luncheon meats, and dried beef. If you are concerned about not getting enough salt due to excessive sweating and high-humidity exercise, choosing foods from this list will help replace that salt naturally. You probably won't need salt tablets. See the following chart on foods containing large amounts of salt.

The exact use of potassium in the body is not clearly understood. Potassium is probably necessary for growth and for the movement of nerve impulses. Potassium is one of the few minerals that is found in your cells as well as in the fluids which surround them. There is less potassium than sodium in the body. But the muscles contain at least 6 times as much potassium as sodium. You lose potassium by sweating, so it is important that when you exercise you be concerned about the loss of potassium. Some of the lesser symptoms of potassium depletion are loss of appetite, nausea, vomiting, distended abdomen, irritability, and confusion.

High Salt Foods

All canned and frozen foods	Meat sauces
Bacon	Milk*
Beets*	Mustard
Bouillon cubes	Mustard greens*

Canned meats
Canned soups or stews
Carrots*
Caviar
Celery salt
Cheese*
Chili sauce
Commercial salad dressings
Commercially made:
 Breads
 Rolls
 Crackers
Dandelion greens*
Frankfurters and sausages
Garlic salt
Gravy
Ham
Kale*
Ketchup
Luncheon meats

Olives
Onion salt
Organ meats
Pickled foods (sauerkraut)
Pickles
Pretzels
Relishes
Salt pork
Salted butter
Salted, dried, and smoked fish
 and meats
Salted nuts
Salted popcorn
Salted margarine
Shellfish
Soy sauce
Spinach*
Tenderizers
Worchestershire sauce

The chart illustrates that almost everything you eat contains salt.
I really don't think you need to worry about salt replacement. My
own feeling is that you should get the salt from the natural, wholesome foods which have an asterisk.*

In its most severe form, potassium depletion can lead to muscle
weakness and even paralysis. Natural sources of potassium are
bananas, lima beans, navy beans, dried peas, kale, lettuce,
parsnips, potatoes, and most sea foods. See the following chart
for some good potassium foods.

High Potassium Foods

Bananas
Beef
Beet greens
Brussel sprouts
Chard
Cabbage
Dandelion greens

Kale
Lima beans
Most sea foods
Mustard greens
Navy beans
Parsley
Parsnips

Dried fruit	Peanuts
Dried peas	Potatoes
Dry milk	Spinach
Endive	Turnip greens

Q: *Do commercial products which are called electrolyte replacements help replace salt and potassium?*
A: Many electrolyte products are available. They are special mixtures of liquids, salts, sugars, and other minerals. They are designed to replace those things your body loses during physical activity. In fact, if they didn't have any flavoring added to them, they would taste just like sweat. Their chemical composition is similar to sweat.

Like any modern attempt to improve a natural process, they have their shortcomings. First, to make them taste good they contain a great deal of sucrose. More than you need. Because of this they tend to make you thirstier. So the beverage may have an initial thirst-quenching effect, but a short time after drinking it you are thirsty again. Second, many contain too much salt. There is no magic formula for every person to follow to maintain an adequate salt intake. For the person exercising vigorously for an extended amount of time in a hot, humid climate, this type of product may replace the correct amount of salt. For the average person who is exercising on a normal day, the electrolyte products contain excessive amounts of salt. The fact that most people find the taste of these products pleasant, encourages them to drink more than is necessary. While the liquid itself will not hurt you, the chemicals and minerals that are in the liquid may be too much for a particular amount of exercise. While these aids may not be harmful, they may be no better than a glass of water and a proper diet. Their benefit is probably mostly psychological. My own preference is to use water.

Q: *Do some people tolerate heat and humidity better than others?*
A: Certainly. Differences in life style and the level of physical fitness are major reasons. Some women do not respond to heat as well as men. Environmental physiologists note that, unfortunately, many women have a lower level of fitness than men. They also have a higher level of fat—around 9 to 12% more than men.

Studies have shown that properly trained women with a low percentage of body fat acclimatize to heat more successfully than sedentary women. Adaptation to heat has to do more with life style and body fat than with gender.

Q: *Can steam rooms be dangerous?*
A: The steam room, in my opinion, is a potential health hazard. The door should state: *Warning—The use of a steam room is hazardous to your health.* It may cause sudden death. The theory behind their use is that you can sweat your weight away. The theory is all wet literally and figuratively. True, you can walk into one of those hot, humid rooms weighing 150 pounds and walk out a while later weighing 146, 147 or so, but you have lost valuable fluid that your body desperately needs. If you don't replace that fluid you will eventually become dehydrated, a serious condition. As soon as you replace the fluid, you'll return to your normal weight. So you really haven't lost any weight at all and you haven't gained anything valuable.

One of the biggest dangers connected with steam rooms is the exposure to such extreme heat and humidity. It is just not a normal condition for the body to face. Look at how much you complain when the outside temperature rises to 95 or 98° with the humidity almost 100%. A steam room offers higher temperature with 100% humidity. Because of that very high humidity, the sweat cannot evaporate and cool the body. If you recall, that's the purpose of sweat. Without this cooling effect, body temperature can rise to dangerous levels. The heat alone can be detrimental to most middle-aged people and can lead to heat exhaustion.

These dangers are increased if you go into the room after exercising, for that's when the body really needs to cool down. Such conditions could easily lead to heat stroke which is a medical emergency requiring prompt first aid to sustain life. I find it ironic that people are willing to put themselves through such an ordeal just to lose a couple of pounds that they will put right back on anyway.

Q: *Why do people use steam rooms?*
A: People figure if they're sweating they're working hard. It's

false. Completely worthless. DO NOT USE A STEAM ROOM—EVER!

Q: *Are there as many dangers connected with the sauna as there are with the steam room?*
A: If you were forced to choose between the two you should go with the sauna for one reason: the humidity is kept low, allowing your sweat to evaporate and maintain proper body temperature. But I would still caution against using the sauna as a means of achieving physical fitness. Initially it may make you feel better or more relaxed (and those are two important health objectives), but it won't improve your physical fitness level.

Q: *What's the best way to use a sauna?*
A: Try to keep the temperature below 185° and stay in it no longer than 8 to 10 minutes for the beginner; and 15 minutes for the veteran. Staying in longer will increase the possibility of heat exhaustion. Try not to use the sauna right after a vigorous work-out as this will place an added burden on your body that may be harmful to heart and cooling mechanism. It should not be used right after a workout. Cool down properly first.

Wearing a shirt or towel or any type of clothing reduces the air's ability to evaporate sweat. Hence body temperature can rise to dangerous levels. Some sauna sponsors list the raising of body temperature as a benefit. What that benefit is I don't know. Finally, saunas aren't for everyone. Elderly people, people with heart disease, high blood pressure, and people under the influence of alcohol or narcotics may suffer adverse effects from using a sauna. How many times does an overweight, slightly inebriated businessman with a history of heart ailments relax in a motel's sauna at the end of a busy day on the job? As far as I'm concerned, there are too many risks involved in using saunas.

Q: *Can rubberized sweatsuits be dangerous?*
A: Yes. In fact, I don't recommend their use at all. Some claim to make you look better and some claim to make you feel better. But they're outright dangerous. They don't let your body be exposed to the air and as a result, your body temperature starts to escalate. I panic when I see athletes and coaches wearing them in

gymnasiums. They think they're getting into shape. They're really setting themselves up for heat exhaustion or heat stroke.

Q: *Are there any dangers involved in wearing a sweatsuit?*
A: Clothing during exercise should be worn for protection from cold and other elements. Sweatsuits are excellent for exercising in cold weather. They are soft, loose fitting, and comfortable. They never should be worn in hot weather for the mere purpose of producing sweat. Remember, sweat helps cool your body. A sweatsuit in warm weather impedes the evaporation process. Wearing a rubberized sweatsuit or a very heavy sweatsuit in a hot environment can produce an extreme heat buildup that can lead to heat exhaustion or heat stroke.

Q: *What is heat exhaustion?*
A: This is a condition brought on by loss of body water. If you continue exercising vigorously while sweating profusely, there comes a point when you simply run out of water. When this supply of body water is gone, the blood circulation is reduced and your blood pressure falls. Weakness, fainting, and shock may occur. Heat exhaustion is easily prevented by taking water before, during, and after exercise. The old days of don't drink the water during a workout are gone forever. Small but regular amounts of water during a workout are necessary to prevent exhaustion. If heat exhaustion occurs, the remedy is water, supplemented with salt and potassium taken slowly. Heat exhaustion is a relatively simple condition but if not treated properly, can lead to heat stroke.

Q: *What is heat stroke?*
A: Heat stroke is a life-threatening situation. Far more serious than heat exhaustion. It occurs when the skin is soaked with sweat because of humidity or restricting clothing. Your perspiration cannot evaporate. Eventually, your sweat glands become swollen and close off. Sweating stops and body temperature rises rapidly. The skin becomes warm and dry; mental confusion occurs and coma quickly follows. Treatment must begin immediately by placing the victim in a tub of cold water or under a cold

shower. If treatment is not begun within a few minutes of the onset of the symptoms, death may result.

Heat stroke can be avoided by conditioning carefully (don't try too much, too soon), drinking adequate amounts of water and other liquids during exercise, wearing light clothing, changing sweat-soaked clothing as required, and stopping as soon as you have chills, stop producing sweat, or feel mentally confused.

As a summary on heat, the crucial factor is to allow your body to sweat, get into better shape, lower your percentage of body fat, make sure you replace lost salt and potassium, and drink plenty of water.

CHAPTER
14

How To Get The Most Out Of The Foods You Eat

Q: *How important is diet in getting the most out of my exercise?*
A: A well-rounded diet is essential. Your prime concern in picking up this book was your body, and you are hoping that exercise will do something for that body of yours. You want to make it look better, feel better, or do things better. Exercise can and will do all these things and more. But it is always nice to have some extra cards in your hand. You need to make sure your body is getting all the nutrients it needs. You also need to avoid those things which don't contribute to good health. A good analogy is your automobile. You can't put a low-octane fuel into a high-powered engine. It's the same way with your body. You can't put in junk food and expect your body to perform at an optimum level. A jitter-bug diet like that is bound to hurt your health.

I'm talking about nutrition, not "a diet." You have probably gathered by now that I am not exactly in favor of the many diets that are supposed to help you lose weight. Most are based on erroneous concepts. They tell you not to eat certain foods—many times foods your body needs.

Good nutrition is the prudent consumption of foods from *all* the food groups and goes hand-in-hand with exercise. To get good nutrition you need carbohydrates, fats, proteins, vitamins, minerals, water, and fiber. The first six of these are called nutrients. Fiber is not a nutrient, but it is essential for good health.

Q: *Are fats really good for you?*

A: Absolutely. Fats have an undeservedly bad reputation in America. Most people think that if they eat fats, they'll get fat. But this is equally true of proteins and carbohydrates, if enough of them are eaten.

The very important nutritional role played by fats is often overlooked. Pound for pound, fats provide more usable energy fuel than either carbohydrates or proteins. They also take longer to digest, so you feel fuller after a meal or snack containing some kind of fatty component.

Nevertheless, there are good fats and bad fats. Fats are made up of fatty acids. And there are three general kinds of fatty acids. They are called saturated, unsaturated, and polyunsaturated. These terms refer to the manner in which the hydrogen and carbon atoms of the fat are fastened together. If you looked at a saturated fat under a microscope, you would see the hydrogen and carbon atoms linked together as in the following chart.

Three Types of Fat

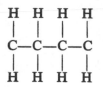

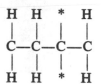

Saturated	*Unsaturated*	*Polyunsaturated*
beef	almonds	corn oil
butter	cashews	fish
cheese (whole milk)	chicken	herring oil
chocolate	duck	margarine (special)
coconut	olive oil	safflower oil
cream	peanuts	soybean oil
ice cream	peanut oil	walnuts
lamb	pecans	wheat germ oil
margarines (ordinary)	turkey	
milk (whole)		
pork		
shortenings (hydrogenated)		
veal		

When a fat is saturated, it is saturated with hydrogen. The carbon atoms are saturated with hydrogen. When a carbon atom has some free space for hydrogen atoms to hook on, it is called unsaturated. And if there are several carbon atoms that are not attached to hydrogen, it is a poly- or many-unsaturated fat. The fewer hydrogen atoms present, the more unsaturated the fat is.

This distinction between unsaturated and saturated fats is very important. A diet high in saturated fats tends to raise the level of fat in the blood. A higher level of fat in the blood will mean a person is more likely to develop heart disease. So, when you are choosing fats to eat, it's good to know whether they are saturated or unsaturated.

Q: *Should you try to eat less saturated fats?*
A: Personally, I'm not in favor of manipulating fat intake to include only polyunsaturated or unsaturated fats. There is no conclusive evidence indicating that small quantities of saturated fats (the kind found in butter, beef, pork, and milk) contribute to heart disease. I think a well-balanced diet should include a diet of around 30% fat. And of this 30% fat, ⅓ should be polyunsaturated, ⅓ unsaturated, and ⅓ saturated. If you'll look at the list closely you will see, however, that most Americans get a large percentage of their fat in the saturated form. And this is what is bad.

Q: *How can you tell if commercial products contain saturated or unsaturated fats?*
A: Many unsaturated fats are made into saturated fats by food manufacturers. The change is made through a process called hydrogenation. Hydrogenated fats are those in which additional hydrogen has been forced to hook up with the carbon atoms. Oxygen would normally hook up with the open-handed carbon, but oxygen can cause fats to spoil. Since hydrogenated fats don't spoil rapidly, they last longer on the shelf. So manufacturers extend the shelf life of a product by hydrogenating their oils. You must read labels and make sure they don't say partially hardened, hardened, or hydrogenated.

Don't be misled with the word vegetable oil. Vegetable oil may be something other than safflower or corn oil. It may be coconut oil. Coconut oil is very high in saturated fat and should not be used at all. Most non-dairy creamers have more saturated fat than whole milk or cream. Ironic, isn't it? Soon government regulations will require that the type of oil be identified.

Q: *Why is protein important to the diet?*
A: While you're sitting there reading this book, you are losing several hundred cells each second. Millions of cells in your body are destroyed daily. If you had no way of replacing those cells, you would waste away and die very shortly. Thank goodness for protein, because it builds and repairs body tissues.

Proteins are the building blocks of the body. They are composed of many nitrogen-containing compounds called amino acids. The digestive system breaks the protein molecules down into usable forms of amino acids. Different kinds of cells need different kinds of amino acids. The cells use the amino acids to form their own protein and use them to carry out the task of building and repairing body tissue.

Protein can be used to supply energy, though not for very long. When used to generate energy, proteins cannot do their normal job of building. Eventually, the building process would fail and the body would begin to deteriorate.

Although proteins are necessary for continued life, you do not need them in large amounts. Most Americans get plenty. Foods that are rich in protein include meats, fish, eggs, and milk. Other foods which contribute lesser amounts of proteins are dry cereals, breads, beans, rice, and peanut butter.

Q: *What is the difference between high-quality protein and low-quality protein?*
A: Proteins are really made up of amino acids. And amino acids can be broken down into essential and nonessential amino acids. Nonessential amino acids can be made by the body, but essential amino acids are those which must come from the food you eat. While all amino acids are essential for building and repair of the body tissues, more than one-half of the number you need can be made by your body, if not enough are found in your food. But the remainder (the essential), are those which you must get from your food.

There are 8 known essential amino acids and 14 non-essential amino acids. Foods that contain all eight essential amino acids are called complete or high-quality proteins. The foods that don't have all 8 are called low-quality proteins. Dairy products, meats, eggs, fish, and fowl are complete or high-quality proteins. Nuts, soybeans, etc., are low-quality proteins. Of course, with the low-quality proteins it is possible to eat combinations of foods to get the essential amino acids. For example, combining soybeans, rice, and wheat, or beans and wheat, or rice and legumes, or corn and legumes will provide all essential amino acids.

Q: *Do you recommend a vegetarian-type diet?*
A: I see nothing wrong with vegetarianism provided you know what you're doing. If you lean toward vegetarianism or would like to cut down on your animal protein intake, I suggest you get a copy of Frances M. Lappe's book *Diet For A Small Planet*. Most books on nutrition are either too simple or too complex. This book isn't. *Diet For A Small Planet* has a series of tables which tell you how to plan good meals that have plenty of protein, yet are meatless. This book convinced me to cut my red meat eating substantially. I now eat mostly fish, fowl or plant protein. I eat red meat about once or twice a week, and then only a small amount.

Q: *Isn't animal protein necessary for good health?*
A: Four ounces of high-quality protein is all you need a day. The average American gets a lot more. Joan Ulloyt, M.D., says that the healthiest blood chemistries are found in runners who are vegetarians. This group is followed by sedentary vegetarians, followed by meat-eating runners. All three are significantly better than the average sedentary, meat-eating American.

A study done in Boston on 200 vegetarians supports Dr. Ulloyt's contention. Investigators found that these vegetarians had excellent blood chemistries. Almost all had extremely high HDL and LDL ratios. Remember, that type of ratio reduces your chances of a heart attack significantly.

Dr. William Castelli, from Framingham, Massachusetts, whom I introduced to you in Chapter 4, agrees. He found that a low fat, low cholesterol diet can have a very good effect on HDL and LDL ratios. His investigations showed that a prudent diet which emphasizes vegetables and vegetable oils, cereals, fish, little meat, and no junk foods (such as fatty hot dogs and potato chips), can do just as well as vegetarianism in producing positive HLD and LDL ratios.

Quite frankly, the research is not definitive in respect to how much animal protein we should eat. Ten percent of your diet seems to be plenty.

Q: *Why are carbohydrates important to your diet?*
A: While fats provide sustained energy and protein helps build tissues, carbohydrates provide "quick" energy. This class of nutrients has been called the "body's most preferred food" because carbohydrates are easiest for the body to digest and use. Aside from providing quick energy, they also furnish some important proteins, minerals, and vitamins. In addition, they usually taste good.

Basically, carbohydrates are either simple sugars or complex combinations of sugars. The sources of carbohydrates are fruits and vegetables, specifically beets, carrots, onions, turnips, and sweet potatoes. The sugars that the plants do not use are stored as starch. When we eat those starches (grain products and some vegetables), our digestive system easily changes these starches back into simple sugar components for quick energy food.

If you are physically active, you need larger amounts of carbohydrates. If you do not get enough carbohydrate fuel to meet your energy needs, a condition called hypoglycemia (lack of sugar) exists. That condition produces a feeling of extreme fatigue. For that reason, at least 50 to 60% of your diet should consist of carbohydrates.

Q: *What is the difference between simple and complex carbohydrates?*
A: Simple carbohydrates, many times called sugars, are found in such foods as beet sugar, corn syrup, cane sugar, milk, grain products, and fruits. Complex carbohydrates take a little longer to digest and are usually found in vegetables, potatoes, and corn.

Q: *Does table sugar contain carbohydrates?*
A: Table sugar does supply carbohydrate energy, but table sugar contains no vitamins, minerals, fats, or proteins. Nu-

tritionists call this kind of food "empty calories." Numerous books and articles that elaborate this perspective have been published.

Naturally, the sugar companies are up in arms over this new controversy surrounding their product. The president of one said, "Most authorities agree that sugar, in moderation, is one of the most useful foods as well as an economical source of energy. Yet sugar is frequently accused of being detrimental to health. Some of these accusations come from food faddists and non-scientists with an ax to grind. And some come from physicians and researchers whose views are not generally accepted."

Well, I'm not a food faddist and I agree that using sugar in moderation is not harmful. But the question is: What is moderation? Certainly, sugar (sucrose) is being used in excess when it constitutes 15 to 20% of your total caloric intake, which is the average in the United States.

You may not think you're consuming that much sugar, but it's often forgotten that sugar is a basic ingredient in foods such as candy, soft drinks, pastries, and desserts. It is also added to commercially prepared soups, rice, peanut butter, baked beans, crackers, catsup, chow mein, blue cheese, cereals, fruit drinks, juices, frankfurters, bread, vitamins, medicines, and almost anything else you can think of.

Q: *How can I cut down on my sugar consumption?*
A: There are seven steps that I recommend that would cut your sugar consumption in half:

1. Don't put sugar on cereal or in coffee or tea. (If you can't do without it, compromise by using only one teaspoonful.)
2. Never eat presweetened cereals.
3. Cut your consumption of soft drinks and candy by 50% or more.
4. Drink fruit *juices* rather than fruit *drinks*. Also, check fruit juice labels. They should say "no sugar added" rather than "unsweetened." "Unsweetened" can mean that some sugar, usually in the form of fruit sugar, has been added.
5. Keep sugar off fruit.
6. Use fresh rather than canned fruit.

7. Carefully check all labels and select foods that are low in sugar or simple carbohydrates. If you have a choice, choose the can or box with no sugar listed among the ingredients—or with sugar listed *after* several other ingredients, rather than a product where sugar is listed among the first few.

Q: *Should saccharine be substituted for sugar?*
A: I avoid it. It seems to have a cancer-producing effect on the body. Significantly, it also seems to foster a taste for sweets.

Q: *Isn't sugar also a good source of energy?*
A: Yes and no. It's a good source of energy if you don't eat any carbohydrates for a couple of days. Then the sugar would give you a lift. But since most of us get an adequate amount of carbohydrates, it's not a necessity. It is a problem only for those people on low carbohydrate diets.

Q: *What type of food is the best source of energy?*
A: Carbohydrates and fats. Your body uses carbohydrates for energy most of the time, that is, when you're resting, reading, watching TV, etc. You also use carbohydrates when you run or swim fast for a short period of time. Most of your energy comes from carbohydrates. But when you walk, jog, or ride your bicycle for half an hour or so, half your energy comes from carbohydrates and the other half from fats. And if you walk, jog, or run for longer than an hour, other changes occur. Most of your energy then comes from fats. It's simply amazing how your body makes these adjustments without your having to think about it. Even animals use energy in much the same way. Birds that migrate use fats and carbohydrates just like you. When they are not migrating, most of their energy comes from carbohydrates. But when they begin to fly south, they use fat for muscle contractions. Some birds have lost as much as 40% of their body weight flying for more than 60 hours. And most of what is lost is body fat.

Q: *How does protein rate as a source of energy?*
A: Actually, protein is one of the worst sources of energy. Protein can provide energy but when it does, it ignores its main job of building and repairing tissue. As several million cells are de-

stroyed each day, protein cannot supply energy for very long without the body deteriorating. Carbohydrates and fats are pretty single-minded. Unlike proteins, they are not multitalented. Therefore, you should leave the job of building to proteins and let carbohydrates and fats supply you with energy. That way, everybody stays happy. And that's just another reason why most diets are not recommended. They simply restrict some of the nutrients your body needs. The infamous liquid protein diet illustrates that pretty well. Man cannot live by protein alone.

Q: *Do you need to take vitamins if you exercise?*
A: It all really depends on your eating habits. Vitamins are organic substances that provide chemical control of a number of body functions, including energy production, normal growth and development, reproduction, resistance to infection, and general health. If you were a plant, you could make your own vitamins, but animals have to get them from the foods they eat. If you do not get enough of the various essential vitamins, your health will falter.

The essential vitamins necessary for us to remain healthy are available in meats, fruits, vegetables, milk, eggs, fish, and certain cereals. However, many Americans have erratic eating habits and miss out on certain vitamins. Consequently, concentrated forms of vitamins are commercially manufactured and made available so that such people can keep a balance of the required vitamins.

Many people take vitamins in an effort to ward off what they feel are subclinical deficiencies—to make up for anything they feel they do not get enough of. I feel this is a cop-out. The best solution is to maintain a well-balanced diet. A well-thought-out diet allows you to avoid the pit falls of saying you can make up for low nutrition with a few extra vitamin pills.

You must understand that foods don't contain just vitamins. Citrus fruits, for example, provide vitamin C. But they also provide pulp and cellular material, material which aids in proper bowel function. In addition, they are a natural source of sugar and liquids, all necessary for good nutrition. You do not get the same benefits from taking a couple of vitamin C tablets. It would be disastrous if you relied solely on vitamin pills and capsules for good nutrition.

Cereal manufacturers make the same mistake when they imply through their advertising that if you eat their cereal you'll get all the vitamins and minerals you need. There is more to nutrition than vitamins and minerals. Another problem is the amount of sugar many companies put in their breakfast cereals. If you decided to eat a bowl of cereal every day for the rest of your life and that was it, you probably wouldn't live very long, even though you'd get enough vitamins.

Q: *How are minerals important to a balanced diet?*
A: Minerals are necessary to the structure of bones and other body tissues. The proper functioning of your organs depends upon a proper supply of several important minerals. Some of the essential minerals are calcium, phosphorus, iron, copper, iodine, sodium, and potassium. We talked about sodium and potassium in Chapter 13—Exercise Is Weatherless.

The important thing to understand is that tiny amounts of minerals are necessary for life. Iron and copper are just two common examples. You take in trace minerals in water, food, and even in the air you breathe. Only recently have scientists been able to determine when a person is getting too many or not enough minerals. But there is evidence that even the smallest amount of minerals has a great effect on body health. The question of mineral nutrition for humans will not be answered fully in the near future, but there are certain things that you can do to make sure that you get an adequate supply in your diet. They are:

1.   Put real variety into your diet. Some people think that variety is switching from boiled potatoes one day to mashed the next. They are still potatoes and have low mineral value unless you eat the skins. Instead of eating just meat and potatoes, your family can enjoy fish, vegetables, beans, peas, nuts, whole grains, and a wide variety of fruit. To add fun to your diet you can try new and unusual foods.

2.   You should be careful about foods that come in boxes. They usually contain highly refined flour and sugar. Whenever possible, try to eat fresh, natural foods. Fresh fruits and vegetables should be eaten first.

3.   Besides the beef your family normally eats, try to eat more fowl and sea foods.

This approach will be far better than trying mineral supplements.

Q: *What's wrong with taking mineral supplements?*
A: Supplements are a cop-out. I think people placate themselves with the idea that a vitamin or mineral supplement will make up for disastrous nutrition. It just isn't so. It's a rather expensive way to insure good nutrition. It would be far better, far more palatable, and far more enjoyable to get nourished from food. Good nutrition is really "nature's own way" and is a lot cheaper. I have also found that many people who rely on vitamins approach health from a passive view. They take these vitamins in hope that it will cure their health problem rather than taking responsibility for their own health with exercise, good food, and proper rest and relaxation.

Occasionally I recommend supplements of vitamins C and B, especially for those people who run, cycle, or swim long distances. I strongly suggest iron supplements for women.

Q: *How does fiber fit into a balanced diet?*
A: Fiber is not really a nutrient in the classic sense of the word. It contains no energy or building properties. But it does play a significant role in the health of the digestive tract. Resarch indicates that fiber may be important in preventing constipation and in reducing the incidence of gastrointestinal tract problems, including: appendicitis, polyps, colitis, diverticulosis, and even large bowel and rectum cancer.

Exactly how the fiber works is not firmly established. It appears to be linked to the transit times of the digested food. That is, the length of time the food stays in the large intestine and the bacteria count. Interestingly, ailments such as appendicitis, colitis, etc., are lowest in the underdeveloped countries whose diet contains a good bit of coarse grain. The incidence of these diseases rises in proportion to the decrease in consumption of high fiber foods.

Dr. Dennis Burkitt was perhaps the first man to point out this role of fiber. Burkitt has done extensive research on primitive cultures and modern diseases. He feels the fiber situation is twofold. It involves not only a reduction of fiber content but a tremendous increase in sugar consumption. Dr. Burkitt noted that the Indians who live in urbanized Napal eat 10 times more sugar than the rural village Indians. They also have a far lower amount of fiber intake. Consequently, they have far more diabetes and heart disease. Dr. Burkitt also observes that native Africans who live in Cape Town on sugar-rich diets and low fiber diets have diabetes at a rate 40 times higher than that of Africans living in rural villages.

Q: *How do I get more fiber in my diet?*
A: Bran is your best source. This can be gotten through whole grain cereals and breads. You'll also find it in dried fruits, raw fruits and vegetables, and nuts, to name a few important sources.

To make sure your intake is adequate, eat a whole-grain cereal at breakfast. Also eat whole-grain bread during the day. Furthermore, eat raw fruits and vegetables whenever possible.

Q: *Can you summarize all this dietary advice?*
A: 1.   Try not to eat foods that come in a box or a bag. That way you'll cut down on your sugar, salt, and white flour intake.

2.   Try not to eat candy, sodas, cakes, and pies—that way you'll also cut down substantially on your sugar.

3.   Try to get as much nutrition as you can from wholesome, natural foods, fresh or frozen fruits and vegetables, whole-grain products, low-fat dairy products, small amounts (4 ounces) of meat daily, and more fish.

CHAPTER
15

The Diseases Of Excellence

Q: *Can exercise make you susceptible to certain diseases or ailments?*
A: When you put your body in motion you are more prone to some injuries and ailments; some minor, some disabling. I want to put this whole discussion in a positive vein since many times people look for an excuse not to exercise.

Many of these conditions which I am going to talk about are a small price to pay for a healthier, more productive, and certainly more enjoyable life. Consequently, I have borrowed Dr. George Sheehan's term for these problems—Diseases of Excellence.

Q: *What are the diseases of excellence?*
A: Diseases of excellence are those ailments brought on by the very process of getting back in shape. Examples are the blisters, charley-horses, cramps, and other aches and pains you are bound to get from working out. These really aren't diseases at all, but they are bound to happen to you and you should be aware of them so you know what to do about them when they do occur and won't chuck the whole concept of fitness and tell Charlie Kuntzleman to go take a flying leap.

Ailments usually occur in the early stages of your journey from a sedentary life to an active one. They hurt (about enough to give you an excuse for not working out), but if treated properly they will go away quickly (taking your excuse along with them).

But some ailments happen to those of us in good or excellent shape, usually because we try to do too much and fail to heed certain warning signs our body emits.

You see, getting that machine of yours back in good condition requires a small down payment and a lot of sweat, perhaps a little blood, maybe even a tear or two. But what a small price to pay compared to a heart attack, a stroke, or a life plagued by trips back and forth to the hospital. A life of the blahs. Eugene Greer said it best: "Since I've been exercising my worst days are like my best used to be." I like that.

But ailments do occur, usually because of overdoing, poor body mechanics, accidents, or improper clothing.

Q: *What causes blisters?*
A: A little friction or pinching on some tender skin results in that painful bubble of skin known as a blister. When tender skin is rubbed or pinched for an extended period of time, the outer layer (epidermis) separates from the inner layer (endodermis). Fluid and/or blood fills this space between the layers, causing the bubble-like appearance.

Blisters appear primarily on the feet, since this is an area that receives a great deal of friction. The hands are also great "blister getters" especially in activities involving a firm grip such as in golf, tennis, and squash.

Q: *Why are blisters so painful?*
A: When a blister breaks (either on its own or with your help) it exposes new skin that is extremely tender. Previously, that skin was protected by a layer of thicker, tougher skin, but when the tough skin is removed, you will experience some pain until the new skin is conditioned. This can take anywhere from a few days to a couple of weeks. It depends on how well you take care of it.

Q: *How should I take care of a blister?*
A: The best way is to puncture the bubble or blister not in the center but at the edge, and only if you can observe extremely sterile conditions. Picking at it with your fingers until it breaks is not a sterile condition. A sterilized needle, some antiseptic, and sterile bandaging material is necessary. Otherwise, puncturing

the blister can cause more problems than the blister itself. It might cause infection. So if you're not going to be clean about it, don't try lancing it.

Once you've punctured the blister, allow the wound to drain. This may require a little pressure using *clean* fingers. After the wound has been drained, apply some antiseptic and a sterile gauze pad and ointment such as first-aid cream. Change the dressing daily, and if possible, give the wound some fresh air occasionally. In some cases, extra padding may be necessary to protect the wound and allow you to resume physical activity. In most cases, a blister is a pretty lame excuse to stay away from exercise!

Q: *How can I prevent blisters?*
A: Remember the term diseases of excellence? In the early stages of getting in shape, you can simply count on getting a blister or two occasionally. However, there are some preventive measures that will definitely minimize the possibility. Since blisters occur most frequently on the feet, what goes on and around those feet is important in preventing blisters. That means pay a little attention to your socks and shoes. Socks should be clean, above all. Whether they are made of cotton or wool is a minor point. The recent development of "tube socks" made of cotton gives the exerciser a cheap alternative to wool. You might even try two pair. Shoes should be of good quality. Don't try to save money here. Some people shell out $40 for a fancy jogging suit then spend $9.95 for a pair of cheap "tennies." I would suggest you do just the opposite. I'm not out to push any particular brand, but I would strongly suggest you select a well-known, proven manufacturer and be willing to pay $20 or more. In the long run, your feet will applaud it. That is, if feet do such things.

Whatever shoe you choose, make sure it fits properly. Shoes that are too small, too large, too narrow, or too wide will almost automatically produce a blister as well as other more serious problems. I would also suggest that you take good care of your shoes. If you allow them to get wet, they may lose their flexibility and set you up for more blisters. Even after you get a new pair of good shoes, allow a break-in period. It's a good idea to wear them around the house for a few weeks prior to running in them—no matter what the manufacturer tells you.

Check your feet occasionally. If you experience a burning sensation and notice an area that is especially sensitive, you may want to apply a soothing ointment and a sterile pad for protection. At the University of Kentucky, athletes are told to apply ice directly to those areas after their workouts. According to their results, it completely eliminated blisters. It might be worth a try.

Finally, if a hot spot or blister occurs frequently, try a "doughnut." To make a doughnut, simply take a piece of felt and cut a hole in it. The hole in the felt is then placed over the hot spot or blister. The felt pad (or the outer part of the doughnut) surrounds the sore spot. Of course, the felt pad must be taped to the foot.

Q: *Is it good to wear shoes without socks?*
A: Good question. Also a good way to get blisters. You've probably seen world-class track and field athletes on TV who compete without wearing socks. First, remember that these people are men and women who devote several hours a day to training. In doing so, they have toughened the skin on their feet so that the possibility of blisters is minimal. Also, keep in mind that many of these athletes who appear to be wearing their shoes without any socks actually have on little foot socks or ankle length socks that offer protection, but from a distance make it appear that they are wearing no socks at all. Finally, the shoes that these runners wear are among the most expensive money can buy. If you looked at the insides of these shoes carefully, you would see that they look better than a velvet-lined Cadillac and protect the foot much like a sock would. Moreover, you will probably find that they too have blisters.

If you or I laced on our shoes without any socks and ran for a half hour or played tennis for an hour, we would probably have blisters on our blisters. For the average exerciser, wearing shoes without socks just doesn't make good sense. Socks not only protect your feet from blisters, but help absorb the sweat that is a natural by-product of exercise. My advice: keep your socks on.

Q: *Should I ever go barefoot when I exercise?*
A: My answer is an emphatic NO. You run too great a risk of injury from stepping on sharp objects or having someone step on you or stubbing your toe. But when it comes to walking around

the house or yard, kick your shoes off and give your feet a lift. Walking barefoot can strengthen all the foot muscles. In addition, it keeps the achillès and hamstrings flexible.

Q: *What is a charley horse?*
A: This is a painful condition that results from a bruise of the muscle between the skin and the bone. It is most common on the thigh area and usually does not show up until the muscle has had a chance to cool down. A charley horse is caused by a direct, severe blow to a relaxed or fatigued muscle. Contact sports such as football, soccer, basketball, martial arts, or hockey are known producers of charley horses. So are little kids who like to punch their sisters in the thigh.

A charley horse is not serious, but if not treated properly it can seriously impede your physical activity.

Q: *How can I prevent charley horse?*
A: By wrapping your entire body in foam rubber and sitting in the closet all day. In those contact sports mentioned, it is almost inevitable that you will get one sooner or later. Of course, strengthening the muscles and avoiding overfatigue will help. A fatigued athlete runs the greatest risk of receiving an unexpected, perhaps unguarded blow. When such fatigue sets in, take a break. No sense in spoiling all the fun with a painful charley horse.

Q: *How do you treat a charley horse?*
A: Even while you're groaning, treatment must begin immediately, while the affected area is still warm. First, stretch the muscles in the area to improve flexibility and help keep tightness from setting in. Then apply cold packs (ice cubes in a plastic bag will do) for at least 15 to 30 minutes. The cold prevents the damage from spreading by limiting the swelling. After a half hour of cold packs, wrap the area with a wide elastic bandage and walk around for 5 to 10 minutes. The next day, apply heat and then massage the area. The combination of heat and massage tends to break up the resultant blood clots. This should be done twice daily until the pain leaves the area and you are ready to go again.

Q: *Should I work out while I'm treating a charley horse?*
A: By all means! Don't let a little thing like a charley horse stop

you. I would suggest you stay away from the more vigorous contact sports, or at least keep the area protected if you just have to play that game of hockey or touch football. Keep in mind that activities involving stretching and flexing of the injured muscle will help speed the healing process. Swimming is always a good rehabilitative activity for a mildly injured person and will keep your cardiovascular fitness level up where it should be.

Q: *What's the difference between a charley horse and a muscle cramp?*
A: Have you ever awakened, looked at the clock, and felt good? You had an hour or more to sleep so you decided to take a nice big stretch and then roll over and get back to sleep. And then all of a sudden right in the middle of that luxurious stretch, your calf was hit with an outrageous pain that sent you screaming. That, my friend, is a muscle cramp or spasm. A cramp is a relatively minor problem. It results in severe pain and short-term loss of mobility.

There could be any number of causes for muscle cramps, including fatigue, cold, imbalance of salt, potassium, and water levels, a sharp blow, or overstretching of unconditioned muscles. The cramp experienced while stretching in bed is brought on generally by a combination of fatigue and overstretching of unconditioned muscles.

Your chance of getting a muscle cramp may be reduced considerably by maintaining a proper diet, proper warm-up prior to vigorous activity, ceasing activity prior to extreme fatigue levels, and tapering-off exercises.

Once a cramp occurs, it can usually be stopped by simply stretching the muscle affected and firmly kneading it. Normally, a sense of tightness or dull pain will follow, making it necessary to apply heat and massage to the area to restore circulation.

If muscle cramps occur frequently, drinking adequate fluid and eating foods high in salt and potassium, along with muscle strengthening and stretching exercises, will usually eliminate the occurrence of the problem.

Q: *What's the best way to relieve overall soreness and stiffness after a workout?*
A: This is a frequent complaint of the novice exerciser. The

soreness probably causes a great many people to quit exercising. Muscle soreness and stiffness results from an abrupt change or departure from your regular activity level. If you never exercise, raking leaves on a Saturday afternoon or a weekend canoe trip will send you back to work on Monday with sore muscles. On the other hand, even if you run 2 to 3 miles a day, a short game of basketball may leave you groaning the next day when you climb out of bed. These things happen because you have called upon new muscles to do new jobs.

The key to minimizing muscle stiffness and soreness is a regular and complete warm-up and cool-down with each exercise session. Whether you jog, swim, ride a bike, or play tennis, it is always wise to do some stretching exercises first. Then, after you've completed your workout, walk around, stretch, swing your arms, twist your trunk, etc. The few minutes you devote to this will help reduce soreness the next day.

One other thing! You can always count on soreness and stiffness if you are not regular in your exercising program. Exercising sporadically can almost be more harmful than helpful. Once or twice a week is *not* enough. Try for a minimum of 3 times a week with 4 to 5 times being the best.

Q: *Why does it seem that some days I get sore immediately after exercise and on other days it happens a couple of days later?*
A: First you must realize that medical authorities have been unable to prove conclusively the physiological causes of soreness and stiffness. Two theories are widely accepted and probably both are right. One theory is that lactic acid remains in the muscles for a few hours and causes pain. This seems to hold true and explains why the experienced exerciser has less soreness than the beginner. His improved circulatory system gets rid of the lactic acid more easily.

The other theory is that soreness may be the result of tiny muscle fiber tears that occur during severe muscular activity. Since the fibers involved are very small and relatively minor, the effects of the injury are not readily noticeable, but surface 24 to 48 hours later. That would explain the soreness you might feel a few days after exercising.

Q: *What are shin splints?*
A: Shin splints are a painful condition of the lower front shin. If

you have shin splints, you will feel pain in the lower leg when you put weight on your foot and your shin will be tender to the touch. If you run your fingers along the shin you may feel a roughened area along the bone. Though the name implies a splintering or damage to the shin bone, it may any of several conditions. Here are a few possibilities:

1. Your arch may drop somewhat, thereby irritating one or more of the tendons of the lower leg.
2. The membrane between the two bones of the lower leg may become irritated.
3. The tendon which inserts one bone of the lower leg may be inflamed.
4. This same tendon or the muscle (anterior tibialis) may be torn from the bone.
5. A muscle spasm may occur because of a swelling of the anterior tibial muscle.
6. A hairline fracture of one of the bones of the lower leg.
7. A muscle imbalance caused by a "toeing out" of the feet or other improper body mechanics.

Q: *How can I prevent shin splints?*
A: Lately, a lot of attention has been placed on improper footwear and a hard running surface as major causes. For the solution, we have to look at those two. Preventive measures include: exercises to strengthen the anterior chamber muscles and avoiding some of the known factors that lead to shin splints.

A good exercise to include in your warm-up is the foot flexor with weights, or an isometric exercise. The idea is to flex your foot up and down against resistance. If there are no weights handy to strap on, sit with your legs dangling, feet not touching the floor and have a friend hold your feet while you try to life them. Doing this for 3 sets of 10 each day will help prevent shin splints from occurring by strengthening the muscles involved. This exercise must be done since running tends to strengthen the muscles at the back of the legs. So a muscle imbalance occurs. The muscles in the back of the leg are a lot stronger than the ones in the front. This sets you up for shin splints.

There are other precautions you might take that would help prevent shin splints. First, look at your shoes. A good pair with a ripple sole and heel is best. Shoes with cushion soles are a must. Next, switch from a hard to a soft running surface whenever possible. A golf course or a local park offers the runner a chance to work out on grass which is much softer than pavement or a gym floor. Another thing you might try is to reverse the direction that you run on a track. Instead of always going counterclockwise, switch back and forth so that you do not place a great deal of stress on the inside leg as you go around the turns. Other suggestions for runners and non-runners alike are: Try to avoid running on your toes, for this has been cited as one of the causes of shin splints. Put a sponge heel pad in the heel section of your shoe to help absorb some of the stress from running on a harder surface. Dr. George Sheehan, also recommends placing a molded crest under the toes.

Q: *How would I treat shin splints?*
A: Unlike cramps and charley horses, shin splints can be so painful you must stop exercising. Almost any activity requiring even limited running, jumping, or walking may be impossible. For this reason, quick, effective treatment is crucial.

First, rest the affected leg. This means ceasing activity that uses that leg. This usually takes care of the problem. As an alternative, you might try swimming. You simply cannot "run out" shin splints. Second, a good pair of shoes is a must (accept no alternatives). No $9.95 specials. All the measures mentioned under prevention will also help, especially rehabilitation of the weakened anterior tibialis.

Q: *Can cortisone shots help in the treatment of shin splints?*
A: That is probably the worst thing you could do. Repeated cortisone shots may weaken your connective tissue. The real tragedy is that cortisone treats the symptom, it doesn't provide a cure. Cortisone shots provide temporary relief. But because you continue to run on hard surfaces, wear improper shoes, or not run properly, the shin splints will reappear. By the way, those shots won't exactly be cheap. The best cure is rest initially, followed by an analysis of what caused the ailment, and then doing something about it. Your best bet for avoiding this and other foot and leg problems is your choice of shoes.

Q: *Why is the choice of shoes so important?*
A: Many of the diseases of excellence are simply symptoms of foot problems. The runner's foot strikes the ground about 5,000 times an hour. Many so-called running shoes can't protect your feet from that kind of punishment. Usually, the arch flattens. When that happens, watch out! Just about any problem from the trunk down can be caused by the lack of arch support.

Dr. George Sheehan, the "runner's doctor," lists such ailments as shin splints, knee problems, pulled calf muscles, and achilles tendonitis as being directly caused by improper footwear.

And I think it extends beyond running. I think the walkers, tennis players, and handballers who are serious about their sport will find that an investment in a good pair of shoes will go a long way in preventing leg injuries. All you have to do is remember how many times your feet hit the floor in an hour. You'll get some idea of what I'm talking about.

Q: *What kind of problems affect the Achilles' tendon?*
A: Reach down to the back of your heel, then run your fingers up along the back of the foot. That stiff cord-like thing you feel is your Achilles' tendon. Now, *gently* pinch that cord. Hurt, didn't it? It should, because it is vulnerable and just loaded with nerve endings.

The Achilles' tendon helps to control the movement of the foot. As with any tendon, it's susceptible to injury. A direct blow to the tendon can cause an injury, though this type is not too common. The tendon can receive 600–800 individual blows each time you jog a mile. It must also absorb a lot of blows on the handball, racquetball, squash, and tennis courts. The heel accepts the blow and sends shock waves on up the back of the leg. Constant pounding on hard surfaces, then, is one of the major causes of Achilles' tendon injuries.

You can prevent Achilles' tendon problems by staying off the pavement entirely or by placing some firm sponge padding in the heel of your running shoes and making sure you have a good arch support. Your goal is to minimize the shock of pounding on a hard surface. Make certain you do stretching exercises in your warmup and cool-down. These exercises help stretch the tendon. Don't forget, the slow stretch is best.

Q: *Why do exercisers get these leg ailments?*
A: Because they are *doing* something. One sure-fire preventive measure for all of these diseases of excellence would be to come home from work, grab a beer, sit down in front of the TV until dinner, eat, light a cigarette, plop down on the couch, have a couple more beers, then go to bed. Doing this regularly (as many millions do) will assure you of a life (however short) free from blisters, muscle soreness, and shin splints. Of course, such a life style may have you facing heart disease, hypertension, emphysema, etc.

The point is, getting in shape and staying there costs something. I personally feel the price is minimal compared to the cost of sedentary living. Like the man said, "You can pay me now or you can pay me later." An occasional blister seems mighty small to the bed-ridden heart patient who is not allowed to sit up without assistance. A shin splint is minor to a person so obese that appearing in public becomes a nightmare of embarrassment and ridicule. If you are pursuing the task of getting your body in good physical condition, you can expect a few aches and pains along the way. But the satisfaction of feeling good is hard to beat.

Q: *What are some other kinds of diseases of excellence?*
A: Tennis elbow is an example. It is a steady dull ache on either the inner or outer side of the lower end of the elbow. It is a persistent pain which people seem to have a difficult time getting rid of. The standard therapy has been rest, lots of cortisone, playing with less vigor or switching to your other hand. The last two are completely unsatisfactory recommendations for most people.

Q: *What can be done to prevent tennis elbow?*
A: To keep tennis elbow from putting you on the sidelines, ask a coach or trainer to take a close look at how you use your racquet. You may be putting an unnecessary strain on your elbow by using faulty technique. You may also be using a racquet handle which is too large for you.

If it is to strike the ball properly, your racquet must fit your hand. The circumference of a racquet grip ranges from about 4⅜ to 5 inches. Too large or too small a grip leads to excessive strain on the forearm muscles when they are rotating. Too large or too small a racquet head can also cause faulty strokes which increase the elbow's exposure to trauma. An out-of-balance, top-heavy racquet has a similar effect.

Although there are some exceptions, tennis trainers and tournament class players are in general accord that the resiliency and flexibility of the metal racquets, particularly the stainless steel alloys, produce the least strain on the elbow.

Attention should also be paid to the shock absorbing qualities of the racquet's string. Gut strings are preferable to nylon for this reason, and a string tension of 50 pounds should be tops.

The pain of tennis elbow comes from the repeated forceful pronation (palm down) and supination (palm up) of the forearm with an extended elbow. Therefore, how you grip the racquet, your stroke technique, and how you meet the ball all play a crucial role. Another factor is your warm-up. It is necessary to take a few minutes of limbering up before going all out. This applies in both warm and cold weather. It's also a good idea to warm up on a wall or backboard before moving to the court for practice serves and warm-up volleys.

The other important thing is to remain fit. The muscles of your arms should be kept in excellent physical condition. So you may want to do both aerobic work and weight training as outlined in Chapter 10.

Q: *What's the difference between tennis elbow and tendonitis?*
A: Tendonitis can occur at any joint or wherever there is a tendon. Tendonitis may reflect an irritation of the muscle, tendon, bursa, or ligament.

Q: *How would I know if I have tendonitis?*
A: By analyzing the pain. Tendonitis usually appears slowly over a period of days. The area is usually quite tender. Surprisingly, there seems to be less pain when active and more after prolonged rest.

Q: *What's the best treatment for tendonitis?*
A: Aspirin and cold packs seem best. The ice packs are to be kept on for about a ½ hour after exercise. You can continue

exercising, but try not to go with more intensity—go slowly. *Do not* increase the length of your training during this period of pain.

You should analyze your techniques. No matter whether it's running, walking, tennis, or golf. You probably did or are doing something wrong. If you can't blame it on increased training or improper foot wear, it's probably due to faulty technique. Get a pro or expert to analyze your stroke, swing, or stride.

Q: *What is a side stitch?*
A: The side stitch has many names. It is also called side sticker, pain in the side, stitch in the side, side ache, or just a plain stitch. No matter what it is, it sure is a pain. And it hurts. Doctors disagree on what causes it. There are probably two reasons. The first is improper breathing. Improper breathing causes a spasm of the diaphragm. To reduce the problem, belly breathing is suggested. That is, when you inhale, the diaphragm should descend, pushing the abdominal wall out. When you exhale, the diaphragm should be pushed in or the belly flattened. It's just the reverse of what you normally do. That is, push your belly out when you inhale and push your belly in when you exhale.

The second cause, which I feel is more valid, is a spasm of the ligaments that attach themselves to the liver, pancreas, stomach, and intestines. These ligaments are put under stress when you run or jump up and down. The bouncing action causes these ligaments to stretch, thereby causing pain. I've had success with myself and others by simply gripping my side and pushing in. It works. In severe cases, lie on your back and raise your feet in the air or even try standing on your head or hands. That may seem crazy, but it's my contention that the side stitch is due to the ligaments which hold the abdominal viscera. Because of repetitive bouncing, these ligaments go into spasm. The inverted position takes these ligaments out of stretch and relieves the spasm.

There are some general rules:

1. Do not eat or drink within 3 hours of an activity.
2. Increase your fitness level.
3. During an attack, bend forward at the waist and place your hand on the affected area.
4. Inhale deeply, provided the belly is pushed out.
5. If the pain is intolerable, lie flat on your back, raise your

legs over your head, and support your hips. Keep your legs moving. Even standing on your hands will bring relief.

Q: *What is a sprain?*
A: A sprain is one of the most common injuries that afflicts active people. It is usually the result of a violent twist of a joint that produces a stretching or tearing of one or more ligaments surrounding the affected joint. Many times other tissues such as tendons and nerves may be affected.

Any time a sprain occurs, it is important to follow the principle of ICE. The three letters stand for ice, compression, and elevation. If the ligament is torn, surgery is necessary.

Q: *What's the difference between a strain and a sprain?*
A: A sprain is an overstretching or tearing of a ligament. A strain is an overstretching or tearing of a muscle or, in a few instances, a tendon. The tear is usually the result of an abnormal muscular contraction. The strain may range from a small separation of connective tissues and muscle fiber to a complete muscle rupture or tissue tear.

After the rupture or tear, there is usually a hemorrhaging of the blood vessels or capillaries. Clotting takes place shortly thereafter. To prevent too much hemorrhaging, a compression bandage and ice pack should be applied for at least 30 minutes. Overnight, keep ice on the affected area, and elevate the area when possible.

Q: *Why do most injuries seem to focus on the knee?*
A: Any joint can be injured, but the knee is the most vulnerable. The knee is the largest and most complicated joint in your body. Doctors call it a hinge joint. The three main bones of the knee joint are the femur of the upper leg, the tibia of the lower leg, and your knee cap. You have 13 different ligaments and tendons which give support to your knees. If you did not have the ligaments on each side of your knee, your knees would not be stable.

Between the femur and the tibia are two more ligaments. These ligaments cross over each other. They allow your legs to move forward and backward. The main job of your knee is to let you walk, run, squat, and lift. The muscles of your upper and lower leg and your knee let all these things happen.

Common Diseases of Excellence

Complaint	Cause	Treatment
1. "My heart feels funny." (This may be a hollow feeling, fluttering, a sudden racing, or slowing of the heart rate.)	Your exercise is too vigorous.	Slow down level of exercise and see your doctor.
2. "I have this sharp pain or pressure in my chest."	Your exercise is too vigorous.	Slow down level of exercise and see your doctor.
3. "I am dizzy or lightheaded"; "My head feels funny"; "I break out into a cold sweat"; or "I almost fainted."	Your exercise is too vigorous. Not enough blood gets to your brain.	Slow down level of exercise and see your doctor.
4. "My heart seems to be beating too fast 5 to 10 minutes after exercising" or "I seem breathless 5 to 10 minutes after exercising."	Your exercise is too vigorous.	Work at a lower level of target heart rate range, about 70%. In some instances you may need to work below that. If this doesn't correct the problem, see your doctor.

#	Statement	Cause	Solution
5.	"I feel like vomiting" or "I vomit right after exercising."	Your exercise is too vigorous or you need a better cool-down.	Work at a lower level of target heart rate range, about 70%. Take longer for a cool-down.
6.	"I'm tired for at least a day after exercising" or "I'm tired most of the time."	Your exercise is too vigorous.	Work at a lower level of target heart rate range, about 70%. Work to a higher level more gradually or you may need more sleep/rest.
7.	"I can't sleep at night after exercising."	Your exercise is too vigorous or done too late in the evening.	Work at least 2 to 3 hours before retiring or work at a lower level of target heart rate, about 70%.
8.	"Even though I'm exercising my nerves seem shot"; "I'm jittery"; or "I'm hyper all the time."	Too much exercise or too much competition.	Lay off the competition, cut back on your intensity, and/or switch to another activity for a short time.
9.	"I've lost my zing" or "I'm no longer interested in my favorite activity."	Too much exercise or too much competition.	Lay off the competition, cut back on your intensity, and/or switch to another activity for a short time.
10.	"During the first few minutes of exercise I can't get my breath."	Improper warm-up.	Spend more time in your warm-up, at least 10 minutes, until you get to your target heart range.

247

Your knee is an amazing and beautiful structure. Yet, because of the way the bones and ligaments are placed, it is susceptible to injury. Another problem is that the only real support of your knee comes from the soft tissue of the ligaments, tendons, and muscles. To add to its work, your knee must support all of your body weight. So while the knee is great for movement, it can easily be injured.

Ligaments and tendons are tissues that can be torn or stretched. When that happens many times doctors must operate to correct the problem.

The best thing to do, however, is to prevent the injury from happening. Prevention of knee injuries means strengthening the leg muscles with proper exercises. Three exercises you should *not* do are deep knee bends, duck walks, and squat thrusts. These exercises can actually do more harm than good. They stretch your ligaments and tendons and make them more likely to be injured.

Two good exercises, which I described in Chapter 11, are the one-half knee bend and the sitting leg raise.

Q: *Are exercisers more susceptible to colds and infections?*
A: This is a tough one to answer. My personal feeling is that the fitness enthusiast has an edge against colds, respiratory illnesses, and infections. Furthermore, if he gets a cold he is better able to handle it. It just makes good sense that if you're in better health and subjected to less emotional stress, there is less likelihood of your developing a cold.

On the other hand, many times fitness people push themselves unmercifully. They do not listen to their bodies. Even those who should know better. In their zest for more mileage, more time in the pool, and more excellence on the court, they get run down. The results: greater susceptibility to colds, flu, and other respiratory illnesses. Dr. George Sheehan lists respiratory ailments as one of the diseases of excellence.

There are many other ailments which could be listed here. I've summarized a few more on the accompanying chart.

I think if you follow the principles outlined in this book, listen to your body, work at target heart rates, and increase your exercise level gradually, your chances of developing any of these ailments are minimal.

But then, everybody is different. I personally feel that many of the strains, aches, and pulls come from trying to do too much, too soon. The mentality of a lot of people is that if 30 minutes of swimming is good, then 60 minutes is better. If 1½ miles in 11 minutes is good, then 3 miles in 22 minutes is excellent. Don't be like the guy who thought putting twice the amount of fertilizer on his lawn would make it grow faster. He burned his lawn up. So will you. Only that lawn is your body.

If you try doubling, tripling, or quadrupling everything I've told you in too short a time, you're headed for trouble. Proper preparation and a gradual approach are best. Always begin and end each exercise session with some stretching and conditioning exercise. Increase the amounts and severity of exercise slowly. If you do, you will find that the diseases of excellence disappear. Make haste slowly.

CHAPTER
16

Who Shouldn't Exercise?

Q: *Are there some people who shouldn't exercise?*
A: Yes, but not as many as you might expect. Moreover, many conditions are temporary and people may resume activity after successful treatment. It is also important that we recognize what is meant by exercise. In many instances, traditional types of exercise are contra-indicated for people with certain conditions. That is, no jogging, calisthenics, or vigorous sports. For them, mild walking may be beneficial.

Q: *What are some of the ailments that preclude people from engaging in more vigorous types of exercise?*
A: I think it will be best for me to list and explain what these conditions are. Non-heart ailments include:

1. The acute stage of arthritis. During the acute stage of arthritis, rest and medication is necessary. Any exercise during this period will probably aggravate the arthritic condition. But during the quiescent stage, exercise is recommended, provided the disease has not caused too much deformity of the joints. Even then, swimming is a good activity, with bicycling as a possible alternative. Easy range-of-motion exercises may also be helpful.

2. Chronic low back pain may be aggravated by jogging or calisthenics. Low back pain may increase with obesity, running

on an uneven surface, poor running shoes, or sudden twisting movements of the spine. Once over the acute pain, you should stretch the low back, condition the abdominals, stretch the muscles in the back of the legs, and engage in go-slow exercise.

3. Anemia is another condition which is usually aggravated by exercise. With anemia there is a lack of protein hemoglobin in the blood so there is not enough oxygen getting to the organs and muscles of the tissue. The result is severe fatigue, breathlessness, and even on occasion anginal pain. There are several causes of anemia. Anemia is usually due to loss of blood from such things as an ulcer, hemorrhoids, or excessive menstrual loss. It is important that the hemoglobin levels return to normal before exercise is introduced. Since ongoing exercise is dependent on the oxygen supply, little is going to be gained by having people exercise and have greater amounts of fatigue, breathlessness, and anginal pain.

4. Diseases of the lungs, kidneys, and liver. If a person has tuberculosis, exercise may cause complications. Likewise, exercise may be harmful to people who suffer from severe kidney or liver diseases.

5. Uncontrolled diabetes. If you suffer from uncontrolled, severe diabetes, it is best to avoid exercise. This condition requires medical supervision. Uncontrolled diabetes refers to unstable blood sugar levels. While milder forms of diabetes are usually helped by exercise, people who do not have it under control will find that their condition is aggravated by exercise. Exercise uses up the blood sugar supply in unpredictable amounts, giving the diabetic patient too little basis on which to set up an exercise program.

Q: *What are some of the heart conditions that would prevent someone from exercising?*
A: Again, let me list these.

1. A recent heart attack. It takes a good six weeks for the scar from a heart attack to heal. So no vigorous activity should be permitted before that time, though a doctor may permit casual walking within a week of the heart attack. A regimented exercise program is not recommended.

2. Acute heart failure. In acute heart failure the heart is not

able to pump blood efficiently around the body. Exercise makes this condition worse. When heart failure occurs because of a heart attack, the condition usually corrects itself after the scar tissue is healed. So exercise is permissible later on.

3.   A bubble on a major blood vessel (aneurysm). A person with an aneurysm should not be permitted to exercise since the added pressure during exercise may cause the vessel to burst.

4.   Heart muscle infection. When the heart muscle has an infection causing an inflammation of the muscle or the sac that surrounds it, it is called myocarditis. No exercise is recommended until you are over the infection. In fact, it's a good idea to avoid exercise any time you have the flu, influenza-type conditions, or a cold.

5.   Extremely abnormal heart beats or heart action. Some of these are not dangerous, but only your doctor can tell you if you suffer from a dangerous form. If so, exercise is not recommended. Generally, people who have the dangerous forms have pacemakers and their recommended form of exercise is walking.

6.   Uncontrollable blood pressure. Most people with high blood pressure do quite well with exercise. But if the blood pressure cannot be controlled by medication and diet, then a person should not exercise because it will make his blood pressure go up even higher. The end result could be a stroke.

Of course, there are other conditions which may preclude a person from engaging in exercise and these include: badly defective valves, rapidly progressing anginal pain, active blood clot(s), general heart defects, and certain congenital heart defects. Again, it will depend primarily on the doctor's recommendations.

Q: *What is considered to be high blood pressure?*
A: A normal reading for blood pressure in men is from 110–140/60–90. If your blood pressure is much higher than that, you may have high blood pressure or hypertension. This condition may be mildly serious (175/100) or quite serious (300/180), but should be cause for concern to the exerciser.

Q: *Why is high blood pressure of such immediate concern for exercisers?*
A: Because vigorous exercise tends to raise blood pressure.

During exercise there is a greater demand for oxygen. Your body craves it, screams for it! To meet this demand for more oxygen, you have to increase the amount of blood passing through the lungs (to get more oxygen) and muscles (to get rid of carbon dioxide). There is more peripheral pressure surrounding the arteries, making it necessary for the blood pressure to be increased. So when you exercise, your blood pressure rises. If you start out with high blood pressure, you may place your system in great danger by forcing your pressure up beyond a safe point.

High blood pressure can increase the chance of a blood vessel breaking. The extra pressure during exercise can cause a weak spot in one of the vessels to break. Much like a weak spot in a hose, when the water pressure is increased dramatically. If a large vessel ruptures in the brain, a stroke would result. If a large vessel in the heart breaks, a heart attack will occur.

Q: *Should you exercise if your blood pressure is slightly high?*
A: Of course you should exercise. In fact, failure to exercise will allow the condition to worsen. Some studies have indicated that exercise may reduce blood pressure of hypertensive people. Two men, Drs. John Boyer and Fred Kasch, chose 23 middle-aged men with high blood pressure and put them on a fairly mild exercise program for 6 months. Their routine consisted of 15 to 20 minutes of warm-up exercises followed by walking and jogging. All these men had previously been inactive and no attempt to change their diets was made. The result: after only 6 months there were significant reductions in their blood pressures.

No one study makes a very sound case, but other studies have shown similar results and are lending credence to this study. So more and more physicians are prescribing exercise for their hypertensive patients. It is important, however, to keep in mind this is for people whose high blood pressure is controllable. Some have advanced to what is known as the malignant or uncontrollable stage and have very little hope of turning their condition around. Though it is a sad fact to face, the price of regaining one's good health may simply be too high.

No one with high blood pressure should begin an exercise program on his own without first checking with his or her physician. Your doctor will advise you on the types of exercise and the degree of vigor at which you should undertake that exercise. He can give you the proper dosage. In all probability, he will make similar recommendations to those outlined in this book. Those with uncontrollable high blood pressure should not exercise at all, since the increase in pressure while working out may simply put too much stress on their arteries.

Q: *Should people who have already suffered a heart attack exercise?*
A: Unfortunately, this is a difficult question to answer. You are talking about diseased conditions that always create unpredictable results. That is why so many times in this chapter I refer you first to your personal physician. Your doctor alone knows the severity of your case and can advise you on the amounts as well as types of exercise that will be best for you.

But my answer here is that, yes indeed, heart attack victims should begin exercising as soon as their condition permits. The American Heart Association says that a person who does not have any complications after a heart attack should be encouraged "to perform activities of daily living that can be done with minimal or no discomfort." Furthermore, it is generally anticipated that by 6 to 8 weeks after the heart attack a person will be able to walk comfortably ½ to 1 mile twice a day. The only caution is that you don't do too much too soon. Be patient. If your doctor gives you walking privileges, then walk. Maybe it will only be from your front door to the mail box, but it's better than letting someone else do it for you while you sit in an easy chair. That is probably one of the reasons why you suffered your heart attack in the first place.

Naturally, you'll have to learn to listen to your body and stop when it tells you something is wrong. It does this by giving you signals. These include: lightheadedness (your heart simply cannot keep the blood pumping quickly enough to supply your brain with oxygen), pain in the chest, nausea, inability to catch your breath, etc. The Talk Test is also important.

Q: *Should heart attack victims exercise with someone else?*
A: Yes, especially for the first 3 months. Just in case you get too weak, too dizzy, or too out of breath to carry on. Besides, it's

always more fun to have smoeone to talk to. Sometimes heart attacks are a boon to Americans. They force you to slow down and enjoy life a little more.

It's ironic that it is only after a person has had a heart attack that many doctors specifically recommend types and amounts of exercise. Prior to the attack the recommendations may have been rather casual. One physician, Dr. Per-Olaf Åstrand, has said that a heart attack victim should be indignant with his physician if he did not specifically recommend exercise before his heart attack. In fact, some heart attack victims have run marathons.

Dr. Terrence Kavanagh, Medical Director of the Toronto Rehabilitation Centre and Assistant Professor, Department of Rehabilitation Medicine, University of Toronto, has an interesting story to tell. On April 15, 1973, Dr. Kavanagh took 7 men to the Boston Marathon. It was not an easy day for a 26 mile 385 yard run, for temperatures were in the low 80's. But all 7 of Dr. Kavanagh's group completed the 26+ mile run. So what, you say? Interestingly, all 7 men were heart attack victims. Each of these men had sustained a fully documented myocardial infarction (heart attack) one to four years previusly. In fact, three of the men had had two heart attacks.

Too many people wrongly believe that having a heart attack means the end of an active life. Consider John. At age 35 John led a fairly normal middle-aged life. He played softball regularly every summer and had smoked a pack and a half of cigarettes a day since he was 17 years old. After one of his softball games, John was rushed to the hospital with a massive coronary thrombosis. He was placed in intensive care and within a week, while in intensive care, suffered another massive heart attack. He was released, only to be sent back to the hospital with a third major heart attack.

When he finally got out of the hospital, John, as you can well imagine, was scared to death. He was afriad to do almost anything for fear of having another heart attack. At about this time he was promoted to a job that required a considerable amount of walking and though he was fearful of the results, he took the job anyway. In retrospect John figures that this new job is what began to rehabilitate him so that he can now face a normal, productive life, for this job required that he walk 5 miles a day, 5 days a week. And he did that for 6 years. At first it was difficult and he had to stop and sit down every so often.

At his doctor's advice, John enrolled in a local fitness class at a university and began an aerobics exercise program. Everyone in the class was required to run for 20 minutes at least 3 times a week. Skinfold measurements were taken as well as weight, height, resting pulse rate, and pulse rate after the Modified Harvard Step Test. In short, John was placed on a vigorous cardiovascular endurance-type exercise program that slowly improved his ability to live life more fully and less fearfully of heart disease.

That was 14 years ago. Today John is 49 years old, runs 4 times a week, 3 of those days he runs 3 to 4 miles and on the fourth day he runs 5 to 6 miles. For a man who once faced the very real possiblity of an early death, he's made quite some progress.

No, having a heart attack does not mean the end of an active life. What it means is that you probably never had an active life to begin with. Or at least not one with the proper types of activities at the proper times. Shoveling snow once or twice a year or even playing softball once a week in the summer is not such activity.

Q: *When should people who've had heart attacks resume exercising?*
A: As soon as the doctor says it's ok. Remember, if you've had a heart problem, you should always consult your physician first because each case is unique. If there was not a great deal of damage done, you may be able to start walking regularly after 3 to 4 weeks. In some instances the doctor has the patient up and moving about within a week of the attack. You may be able to start walking regularly after 3 to 4 weeks and then be at the ½ mile to 1 mile point around 6 weeks after the attack. Naturally, if more damage was done, the doctor will hold you off longer.

I can't stress enough the importance of two elements of your exercise program. First, it should start slowly and gradually increase; second, it should be regular. If your doctor gives you a green light for mild activity and you jump into a basketball game at the Y, you are flirting with death. Furthermore, you should not be worried about how fast you exercise. Competition is irrelevant here. It probably was a factor that caused your heart attack. Go slow, go long, go easy. Enjoy it. The motto has been overworked but it is still solid—train—don't strain.

Q: *What types of exercises would be best for the recent heart attack victim?*
A: I've already mentioned walking which is one of the best overall exercises for heart attack patients to improve fitness and control body weight at the same time. Almost everyone can walk; it's cheap, and it burns off calories. Besides, when you get right down to it, it's fun.

Q: *How can walking be fun?*
A: The problem here is the traditional concept of walking. Many people look at walking as being a negative thing. It's always the last resort. When the elevator doesn't work, you *have* to walk. When the car doesn't start, you *have* to walk. When the taxi cab is late, you *have* to walk. It's no wonder people think of walking as something that's unpleasant. What you need to do is change your perspective a bit and look at the brighter side or the better aspects of walking. Walking lets you see and hear things you've never seen or heard before. Quick now! Tell me what lies between your front walk and the post office. What kinds of trees would you see along the way? How many squirrels have their homes along your route? Who's practicing their piano lesson? Who waves? Who do you meet along the way? Who is also walking? How many cars pass by with only one occupant?

Get the idea? Those quiet moments of walking give you time to see, to hear, to think, to enjoy! If you walk in the morning, you can plan your day. If you walk at night, you can reflect on the day's activities. If you walk with your husband or wife, you can get to know him or her better. If you walk with a neighbor, you can walk to a deeper friendship.

Q: *Are there other exercises besides walking for the recent heart attack victim?*
A: There are lots of exercises you could do. Walking just happens to be one of my favorites. Spend at least 6 to 12 weeks on walking. With your doctor's ok you may progress to riding a bicycle. Don't go up hills at first. In fact, a stationary bicycle is

best. Here you can control the terrain. Swimming in a pool is also ok. Go easy and work up to it by holding on to the edge and kicking or by floating on your back and paddling gently with your arms and legs.

Start with walking. Later, swimming and bicycling can be added. Much later, you can jog. As you progress, you may want to use a sport as a change of pace. You may play golf, shuffleboard, or ride a horse (walking). Shortly thereafter, you may play horseshoes or bocce, and you may bicycle.

But let me repeat, these are recreational activities that are to be done only in addition to your walking, bicycling, or swimming.

Q: *How hard should I exercise if I have had a heart attack?*
A: It's really better to think in terms of how long you should exercise. Nothing that you do when recovering from a heart attack should be "hard." If, for example, you plan on walking, don't walk fast. Instead, walk normally for 10 to 20 minutes if possible. If you feel winded or exhausted after walking for that length of time, it's not that you walked too far, it's probably that you walked too fast. Your goal here is continuous, rhythmic exercise. Fifteen minutes a day of non-stop, light exercise will do you far more good than 3 to 5 minutes of tough, all-out strenuous exercise. In fact, that 3 to 5 minutes of hard work may be dangerous to a heart attack patient. Follow the Starter Walking Program on page 134. If 20 minutes is too far, 5 or 10 minutes may be better.

Remember, if you've had a heart attack, some damage has occurred. On top of that, you probably weren't in the best physical shape before you had the heart attack. So now your approach must be much slower than that of the "normal" inactive person. You just walk the fine line between overexertion and inactivity. Keep it light at first and gradually work up to a level that you are more satisfied with.

Q: *But what if I get discouraged from going so slowly?*
A: Unfortunately, recovery from heart attack *can* be discouraging. It's a sobering fact to suddenly realize that your life is so drastically changed. Before you had your attack you *thought* a 20 minute walk was child's play. Even after your attack it seems like

it should be easy, and that a short walk won't do you any good. Of course you have an alternative. Don't do anything. Sit and wait for "it" to happen. And the result will be depression, anxiety, resentment, low morale, decreased stamina and vigor. No joy in life. You might as well be dead. Here's where positive thinking must come in. Constantly remind yourself of the following facts:

1. Complete inactivity will not help you live longer. You cannot entirely escape activity. Sooner or later your body will be called upon to perform a task. Whether it's a seemingly routine romp with your grandchildren or an unexpected emergency, you will be forced to perform duties that present physical stress.

2. Your body will not be able to undergo vigorous activity in the first several weeks of recovery—to do so would be suicidal and you don't want that.

3. Mild regular exercise is the only way to eventual good cardiovascular fitness. No gadget or device will get your heart back into shape. Your heart muscle has to be retrained. By proceeding gradually, it will become stronger and will work more efficiently.

4. Though progress is slow, you're alive! Over 600,000 people die each year of heart disease. You didn't. You were one of the lucky ones given a second chance. Celebrate that fact by reaffirming life itself. Give your heart an edge by slowly forcing it to work a little harder each day. Both your heart and your family will thank you.

Q: *What should I do if my doctor won't recommend exercise?*
A: Your doctor might have good reason for restricting your activity somewhat. Perhaps tests have shown that your cardiovascular system has deteriorated to the point where increased activity, however slight, may be dangerous, though chances of that happening are minimal.

Unfortunately, it could be the doctor. Some physicians aren't ready to admit that regular aerobic exercise can be beneficial for overall good health. Or they may have graduated from high schools or colleges where physical education was not emphasized or was taught so poorly that they have negative feelings about exercise. Moreover, until recently the preparation of the doctor involved practically no presentation on physiology of exercise. Even today, most doctors receive about 4 classroom hours on the subject. That hardly qualifies them as experts in this area.

A doctor may be a fantastic surgeon or bone specialist and yet may not be competent in evaluating your ability to withstand exercise.

To deal with such a situation, you must first share your concerns with your doctor. If you've read this far you probably feel that exercise may be just what you need. Tell your doctor that you would like to spend the rest of your life doing rather than sitting. Sometimes the doctor just needs to be aware of your commitment to that type of recovery. Ask your doctor's honest opinion of what exercise will do for you as you recover from your heart attack. If the doctor still says no, ask on what basis he or she made this decision. If the doctor can show you the results of tests and evaluation procedures, he most likely is giving you a sad but accurate picture of your condition. If he says no without giving you any reason, he is probably against exercise. He is no longer practicing medicine. He's just imposing his biases. If that's the case, look for another doctor. That's tough to do these days. But it will be worth the time and effort. Having a doctor who includes a dose of exercise in his prescription will add life to your years. The doctor should make you responsible for your own health. The doctor who doctors least, doctors best. Dr. George Sheehan writes down 14 to 15 things for his patients to do to get the most out of what they have left. He does this whether the patient is in good health, an athlete suffering from asthma, emphysema, heart disease, or whatever. I like that. Interestingly, his list does not include medications. It includes good preventive measures.

Q: *How do I make sure I don't end up with a doctor who's not keen on exercise?*
A: Check to see if your prospective doctor exercises. Also find out if he is a non-smoker or forbids smoking in his office. They usually go hand-in-hand. If you're still not sure, check his waistline. Dr. George Sheehan says, "Never trust a politician with a waistline larger than 34 inches. The same applies to doctors."

If your doctor practices what he preaches, then you *know* his advice will be sincere. By the way, golf, that well-known pastime of doctors and other professional people, is *not* good exercise. So if your doctor tells you he exercises every afternoon on the golf course, ask him if he carries his own bag. If he doesn't then he doesn't exercise. If you do feel you must choose another doctor, it's important at the outset to let your feelings be known about exercise in order to find out your doctor's position. More and more physicians today are recognizing the value of exercise and are prescribing it as part of a person's total rehabilitation plan after suffering a heart attack.

Epilogue: Putting Exercise Into Perspective

When I started this book I mentioned that more and more people are exercising. They recognize the importance of physical activity for a healthy and productive life. I trust that in these pages you have learned what it takes to get into good physical condition. I hope you have learned how to get more out of the physical activity you have selected for better physical fitness. Your questions should have been answered.

As a writer and fitness consultant, I had a strong motive in writing this book. I want you to be more active and remain active. Since you have stayed with me this far, what I have said has probably intrigued you. I would like one last shot. It may help you answer any future questions on exercise.

Whenever it comes to health and fitness, I think anthropologically. I look at how man was created and the type of world in which he was supposed to live. Quite frankly, it was not the sedentary, smoke-filled, concrete jungle of today.

No, he was designed to live in an environment that tested his physical being. A world that forced him to use his strength, stamina, dexterity, and brain to survive.

Modern man has drifted from the physical arena. Most Americans today are surviving by their wits. The physical challenge is gone.

But we must return to our physical heritage. We must build

activity into our lives if we want to enjoy the true pleasure of living. We are, however, more fortunate than our ancestors. Their physical activity was limited. They could walk, jog, or do physical labor. We have many choices. We can reestablish our physical heritage with many different kinds of exercise. Skiing, bicycling, tennis, jogging, swimming, handball, walking, and ropeskipping are ours to enjoy. Enjoy! Yes, we have another advantage over our ancestors. We can do it for pleasure. The activities are there. All we have to do is do them.

Every living thing seems to have a maximum life span. In the fish family, the flounder lives 10 years, the goldfish, 25. Among birds, the blue jay lives a short 4 years, the Canadian goose 32 and the raven 69. Among the reptiles, the alligator may reach 56, and the quiet turtle 123 years. The life span among mammals also varies widely. The humble mouse lives one or two years, the horse 20 to 30 years, and the elephant about 60 years. But the longest living mammal of all is man. One hundred to 120 years is possible.

Despite this potential few of us live that long. The latest research seems to indicate that each of us begins life with a certain potential for longevity and fitness, a potential inherited from our parents. Then, circumstances and the choices made every day chop away months or years from that allotted life span. They also influence the degree of fitness. For example, your parents may have had the capacity to live to be 100. But their circumstances and their habits caused them to die much younger. Likewise, you may have inherited the capacity to live to be 100. But your environment and your habits—many of which were learned from your parents—may diminish your years to 65 or 70. If you live in noisy, polluted surroundings, eat the wrong foods, do "head work" all day, and fail to exercise, your potential for longevity will be reduced.

Your actual fitness will also decline. The rule of life seems to be "use it or lose it." So, our legs are becoming weaker as we depend on them less.

Humans have walked on the moon. But we are walking on earth less and less today. Yet the human potential for locomotion is surprising. Running short distances, humans at their best can reach a speed of 25 miles per hour—a lot less than the 60 mph possible for the cheetah and pronghorn antelope, or the 44 mph of a race horse. The longer the race, however, the better is human performance. In the 26-mile marathon, a human will outrun the elephant and has a speed only 5 mph slower than a race horse. In a race of 100 miles, featuring the camel, race horse, reindeer, antelope, and the gazelle, only the human, the camel, and the race horse would be able to cross the finish line. The pronghorn antelope, which can run up to 60 mph over 200 meters and at about 35 mph over 26 miles, would at last be defeated by man's greater endurance.

Most of us have this potential within us. The caliber of achievements of our finest athletes and primitive peoples show this. As a species the human has a remarkable blend of strength, stamina, and speed. Humans are incredibly versatile. We have come to dominate the earth because of the variety of functions we can perform. After all, what other creature can run, climb, jump, swim, lift, push, pull, and throw,—and also invent machines to do these things for him?

As René Dubos has noted, however, the tragedy of humans has been that in developing minds to achieve greater control over the environment, humans have consented to the impoverishment of our physical and emotional lives. Many of us have lost sight of our physical heritage. We are lauded for our IQ, SAT scores, grade point averages, and cerebral success. We have forgotten our physical attributes. We have forgotten that we are still physical beings. And we must strive to maintain that physical heritage.

The potential for a greater degree of fitness still lies within each of us, waiting to be fulfilled. Sedentary people can and do train themselves to run a six-minute mile or to finish a marathon that would do credit to the famous long distance running Tarahumara Indians of Mexico. But unfortunately, many of us have never known the ultimate sense of well-being that comes with functioning at peak physical efficiency. We need to realize how little our biological needs have changed over 10,000 years.

The people who used the slogan "Grab all the gusto you can get," knew what people wanted. You want it. I want it. It's great to have. But it doesn't come in a can. In fact, you can't buy it. Yet it's right there in front of you. So I'm inviting you to grab some yourself. Get started today. It's more fun than you think and you'll enjoy many dividends.

I've said it before and I'll say it again. Regular physical activity is not a panacea—it doesn't cure warts, grow hair on a bald head, or do away with cavities. It does strengthen and condition the body and thereby reduce the risk of falling prey to any number of physical and mental ailments. It's just about the best preventive medicine going.

It's also probably the best package deal ever invented. With it, you'll lose weight, firm up muscles, gain a more attractive body, have greater energy, feel less stress and tension—and all these benefits add up to a whole new lease on life. But you'll have more. You'll have the satisfaction of learning or playing a favorite sport, a sport you can do with your friends or alone. You'll be you.

Any way you look at it, regular physical activity is great stuff. If there's anything else that can do half as much for you, I've yet to hear of it.

Appendix A

Warm-Up Exercises

These are exercises to be done before doing target heart rate exercise. Do these exercises in the order listed. These activities will loosen muscle groups, prepare the joints for more vigorous exercise, and help the cardiovascular system adjust to a greater intensity of exercise. With the first five exercises, go to the point of pain. That is, if you went any further, you would feel pain. Once you're at that point, do not bounce. Hold for 10 seconds. Over the weeks, you can increase to 30 seconds maximum. While stretching, concentrate on relaxing the muscles being stretched. The first five exercises will stretch the muscles on the back of your legs.

1. Sitting Toe Touches—Sit with your legs extended in front of you. Feet together and legs on the floor. Reach for your toes with both hands, bringing your forehead as close to your knees as possible.
2. Calf Tendon Stretcher—Stand about 2 to 3 feet away from the wall. Lean forward, body straight. Place your palms against the wall at your eye level. Step backward. Continue to support your weight with your hands. Remain flat-footed until you feel your calf muscles stretching.
3. Calf Stretch—Assume a stride position, have one foot

forward and your hands on your hips. Lean forward, bending your forward leg as much as possible, keeping the heel of your extended foot on the floor. Return to the starting position. Repeat with the opposite leg forward.

4. Sprinter—Assume a squatting position. Then extend one leg backward as far as possible. Hands are to be touching the floor. Hold. Then repeat with the other leg.

5. Standing Leg Stretcher—Find a chair or table approximately 3 feet in height. Place one foot on the table so that the knee is straight and the leg is parallel to the floor. Slowly extend your fingertips towards the outstretched leg on the chair. Eventually you should be able to get your forehead to the knee. Repeat with the other leg.

After these five exercises are completed, you may then progress to the following exercises. Exercises 7 to 10 may be done while walking.

6. Body Bends—Stand erect with your feet shoulder-width apart, hands on hips. Bend forward slowly at the trunk until your upper body is parallel to the floor. Then return to the starting position. As you return, bend your knees so the pressure is off your lower back. Do 10 times.

7. Side Trunk Bending—Stand erect with your feet spread shoulder-width apart, left hand on your hip and right hand extended shoulder height. Bend your trunk to the left, reaching your right arm over and beyond the head. Return to the starting position. Do slowly. Perform 10 on this side and then repeat 10 on the opposite side.

8. Walk And Swing—Swinging your arms back and forth as far as they will go, walk in place, lifting your toes at least 4 inches off the floor. Do this for at least 1 minute.

9. Neck Rotations—Turn your head so you are looking over your shoulder, stretching your neck as far as you can comfortably go. Turn your head to look over the other shoulder. Repeat 10 times to either side. Do slowly. An alternative is to just hold the position as you turn the neck.

10. Cross Body Arm Swings—Stand erect, arms extended outward at the sides. Swing both arms across the body and then reverse the action, swinging both arms sidewards and back as far

as possible. Do slowly. Keep your arms and hands chest high. Repeat 10 times.

11.   Walk at a gradually increasing pace for 1 to 5 minutes.

This completes the warm-up segment of your exercise program. You are now ready to move into target heart rate exercise.

Appendix B

Cool-Down Exercises

These are exercises to be done after target heart rate exercises. Do these exercises in the order listed. Follow the same direction as for warm-up exercises. These activities will help your body return to its resting state. They will also help promote a circulatory assist while cooling down. The last 5 exercises will help stretch various muscles, tendons, and ligaments.

1. Walk slowly for 1 to 5 minutes. Gradually decreasing your pace.

2. Calf/Achilles Stretch—Face a wall, corner—anything you can lean on. Stand a few feet away from the wall. Rest your forearms on it and place your forehead on the back of your hands. Bend your right knee and bring it toward the wall. Keep your left leg straight. Be certain your left heel remains on the floor. Keep toes pointed straight ahead. Hold. You should feel the stretch in your calf. Then bend the left knee. Hold. You should feel the stretch in your Achilles tendon. Repeat with other leg.

3. Side Stretch—Stand with your feet about shoulder-width apart. Keep your legs straight. Place one hand on your hip and extend your other arm up and over your head. Bend toward the side of the hand on the hip. Move slowly. Hold. Repeat on the other side.

4.   Shoulder Stretch—With your arms over your head, hold the elbow of one arm with the hand of the other arm. Slowly pull the elbow behind your head. Do not force. Hold. Repeat on the other side.

5.   Back Stretch—Stand erect with your feet shoulder-width apart. Bend forward slowly at the waist. Let your arms, shoulders, and neck relax. Go to the point where you feel a slight stretch on the back of your legs. If you cannot go to the floor, place your hands on the back of your legs. That will give you support. Hold. Remember, when you come back up, bend your knees to take the pressure off your lower back.

6.   Spinal Stretch—Sit on the floor with your legs straight in front of you. With your right leg straight, put your left foot on the floor on the other side of your right knee. Reach over your left leg with your right arm so that your elbow is on the outside of your left leg. Twist your upper body to the left and place your right elbow on the outside of your left knee. Hold. Repeat on the other side.

Index